What Economists Do About Values

For Al & Bea Rabin
with best wishes)
L.Z.

What Economists Do About Values

Case Studies of Their Answers to Questions They Don't Dare Ask

Glenn L. Johnson and Lewis K. Zerby

Department of Agricultural Economics
Center for Rural Manpower and Public Affairs
Michigan State University
East Lansing, Michigan

Acknowledgments

The authors wish to acknowledge several sources of institutional and personal assistance. The Department of Agricultural Economics of Michigan State University, when under the chairmanship of Lawrence L. Boger, provided salary assistance for Professor Lewis K. Zerby for one summer to help prepare and conduct a series of seminars on certain of the case studies presented herein. Further, both Lawrence L. Boger and his successor, Chairman Dale E. Hathaway, supported the project with allocations of Professor Glenn L. Johnson's time. More recently, Dale E. Hathaway, as chairman of the department, helped arrange for the Department of Information Services to underwrite the publication of this book as a part of the publications program of the Center for Rural Manpower and Public Affairs. Addiann Hinds provided preliminary editorial assistance. The individual case studies and the more purely philosophic chapters of the book have benefited from criticism by a large number of colleagues including particularly James Shaffer, Glynn McBride, John Taylor, Rainer Schickele, Allan Schmid, and Donald Montgomery.

In addition, a number of students have contributed very helpful criticisms and suggestions over the years. In this connection a special mention should be made of Leroy Quance, Albert Halter, Gerald Trant, Michael Petit, and Ronald Bullock.

Kathleen Schoonmaker, of the University Editor's Office, provided careful, effective, and pleasant editorial assistance on the final manuscript. Kathy Kohl, Nita Campbell, and their numerous predecessors provided excellent typing and, at times, editorial help.

To our wives
for encouragement, assistance, and gentle prodding

Contents

THE GIRLS by Franklin Folger

"The thing is, we worked very hard on our
fund-raising dinner to pay for a speaker,
and philosophers never say anything
that's worth 150 plates of spaghetti."

The Fecundity of Philosophers and Economists Working Together

The cartoon on the opposite page pokes fun at the philosopher and others interested in philosophical issues. Well and good. It is always salutary to leaven serious discussions with a little humor. The title of this book, *What Economists Do About Values: Case Studies of Their Answers to Questions They Don't Dare Ask*, is also humorous and is, of course, a takeoff on Dr. David Rueben's best seller, *Everything You've Always Wanted to Know About Sex but Were Afraid to Ask*.

Economists, like members of women's auxiliaries, often question the value of philosophy. In fact, it is our thought that they treat philosophy, and particularly philosophic value theory, much as a typical person treats sex: that is, they are more deeply involved in their everyday activities with philosophic issues involving values than they care to admit and hence are afraid to ask the questions which they ought to ask about such a subject. Thus, the cartoon and the title we have given this book were chosen not merely for their humor but because they are surprisingly meaningful. In fact, it is their pointedness which makes them humorous.

Philosophy and economics are intimately related and indeed share a common intellectual ancestry. Both economists and philosophers, as the cases in this book will show, are concerned with solving human problems. Such problems are never merely abstract difficulties of a single formal science, or even problems answerable by the sort of knowledge which can be gained from purely descriptive, non-normative science. Mathematics is useful and important; knowledge of a descriptive non-normative sort is necessary; but neither separately nor combined can they solve human problems.

Human problems cannot be solved without reference to

1

values; human problems have at their core normative as well as non-normative dimensions. The philosopher has been concerned with normative questions ever since the early Greeks asked questions about the nature of virtue, goodness, and duty.

However, the profit of a collaborative effort such as the present one—between a philosopher and an agricultural economist—is by no means one sided. The philosopher has much to learn from economics in general and from one of its applied subdisciplines, agricultural economics, in particular. Agricultural economists have, in fact, had considerable success in coping with the normative aspects of practical questions, and ethical philosophers can study with great profit the techniques and principles which they have used. Ethics books are too often filled with curiously sterile illustrations of moral questions. The academics do not lack theoretical problems in value analysis. What philosophers do often lack, and lack painfully, is a realistic grasp of the actual world that men live in. The principle of Plato's *Republic* which required philosophers to come out of their studies from time to time to assume roles of leadership in society seems to us a good one.

The procedure of studying actual cases in which agricultural economists have been instrumental in solving human problems has a number of advantages over a more abstract or theoretical approach. In the first place, it has the advantage of concreteness. What is reported in these cases is history, and from the study of them we can see what sorts of analyses were useful and what sorts were not. Second, it has the advantage of appealing to human interest. These cases are all problems of real people and, as such, hold the interest of other real people. Third, by studying a number of different cases it is possible to derive certain generally useful principles. In other words, we can move inductively from a number of individual cases to principles which they all have in common and which can presumably be applied to cases not yet studied. In this way, we can avoid the a priorism sometimes practiced by philosophers and the excessive empiricism sometimes engaged in by agricultural economists. Finally, a case-study approach makes possible an objective foundation for our knowledge. While analysis of the concept of objectivity is a philosophical problem and is deferred until later, we believe our method can achieve objectivity.

There are other ways in which the collaboration of an agricultural economist and a philosopher can be justified. A problem couched in vague or ambiguous language is often impossible to solve; in order to be answerable it must be stated in clear terms. The philosopher, as logician, is concerned with meaning and clarity as well as consistency, and therefore he is well qualified to impose these qualities on the statement of a problem and its possible answers. We hope that just such a contribution is apparent in these case studies.

Problems must also be expressed in words. But what is meant by the meaning of words? Any word has meaning because it is used in a social situation. To assume that a word has a meaning in itself and apart from society is a most untenable assumption. Like Alice after she had gone through the looking glass, we make words mean what we want them to mean. However, this is not to say that men can use words in any way they choose and still achieve understanding and communication. One of the beauties of mathematics is that the meanings of its symbols have become standard among a large community of scientists. The disciplines of ethics and political science unfortunately do not have such standardization. Words like *good*, *right*, and *justice* are used in numerous ways by numerous philosophers. This has led cynics and sophists to charge that such terms are meaningless. But, in a strange sort of way, they are *too* meaningful. With each use we must specify how we are using such terms or else we will not be understood. Thus, another advantage of our case method will be that it spells out explicitly the kinds of meanings which agricultural economists and others have given to ethical terms.

Before turning to an examination of specific cases for investigation, it may be useful to outline in a preliminary way the kind of procedure which we shall follow. In each case, our first effort shall be to state clearly and precisely the problems with which we are concerned. *A problem exists when an indeterminate situation, present or projected, is regarded as unsatisfactory and a more satisfactory alternative situation is sought.* We shall frequently find it useful to distinguish between practical and theoretical or disciplinary problems. The former result in action and therefore have a definite termination. To act in one way or another or not to act at all is a choice which must, in the nature of things, be accomplished. Thus, practical problems demand resolution. Theoretical problems, on the other hand, are often never finally resolved.[1] In trying to solve them, one may accumulate more and more information without ever deciding in a definitive way what the answer to the question is going to be. We can illustrate these two kinds of problems with one of the cases from the present book: whether it would be right to make a national recreation area out of Michigan's Sleeping Bear Dunes is a theoretical problem; whether or not one should support the act of Congress to accomplish this end is a practical problem. Obviously, the way in which one answers the former question will influence one's resolution of the latter question, but the two are very different problems. To support or not to support an act of Congress is a choice which cannot be avoided; to do nothing is to answer the question in a definite way.

Our first concern, then, will be to decide whether the problem or the subproblem discussed is a practical or a theoretical one. Once this is decided, it will be possible to determine just what solving the problem requires. Usually, in the case of practical problems, one can point to an action or actions as the solution or answer to the question. But in the case of theoretical questions, the sort of answer we seek is not often so obvious. For example, the question of whether it is right to make the Sleeping Bear Dunes into a recreation area has no simple answer. Many people, as we shall see, will say that it is right and many will say that it is not right. Each side will give reasons for holding to its position. Which side has the better reasons? This is a question we cannot avoid. If one takes Voltaire's position that "about tastes there is no disputing," then there is no way to choose *on the basis of knowledge* whether one position is better than the other. We shall attempt, however, to show in this and the other cases we examine that one can and should choose on the basis of knowledge and to examine the sort of knowledge that is relevant.

---

[1] Henry S. Leonard, *Principles of Right Reason* (New York: Henry Holt & Co., 1957), p. 35.

This will lead us to an examination of possible solutions to the questions we have formulated. We shall investigate not only solutions actually arrived at but also solutions that were considered and rejected. Most importantly, we shall concern ourselves with the reasons given for the acceptance or rejection of solutions. How was it decided that certain information was relevant and other information was not? How was the relevant information confirmed? How, if at all, was normative knowledge assembled and confirmed? Were some possible solutions overlooked entirely, and if they were, why were they?

As we investigate the problems of this book, we shall observe a decision technique in action. We shall find that in every case, knowledge is accumulated, institutions are made use of, values are explicitly recognized, and alternatives are considered. But the question of the creativeness and inventiveness of the decision maker is, in some ways, more important than these considerations. In human problems, the investigator cannot afford the luxury of rigidity and dogmatism. The world moves on, and social patterns evolve as inexorably as biological forms. To fail to recognize such movement is to run the risk of becoming an anachronism during one's lifetime. The creative, practical agricultural economist must not be content to be an adjustment engineer whose task is to fit his knowledge into a pattern of society which is given to him. He must judge the actions and goals of the society in which he lives as right or wrong and work to improve them. Thus, we shall find it necessary to look at the institutional setting of our problems and the social setting of these institutions. Failure to do this can lead, as we shall try to show, to solutions that are unsatisfactory because of their abstractness.

Agricultural economists are frequently and properly asked to assist political leaders in making policy decisions. The chapter on U.S. economic aid to Thailand illustrates one such instance. If U.S. technicians are to give the best assistance possible, they must avoid the sort of abstractness and dogmatism which too often characterizes the work of experts in social affairs. If the present book can suggest patterns of decision making which are less abstract and more creative than those commonly followed, it will have justified the effort which has been put into it.

We would like to make a preliminary distinction between (1) problems which can be solved by turning them over to the operation of market mechanisms, and (2) those which cannot be solved in this manner but have to be solved, instead, by technological, institutional, and educational changes generated outside the market.

Generally speaking, a very high proportion of the problems involving economic disequilibria can be left to the market place. Such problems include pricing, the rationing of consumption, the allocation of productive resources, and so forth. If these problems are tackled with control programs instead of being left to a market mechanism that is fairly free, they are (1) capable of consuming almost limitless amounts of research and administrative personnel, (2) likely to create no end of opportunities for corrupt gain, and (3) likely to be mismanaged. About all the research that administrative and research personnel can afford to conduct on problems which can be turned over to the market is research directed at identifying how existing programs and policies interfere with the operation of the market, and, in turn, what policy changes are needed in order to turn the problem over to the market place. The alternative uses for administrative and research talents are generally so important that it becomes prohibitively expensive, in terms of both money and foregone opportunities, to use them to tackle the enormous problems of administering prices, consumption, and production outside of the market. Instead, these resources are needed to solve and execute decisions concerning problems that cannot be solved in the market place—that is, the problems involved in the creation of the educational and technological base for growth and improvement in the human lot. Also included here are the problems of redistributing the ownership of resources and political power and of creating the required fundamental legal, social, and administrative changes in the structure of society. Such changes have to do with the capacity of a society to change its basic nature, whereas those which can be consigned to the market place often deal with the fine adjustment of society within the constraints of a given technological, educational, and institutional setting.

The problems that the market cannot settle are the kinds of problems about which men fight, sometimes ignobly, seeking the self-interests of groups, and sometimes nobly, seeking the capacity to develop superior societies. In any event, these problems are so important, so relevant, and so numerous that they are worthy of the best attention of whatever research and administrative personnel are available. Because of their four fundamental characteristics or difficult aspects, the problems that the market cannot handle are generally the kinds of problems which pure economists qua disciplinarians handle poorly despite the high payoff for working on them.

The *first* of these characteristics or difficulties is encountered when the economist is asked to help recommend an action to be taken by some agency or individual who is faced only with alternatives that impose considerable damage or some person or group of persons in order to confer benefits on another person or group of persons.

The *second* difficulty is encountered when the economist is asked to help with a problem involving a variety of goods being sought and bads being avoided.[2] The variety of goods and bads involved in a particular problem often creates great difficulty for an investigator or decision maker trying to find a common denominator in terms of which these goods and bads can be expressed. Utils, dollars and cents, pounds and pence, or GDP and GNP seem woefully inadequate as common denominators of welfare when questions of political and economic control by minority groups, political parties, and disadvantaged farm groups have created tensions which threaten the stability of society.

The *third* difficulty is encountered by the economist who works in various contexts of risk or uncertainty. Under these conditions he does not know whether it is appropriate to maximize the present value of the future stream of expected net returns from alternative actions, or whether it would be more appropriate to minimize or satisfice, vote, toss a coin, or employ a dictator.[3]

Still further, many of the problems which must be handled outside the market involve the processes of technological change, improvement of the human agent, and institutional

---

[2] The words *good(s)* and *bad(s)* are used throughout the text with the meaning specified in the glossary on page 12.

[3] Kenneth J. Arrow, *Social Choice and Individual Values* (New York: John Wiley & Sons, Inc., 1951).

change. A moment's reflection on this point will raise questions about whether the mathematically necessary, second-order conditions are met for the existence of an optimum to use in selecting the right action among identifiable alternative actions. (The mathematically required second-order conditions ensure that actions can be arranged in an order of decreasing net advantages.) If these conditions are not met, the solver of practical problems cannot define an optimum even if he (1) has a common denominator that enables him to define solutions as the maximum difference between the goods and bads involved; (2) can measure these goods and bads in an interpersonally valid manner; and (3) knows that it would be appropriate, if he could, to maximize the present value (at some appropriate interest rate) of the future expected difference between the goods and bads.

The *fourth* difficulty, then, is that economists and others have not yet established anything like the laws of diminishing returns and diminishing utility that they can apply to the processes of (1) inventing and discovering new technology, (2) inventing and creating new institutional arrangements, or, for that matter, (3) improving human nature. Although it may very well be possible to establish something corresponding to the law of diminishing returns, utilities, or proportionality in these three areas, it has not yet been done.

Eventually solutions of practical problems take the form of decisions on the part of some person, group, or agency that determine the right action to take among a set of alternatives. Researchers working on these problems are not always required to make the actual decision and advocate the selected right action. They are, however, expected to produce results which, at the least, will be helpful to those who will actually make and execute the decision.

Chapter 9 of this book discusses recent fundamental developments in mathematical simulation and systems analysis. These developments are most useful in doing research on the normative and decision-making aspects of problem-solving research. Thus, the next few paragraphs and pages will introduce the reader to these techniques so that he will be able to see how economic researchers use them in less formal, more primitive ways prior to using them in a more formal, sophisticated way.

We have noted four fundamental difficulties in defining

right actions, none of which is present for economists when they define a right action as one which maximizes profits or net utility. However, practicing agricultural economists have sometimes sensed and often recognized the existence of these difficulties and have not always engaged in maximization— not initially at least. In such instances, agricultural economists, in studying choices among alternative policies, programs, and projects or solutions, have long used projections as possible solutions to the problems that were similarly sensitive arising with the development of U.S. agriculture. For instance, during the early months of World War II, the former Bureau of Agricultural Economics conducted many research exercises in which multidisciplinary teams of individuals constructed projections through time of the consequences of following alternative methods of placing price ceilings on agricultural products, alternative ways of rationing inputs and taxing agriculture, and alternative programs for drafting and deferring farm youth. The problems which were then being met and solved involved the same basic difficulties mentioned above. Fortunately, the researchers, administrators, and congressmen were not so foolish as to ask the researchers to find an optimum solution by themselves. Instead, the administrators or congressmen asked researchers to estimate or project the consequences through time of following alternative possible solutions and then interacted with researchers in handling the four difficulties as a prelude to possible maximization.

In the chapters to follow we shall note many instances in which researchers have projected the consequences through time of alternative policies. Such projections are, in actuality, informal simulations and systems analyses and, as such, are precursors of modern mathematical analyses and simulations.

The projected consequences of alternative policies and programs that are considered in the following chapters have to do with conditions, situations, or things of practical significance. As such estimates were produced, both normative and non-normative information improved, the picture of open alternatives was clarified and amplified, and administrators, congressmen, and even the researchers began to envision ways of improving the alternatives under consideration. The projections, too, were continually examined and checked for consistency with each other and with experience. When the projections did not pass the tests of clarity they had to be redone. Then they were checked for workability first by experienced administrators and later by actual application. Thus, a fairly high degree of objectivity was maintained with respect to both the normative and non-normative facts and projections. But the process did not stop there. Decision rules were also examined and studied by the entire team of inter-disciplinary researchers, administrators, and lawmakers. In some instances, this team weighed one or more undesired consequences against one or more desired ones to come to evaluative conclusions, decisions, and a choice among alternatives.

This process differs significantly from the process of defining optima commonly employed by economists. For one thing, the abstract theoretical formation employed by economists who are seeking maxima is almost unbelievably rigorous and, perhaps, unrealistic. For instance, their formulation sometimes uses utils as the common denominator in finding optima for consumers and a monetary unit in finding optima for producers, while problems of interpersonal validity in utility measures are unrealistically but rigorously ruled out by the preclusion of non-Pareto-better adjustments (see page 21), and while the laws of diminishing productivity and utility ensure the existence of the necessary second-order conditions. Even the problem of selecting an appropriate decision-making rule is avoided in the typical optimizing problem by explicitly or implicitly assuming perfect knowledge and foresight and thereby making it unnecessary to do anything but maximize the difference between good (utility or income) and bad (disutility or expenses) in order to define the best levels of production or consumption.

A Glossary of Important Terms

We have suggested that one of our purposes in this book is to clarify the meanings of some important concepts used by agricultural economists. In order to assist the reader in understanding some of the key words in the present study, we shall, at the outset, provide him with a kind of philosophic dictionary in which the terms fall in the order of their complexity.

Concept: we use this term to mean either a word or a sentence that has a specifiable meaning.

Belief: the meaning of a concept about the nature of reality. This reality will include values. There are not only non-normative beliefs related to descriptive states of affairs, past, present or future, but also normative beliefs which include values in all senses that this word is used throughout the present book. In actual occurrence beliefs include psychological imagery and symbolic expression, but these are not relevant to our present concern.[4]

Fact: the meaning of a concept of what is, what has been, or what will be.

A fact concept: a word or sentence which has as its meaning an actual state of affairs, past, present, or future.

Value or normative belief: the meaning of a concept of the goodness or badness per se of a condition, situation, or thing. A *value concept* is a word or sentence which has as its meaning the goodness or badness per se of a condition, situation, or thing.

Instrumental value: the meaning of a concept of goodness or badness insofar as it is derived from more basic values. For example, the concept "it is good for man to have money" may be based on the more basic value concept that "it is good for a man to be able to provide food and shelter for his family."

More basic value: this contrasts with an instrumental value in that it is a good for the sake of which instrumental values are actualized. More basic values may ordinarily be actualized by a number of different instrumental values. In our example above, providing food and shelter for a family might be realized by means other than having money. It should be noted that (1) an instrumental value detached from the more basic value with which it is connected may very well be bad in the sense discussed below; and (2) still more basic values, such as that of life itself, may make the values of food and shelter, which are more basic than money, into instrumental values.

An action: an attempt to establish or attain a specific condition.

A goal: a condition not yet established or attained which some entity is trying or could try to attain.

A right action or goal: an action or goal determined to be best in view of the non-normative and normative beliefs involved, where *best* means that which maximizes human interests and purposes as indicated by the value concepts involved.

A wrong action or goal: an action or goal other than the right action or goal.

---

[4] Leonard, *Principles of Right Reason*, pp. 45-53.

Good and bad: adjectives used to modify the word *value*. A good value exists when a condition, situation, or thing contributes to the attainment of human interests and purposes. Conversely, a bad value exists when a situation, condition, or thing frustrates or detracts from the attainment of human interests and purposes.

Right and wrong: adjectives which will be used to modify the words *action* and *goal* or choices and decisions about actions and goals.

True and false: words applied to sentences when we suppose them to express beliefs which do or do not conform to reality.

Objectivity: a quality applied to an investigator or concept. An investigator is regarded as ideally objective if he is unbiased, fair, impartial, and accurate in the sense that he is willing to subject his concepts, both normative and non-normative, to tests as to their objectivity. A concept is regarded as objective if it has thus far passed the tests of (1) logical consistency with previously accepted concepts and with other new concepts based on experience, (2) clarity, and (3) workability.

Kinds of knowledge:

    I. Nonprescriptive (never practical)
       A. Abstract (theoretical)
          1. Normative (about good and bad)
          2. Non-normative
       B. Descriptive
          1. Normative (about good and bad)
          2. Non-normative

    II. Prescriptive (about right and wrong acts and goals and always both normative and non-normative)
       A. Abstract (theoretical)
       B. Descriptive (always practical)

The distinction between descriptive and prescriptive knowledge is crucial in a consideration of applied ethics. Much of the positivistic and pragmatic philosophy of the twentieth century has failed to provide a philosophical basis for reasonable action because such philosophies exclude from the field of legitimate knowledge types of knowledge used by men of action. The positivist excludes the possibility of normative knowledge either about what is good or bad or about what is right or wrong. This means that the decision maker cannot make judgments which are at one and the same time cognitively legitimate, normative, and descriptive of the real world. Descriptive knowledge about what is good and bad and, thus, about what is right and wrong is disallowed. The pragmatists on the other hand, disallow *all* nonprescriptive knowledge because their philosophy relates all knowledge to problem solving and, hence, conceives of knowledge as a mixture of normative and non-normative components. Thus, pragmatism denounces any theorist who affirms his belief in a purely nonprescriptive proposition whether this proposition is abstract or descriptive. Both of these philosophies, then, are exclusive in a regrettable way. As we discuss decision making in action, we shall note that descriptive knowledge about what is good and bad or right and wrong is present when decisions are made, but that it is possible to have nonprescriptive knowledge as well. Some recent ethical theorists have suggested that moral philosophers need to pay close attention to the actual occasions in which moral judgments are made. They contend that on such occasions most ethical theories turn out to be overly simplistic. We applaud this new look at ethical theory but argue that in giving attention to such occasions the theoretical orientation of the decision maker must be kᴖpt in mind. To paraphrase Immanuel Kant, ethical theories viewed separately from ethical occasions are empty, but ethical occasions viewed separately from ethical theories are blind.

The above vocabulary now permits us to discuss more succinctly both the optimizing solutions commonly reached by economists and the work of economists on problems that do not meet the necessary conditions for application of the static economizing principles.

The high-profit points in static production economies define a right action in terms of the combination of inputs to use and of output to attain. The same is true of the utility maximizing points of consumption economies.

Defining the right action is much more difficult, however, when the assumptions of static economic principles are not met, i.e., when (1) an appropriate common denominator is not readily available, (2) relevant possible courses of action include non-Pareto-better alternatives, (3) the second-order conditions for the existence of an optimum are not guaranteed, and (4) the appropriate decision-making rule is unknown. The research process must then include attempts to establish the four conditions that we have just listed. Until these conditions are established, the right (as defined above), is indeterminate. Finding common denominators of value, choosing appropriate decision-making rules, attaining interpersonally valid welfare measures, and ranking actions so as to establish the second-order conditions for locating the maximum difference between good and bad also presume an ability to work with the normative as well as the non-normative.

Philosophers have many conflicting notions about the possibility of working objectively with normative information. Agricultural economists in general often adhere to one or more of these philosophic positions as a matter of accidental past contact with some particular writing, philosopher, or professor. Thus, in order to see how agricultural economists have used philosophy, it will be helpful to classify and describe five philosophical positions by which they have been influenced. Such a classification and description will permit the reader to identify these five positions as he proceeds through the case studies in the chapters that follow. Because the purpose of the case studies is to provide a basis for drawing conclusions about the relevance of different philosophic positions, this preliminary discussion will describe these positions rather than evaluate them. An evaluation will be deferred until the final chapter.

Five Philosophic Positions

Because the five positions considered here spring out of the activities of economists and agricultural economists, not the activities of philosophers, they are not identified exactly as they would be in philosophic literature.[5] However, most of the positions in philosophy having to do with the nature of inquiry (both non-normative and normative) turn out to be subcategories under the five general positions to be described herein. Whether any philosophers actually have put forward these positions is a historical question that does not concern us. These positions might be regarded as ideal types rather than historical.

The five general positions to be considered can be labeled positivism, outright normativism, conditional normativism, pragmatism, and existentialism. Three of these five positions, namely positivism, conditional normativism, and pragmatism, are held to a greater or lesser degree by large numbers of agricultural economists. The fourth position, outright normativism, is less widely adhered to and is often criticized by modern agricultural economists and others as unscientific and subjective. The criticisms leveled at outright normativism by agricultural economists make it necessary to discuss it as one

---

5 Glenn L. Johnson, "Value Problems in Farm Management," *Journal of Agricultural Economics,* XIV (June 1960); "Stress on Production Economics," *Australian Journal of Agricultural Economics,* VII (June 1963).

of the broad philosophic positions commonly encountered among agricultural economists, even if few agricultural economists would endorse it or knowingly employ it. The fifth, existentialism, has always been of practical though largely unrecognized importance and, in the future, may be of increasing formal importance.

Positivism

Of the five broad philosophic positions to be discussed in this chapter, positivism is the one clearly recognized as a separate position by philosophers as well as by agricultural economists. D. D. Runes' *Dictionary of Philosophy—Ancient-Medieval-Modern*[6] contains the following description of positivism:

> [Positivism was] first associated with the doctrine of Auguste Comte that the highest form of knowledge is simply description, presumably of the sensory phenomena. The doctrine was based on the evolutionary "law of three stages" believed by Comte to have been discovered by him in 1822 but anticipated by Turgot in 1750. The three stages were the *theological*, in which anthropomorphic wills were resorted to, in order to explain natural events; the *metaphysical*, in which these wills were depersonalized and became forces and essences; and finally, the *positive*. It should be noted that the positivistic description was supposed to result in mathematical formulas, not in introspective psychology.

Positivism is closely related to what is sometimes called scientific empiricism. Scientific empiricism originated in logical positivism. Runes' *Dictionary* indicates that scientific empiricism and positivism evolved in three stages:

1. The older empiricism and positivism, especially that of Hume, Mill, Mach

2. Methodology of empirical science as developed by scientists since about the middle of the nineteenth century, e.g., Helmholtz, Mach, Poincare, Duhem, Boltzmann, Einstein

3. Symbolic logic and logical analysis of languages developed, especially by Frege, Whitehead and Russell, and Wittgenstein

---

6 (Totowa, N.J.: Littlefield, Adams and Co., 1961), p. 243.

"Russell," says Runes', "was the first to combine these three trends and therefore had an especially strong influence. . . . The views developed in the Vienna Circle have been called *logical positivism* . . . ; many members now prefer the term 'Logical Empiricism.' "[7]

Scientific empiricism helped logical empiricism find support in all of the major countries of the West and in a number of journals such as the *Journal of Unified Science* and the *Encyclopedia of Unified Science.* International congresses on the unity of science took place in the period 1934-41.

What primarily concerns us about positivism is its denial that knowledge of normative matters qua normative matters is possible. Recalling the definition we gave earlier of value as "the meaning of a concept of the goodness or badness per se of a condition, situation, or thing," the positivist would say that such values have no place in reality. According to positivism, a value concept as we defined it would be a meaningless set of marks and not really a concept at all. The impressive contributions that positivists made in the philosophy of science and logic caused many economists and agricultural economists to adopt the positivists' negative attitude toward ethics. This effect on economics is apparent in such literature as Milton Friedman's *Essays on Positive Economics*[8] and S. V. Ciriacy-Wantrup's article in the *Journal of Farm Economics*[9] entitled, "Policy Considerations in Farm Management Research in the Decade Ahead."

An early form of positivism in U.S. agricultural economics grew out of the adherence of the Cornellian School to Karl Pearson's *Grammar of Science.* Data on the operation of farm businesses were kept, not for the specific purpose of solving any immediate practical problem but, instead, to be able to describe how farm businesses were operated. The fact that such data later turned out to be moderately useful in solving a wide range of problems depending for their definition on normativistic concepts does not detract from the fact that farm records and surveys produce a positivistic kind of data. Generally speaking, the early efforts in farm management were purely positivistic in contradistinction to logically posi-

---

7 *Ibid.*, p. 285.
8 (Chicago: University of Chicago Press, 1953).
9 XXXVIII (Dec. 1956), pp. 1301 f.

tivistic. Pure positivism does not involve interpretation of facts with the use of theoretical relationships not directly observable. Logical positivism on the other hand, involves the use of theoretical constructs (often only useful fictions) to interpret facts. Currently, considerable attention is being paid in certain agricultural economics circles to the positivistic works of Karl R. Popper.[10]

Logical positivism, growing out of the work of the Vienna Circle, has had strong support on the Continent and at Cambridge in England. Logical positivism, as indicated above, involves the use of theoretical constructs to interpret observations of particular events. Both pure positivism and logical positivism limit objective knowledge to what can be observed, however. In addition to avoiding normative concepts, positivists avoid concepts involving purpose, force, and cause in the belief that such events are not observable and, hence, neither verifiable nor refutable.[11] They argue, for example, that the statement "water wants to run down hill" is no more refutable or verifiable than the statement "water runs down hill." Quite to the contrary, they argue that the first statement involves the attribution of animal characteristics to inanimate substances, that such projection retards the acquisition of positive knowledge and, further, that such contrary-to-fact procedures interfere with the objectivity of inquiry. They also reject the use of value or purpose as explanation, arguing that it is circular to say that a man does so-and-so because he wants to do so-and-so. The positivists would say that the only observable evidence that he wants to do so-and-so is that he does so-and-so. Such arguments are regarded as teleological and tautological and of no value.

Substantial elements of positivism are to be found in such economic literature as Lionel Robbins' *The Nature and Significance of Economic Science*[12] and Frank Knight's *History*

---

10 *The Logic of Scientific Discovery*, Torch Books Series (New York: Harper and Row, Publishers, 1965).

11 The argument that a proposition must be verifiable in order to be meaningful was later given up for obvious reasons. No universal generalization was verifiable, yet positivists wanted to allow scientific laws to be accepted as meaningful. Confirmability was, for a time, substituted for verifiability, but even using this as a criterion of meaning has been shown by Carl Hempel and others to be unsatisfactory.

12 (London: Macmillan & Co., Ltd., 1946).

and Method of Economics.[13] Strong criticisms have been offered by Kenneth Parsons[14] and others, particularly the institutionalists.

Outright normativism

Despite its current disrepute, outright normativism has historically played an important role in both general economics and agricultural economics. By outright normativism we mean attempts to answer questions about goodness and badness per se independently of answers to non-normative questions about what has been, what is, or what will be. Although independent answering of questions about the nature of goodness and badness does not necessarily preclude attempts to answer non-normative questions about what has been, is, or will be, some extreme normativists might preclude descriptive knowledge in a manner similar to the positivists' exclusion of normative investigation.

One of the early attempts on the part of economists to answer questions about goodness and badness per se was Adam Smith's *Theory of Moral Sentiments* (1759). In the fields of economics and philosophic value theory, which have common origins (the former also being part of the latter in some senses), one of the important normative positions is hedonism—that is, the identification of goodness with pleasure and badness with pain. Hedonistic utilitarianism, which maximizes the difference between goodness and badness (pain and pleasure) in any situation in which an individual happens to find himself, is commonly found in the early history of economics and agricultural economics. Noneconomists perhaps allege that hedonistic utilitarianism is more common among modern economists and agricultural economists than is the case. Some outright normativists are intuitionists, arguing that man knows intuitively what is good and what is bad. Other outright normativists can be called naturalists, saying that goodness and badness are characteristics of the natural world and are knowable in the same way that

---

13 (Chicago: University of Chicago Press, 1956).

14 "The Value Problem in Agricultural Policy," *Agricultural Adjustment Problems in a Growing Society*, ed. by E. O. Heady, *et al.* (Ames, Iowa: Iowa State College Press, 1958).

other phenomena of the natural world are knowable, i.e., as a result of logical inquiry on the basis of experience. Still other outright normativists argue that knowledge of goodness and badness is obtainable by revelation and by reading Holy Scripture.

The increased productivity of the physical and social sciences brought about by positivism has tended to cast a veil of suspicion over all attempts of social scientists to answer questions of goodness and badness per se. Social science investigators, as a result, have tended to confine their scientific endeavors to attempts to answer non-normative questions about the social processes. In effect, this has driven these investigators toward the camp of the positivists.

Conditional normativism

The field of agricultural economics, in sharp contrast to general economics, is expected to be oriented toward the solution of practical problems. Although they tend to be positivists, researchers in agricultural economics would have difficulty in defining and solving problems without abandoning their positivism. Yet the importance of positivism, with its claim to be *the* philosophy of science, has dictated that practical problem-solving agricultural economists pay attention to it. Positivism's claim that nothing objective can be known about purpose, values, and cause has tended to make agricultural economists wary about attempting to answer such questions. Yet agricultural economists have been forced by the practical nature of their work to take values into account. This impact of positivism upon the philosophic thought of agricultural economists concerning the nature of inquiry has been further enforced by the ethics of Western societies, which emphasizes subjective individualism and personal freedom and looks with suspicion on those who believe one can gain *knowledge* of values. To have knowledge of values suggests the subordination of the individual and his freedom to some universal principle. Such opposition to outright normativism has been particularly strong in the United States, where agricultural economics has reached its fullest development.

A reasonable way was needed for researchers in agricultural economics to accommodate themselves to the conflict between the *claims* of positivism, individualism, and personal freedom and their *responsibility to solve problems*. Agricultural economists could compromise by regarding it as their duty to help decision-making units attain what the decision-making unit wanted to attain without trying to answer questions about what should be attained or, more fundamentally, what is good and bad per se. Methodologically, this amounts to assuming or taking as given a set of normative concepts about the goodness and badness of situations, conditions, and things and then seeking ways to maximize the differences between the goods and bads as a solution to any particular problem. This methodological procedure makes it possible for the investigator to proceed positivistically in answering factual questions without addressing himself to questions of goodness and badness in reaching a solution to any problem so defined. The assumed or given ends in the situation have the practical advantage of permitting the investigator to define more completely the problems that he is going to solve. This general approach in agricultural economics is referred to in this book as *conditional normativism*.

In the field of agricultural economics, John D. Black and his followers were early conditional normativists. Earl Heady has also adhered to this position. So have some of the prominent agricultural economists at the University of Chicago. The agricultural economist who is a co-author of this book has done and still does a considerable amount of conditionally normative research work. Much of the research work done in the Division of Statistical and Historical Research of the former Bureau of Agricultural Economics in the Department of Agriculture was conditionally normative, although there was a period in the late 1930s when a considerable amount of research tending to outright normativism was done.

Both conditional normativism and outright normativism have been criticized by Kenneth Parsons.[15] Difficulties encountered by the outright normativists in the Department of Agriculture in dealing with Congress further strengthened the case of positivism against outright normativism.

---

15 *Ibid.*

Agricultural economists have not always recognized the arguments of Vilfredo Pareto (further developed by J. R. Hicks) about the lack of interpersonal comparability of utility measurements. Pareto, bowing in part to positivistic ideas, recognized that great difficulties attend attempts to say whether a bad imposed by a public choice on one individual in order to confer a good upon another represents an absolute magnitude greater than the good imposed upon the other. His recognition of this basic problem of measurement led to the inconsistency of defining certain adjustments as increasing welfare while refusing to judge whether or not welfare was increased in other instances. Adjustments which make one or more people better off without making anyone worse off were regarded as increasing welfare. These welfare-increasing adjustments were referred to as Pareto-better adjustments. Judgment was reserved if anyone was made worse off on the grounds that it is impossible to measure the bads conferred upon that person in terms comparable with the goods conferred upon another.

Pragmatism

The pragmatism of Charles Sanders Peirce found staunch developmental support from John Dewey and George Mead. John R. Commons, in turn, based his methodologies for institutional economics upon John Dewey's pragmatism. John R. Commons' institutionalism, which flowered at the University of Wisconsin, had its impact in turn upon the very strong agricultural economics school developing there. Thus, Peirce's and Dewey's pragmatism was transferred into agricultural economics via Commons' institutionalism. Wisconsin's land economics, of the institutional variety, has spread throughout the profession, with its most effective current expositor being perhaps Kenneth Parsons. Many agricultural economists working on institutional problems having to do with land tenure and land reforms still follow the pragmatic institutionalist tradition of Wisconsin.

There are two characteristics of pragmatism that distinguish it from the other three positions. Pragmatism is based upon two metaphysical presuppositions. The first is that the values of means and ends are interdependent, i.e., that the value of the means depends upon the value of that which it can be used to attain, and that the value of that which is attained depends upon the value of that which must be sacrificed in order to attain it. This metaphysical presupposition implies that normative and non-normative concepts are interdependent for, it is argued, one observes and develops concepts about that which he values either positively or negatively and then forms non-normative concepts about that which has importance to him in attaining goods and avoiding bads. The second presupposition of pragmatism is that workability is a valid criterion for determining the acceptability of the interdependent normative and non-normative concepts generated by the pragmatic approach to inquiry.

Pragmatic researchers in agricultural economics have been primarily on the American side of the Atlantic, whereas the force of logical positivism and the Vienna Circle has been strongly felt on both sides. It was in America that Dewey's pragmatism had its great effect on public education, which helped establish its place in the methodology of agricultural economics research despite the heavy inroads positivism had made upon methodology in the social sciences.

Existentialism

Recently, in Europe as well as in North America, existentialism has become important in universities. Beginning with the proposition that one's existence is the one indisputable fact he has, existentialism places great importance on the establishment of self-identity by individuals. It thereby contrasts sharply with the positivist's interest in the non-normative characteristics of things, conditions, and situations and with the normativist's interest in the goodness and badness of conditions, situations, and things. The existentialist emphasis is on the individual and on the identity of individuals—on existence rather than on the essences of things, situations, and conditions. The importance of establishing identity, in turn, elevates the importance of freedom to existentialists. To some of them, knowledge, both normative and non-normative, is a source of greater freedom for the individual because it helps him to establish his identity by making better choices over a wider range of alternatives. By contrast, in a special and, some might say, perverted extreme form of lay existentialism, logic and experience or observation are viewed as constraints on the freedom of an individual to establish self-identity. For example, all of us are acquainted with certain people including, unfortunately, some faculty members who are so concerned with personal and academic freedom that neither logic nor appeal to experience is permitted to interfere with their quest for freedom and who lose their freedom by ignoring logic and experience.[16] The consequences of existentialism are a greater emphasis on problems of people and on action to solve those problems and a lesser emphasis on knowledge about the essences of conditions, situations, and things.

Historically, and in practice, existentialist ideas have been important in agricultural economics, particularly in policy, farm and rural business management, advising, and consulting work. Land grant philosophy embodies individualistic ideas that have been expressed by agricultural economists (and others) in their extension work and teaching and in their emphasis on problems. However, more formal existentialist ideas are just now becoming influential, although they are rarely found in research methodology courses and project proposals.

Is Agricultural Economics Dead?

In addition to the widespread discussion of whether or not God is dead, there is significant, although less important, current discussion of whether or not agricultural economics is dead. At a recent meeting, Roger Gray presented a paper entitled, "Agricultural Economics: an Orientation for the 70's." He used an allegory that likened farmers to prairie dogs, which the U.S. Department of Interior is trying to exterminate, and agricultural economists to black-footed ferrets, an endangered species which the Department of Interior is trying to perpetuate but which feeds on the prairie dogs

---

16 This was discussed by Glenn L. Johnson in "The Role of the University and Its Economists in Economic Development" (presented as the J. S. McLean Visiting Professor Lecture, University of Guelph, Ontario, March 23, 1970, Publication No. AE-70/2), p. 9.

that are being exterminated. The question Gray posed was whether or not there are, in fact, any true black-footed ferrets left, and whether they ever do anything for, as contrasted to on, prairie dogs. It is our contention that agricultural economists have done much for farmers and others and that they will and should be expected to continue to do so as they attack (1) agricultural development problems at home and overseas; (2) problems of environmental quality; (3) poverty problems; (4) problems of racial equality; (5) nutritional deficiencies; (6) deficiencies in rural public services; and (7) the problem of finding a more appropriate combination of public and private controls over agricultural investments and production. However, the question of whether or not agricultural economics is dead is not very pertinent for this book. Whether agricultural economics has solved all of the problems in its domain and is now dying, and whether the problems with which agricultural economists can assist have disappeared are not the concern of this book. Instead, we are concerned here with the generally useful lessons that can be gained from the highly productive experiences which agricultural economists have had in working on practical problems.

Conclusions

It is hoped that the above discussion, glossary, and description of various philosophical positions will help indicate how value studies can contribute to the solution of selected human problems. Our approach, as is obvious from a glance at the table of contents, is both descriptive and philosophic. An examination and analysis of how certain problems have been solved in the past will serve to make explicit certain assumptions, procedures, and difficulties which may be involved in using the results of value studies to solve public problems. Our analysis will lead to suggestions which, it is hoped, will increase the contribution that normative studies can make to the solution of problems encountered by agricultural economists. The case study problems range from international relations to the selection of a sampling size in economic research. We shall be examining the various philosophical positions and related methodologies actually employed in these cases. In addition, we shall suggest ways in which such choices and decisions could have been improved had they not been constrained by inappropriate philosophies and consequent methodologies.

In the chapter on Thailand we see one government attempting to help another in formulating a better program of economic development. The selection on the Tennessee Valley Authority illustrates some of the problems that arise when the federal government attempts to improve economic conditions in a local geographical area, and the chapter on the Sleeping Bear Dunes discusses the federal government's involvement in developing land for recreational use. In the chapter on pickles we see the sort of research that can be useful in the relations between government and agriculture and the improvements in an industry that can result from adequate knowledge of the problems involved. In order to show the relevance of our method to the activities of a smaller group, we consider in chapter 7 the problems involved in developing a long-run plan for a department of agricultural economics.

Chapters 8 and 9 describe problems in rural development in the African nation of Nigeria. Chapter 10 deals with some of the methodological problems that social scientists encounter in selecting a sample size. The final chapter presents a summary of the decision-making process which has been illustrated in the earlier chapters and makes some philosophical generalizations growing out of the cases studied. This exploration and consideration of a wide range of topics and a variety of problems faced by groups of different sizes and compositions should appeal to readers with different interests and show the general usefulness of the principles with which we are concerned.

The Problems of Improving
11 | U.S. Military and Economic
Aid to Thailand

In the summer of 1961, a U.S. Department of State team was sent to Thailand to evaluate and recommend improvements in the entire U.S. economic and military aid program to that country in view of the newly developed United States' foreign aid policy. The evaluations were to be made from the point of view of the United States, and the recommendations were to be made to the U.S. government.

The team included Howard Bowen, then the president of Grinnell College and later president of the University of Iowa; Sherwood Fine, Sidney Taubenblatt, and John Blumgart, all of the International Cooperation Agency; Henry Billingsley, a governmental consultant in various continuing capacities as a political scientist who had had experience with NATO; Robert Hirschberg, a Taiwan U.S. Operations Mission (USOM) planning officer; and Glenn Johnson, professor of agricultural economics at Michigan State University.

Broad Criteria
of the U.S. Foreign Aid Policy

The newly developed U.S. foreign aid policy had many key objectives. These objectives, as stated and developed by President John Kennedy's task force on economic development, were (1) the acceleration of economic and social development in the underdeveloped areas of the world; (2) an emphasis on aid for long-run development as distinct from short-run political objectives; (3) the tailoring of aid to the needs of each country; (4) integrated and comprehensive long-run planning; (5) the stimulation of self-help; (6) an

26

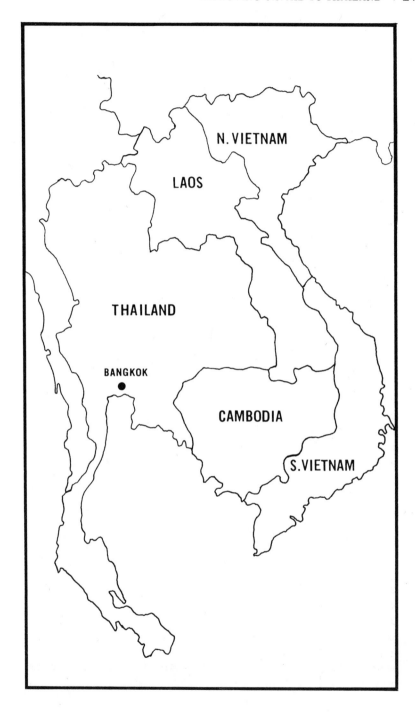

increasing emphasis on loans as distinct from grants; (7) the encouragement of coordinated multilateral assistance; (8) a unified administration of United States' aid: (9) the encouragement of foreign investment by American private enterprise; (10) the use of surplus food; and (11) research in economic and social development.

In addition, it was understood that general and, in many cases, long-standing United States' policies required that, in order not to infringe on Thai sovereignty, U.S. efforts be conceived of as a response to and in support of plans originating in and supported by the recipient countries and that the United States assist Thailand in maintaining its independence and sovereignty against aggression, infiltration, insurgency, and subversion to protect the integrity of its existing borders. Such policies implied a willingness on the part of the United States to promote the economic development of truly neutral as well as prowestern governments. On the other hand, these policies did not imply a willingness to aid the development of any procommunist economy or any admittedly communist government; such aid would only help adherents of expansionist communism interfere with the independence and the right to self-determination of other nations that the United States might help both in maintaining their independence and in developing their nation.

The team was also to be aware of the following admonitions of the presidential task force: (1) "Since almost any kind of assistance can be used in any undeveloped country and since the resources of the developed world to supply such assistance are limited, it is extremely important that the country itself, as well as those assisting it, form at each stage of the process a clear judgment as to what are the most critical bottlenecks to economic and social development and, therefore, what kinds of assistance deserve priority"; and (2) "to insist on a level of performance and programming and budgeting completely beyond the capabilities of the recipient country would result in frustration of the basic objectives of our development assistance to encourage more rapid growth."

In view of what was possible in the existing international and Thai situations, the purpose of the team's evaluation was to maximize some combination of the following and other goods:

1. Long-run economic growth in Thailand
2. Efficiency in the use of resources from
   a. The United States
   b. Thailand
   c. Other countries and agencies
3. The ability of Thailand and other nations to exercise their right to self-determination and independence

However, the team did not perceive its task to be confined to only these goods.

Procedures Followed by the Team

In general, the team followed a common-sense, subject-matter approach. Some members, at least, openly espoused work to establish value concepts and began to explore and extend the meaning of the evaluative criteria furnished by the president's task force. Each man was expected to, and did, mobilize non-normative information in his specialty, i.e., agriculture, military alliances, education, economic planning, public investments, or public administration.

The process of developing and extending both normative and non-normative concepts was made easier by the attitude of both Thai and U.S. governmental officials who both found it politically advantageous to play up the team and its efforts. The Thai government welcomed the team members as official guests, while the U.S. ambassador placed all U.S. resources at the disposal of the team. This ready access to the official opinion, data, reports, and facilities of both the U.S. and Thai governments speeded up the process of extending and developing non-normative and normative concepts.

The team found it easy to hold conferences with scientists, military experts, educators, ministers in the Thai government, rising young Thai civil servants, Changwad (provincial) governors, and agricultural officers. The U.S. ambassador kept in close touch with members of the team and participated in relatively frequent seminars held to report on progress. After the team's initial conference with Prime Minister Sarit, the U.S. ambassador dealt with the prime minister as the necessity arose.

Although the Thai government extended its hospitality to include lodging, food, transportation, translators, and recreation, the team accepted these services only for trips away from Bangkok. The translators were able, young Thai civil servants. Use of these translators on trips to nearby Chang-wads and numerous extended trips to the northeast, north, and south enabled several team members to communicate closely with farmers, villagers, teachers, local governmental personnel, and especially with the competent, articulate translators themselves.

Over several years of cooperation with English speaking countries and international agencies, a considerable body of English literature has grown up concerning Thailand. Some of this literature deals with Thai administrative arrangements. Other literature consists of the reports of consulting teams and missions dealing with such subjects as public investments, farm credit, transportation, ground water exploration, and agricultural extension services. Like the consultations and trips discussed above, this literature provided the team with a basis for developing and extending both non-normative and normative concepts relevant for their evaluations and recommendations.

Another source of normative and non-normative concepts was the team itself. The team members had a wide and varying command over the normative and non-normative information pertinent to their own fields and to the work of the team as a whole. This information was used both directly and as consistency checks on the new concepts generated in consultation, reading, and traveling. Team members engaged in a continual seminar—at breakfast, while traveling, at lunch, at dinner, at scheduled discussion periods, in the evening, and even after retiring, until demand for sleep ended discussion. In these seminars, normative and non-normative concepts were interrelated. Internal inconsistencies were discovered and, if glaringly important, eliminated. In some cases, doubts prompted both non-normative and normative investigations as external checks. In many instances, the need for economy in the use of the team's time made it imperative that inconsistencies among non-normative as well as among normative concepts be tolerated.

Normative and non-normative inquiries were carried out simultaneously but not necessarily interdependently. Although team members often tried simultaneously to develop and extend both normative and non-normative concepts, answers to non-normative and normative questions were not treated as, and did not appear to be, necessarily interdependent.

The goodness of education, electrical power, more food, and sanitary facilities did not depend on answers to non-normative questions. In contrast to answers about the goodness of such items, however, the amounts of education, power, and food that were selected as goals to be attained were treated as dependent on answers to both non-normative and normative questions. For instance, it was agreed that it was wrong for excess population to move to cities to become part of an unemployed, poverty-stricken mass of urban dwellers. Similarly, it was agreed, after much discussion, that the accumulation of underemployed people on farms was also wrong. These concepts of wrongness, while independent of answers to non-normative questions, were nonetheless related to non-normative answers to questions about possibilities for urban industry, the effect of raising the minimum level of education from four to seven years, and the possible effects of birth control. Such answers indicated that industrialization, an increase in minimum educational levels, and birth control measures were appropriate elements of solutions to the problem of excess farm population.

It was important in these analytical seminars to determine the consequences, through time, of alternative policies and programs. In some instances, projections of likely consequences were made verbally. In other instances—for example, in devising repayment schedules for hydroelectric dams—projections were worked out carefully or borrowed from persons who had so worked them out. As the non-normative consequences of alternative courses of action became clear, so too did the normative consequences. Both researchers and investigators became better able to evaluate the total consequences of alternative actions.

Some Relevant Non-normative
Concepts about the Thai Economy

It was a judgment of the team that Thailand had potential in both agriculture and industry and that the future of the country lay in the balanced development of both. Further, it was judged that Thailand had a great potential for total growth.

The country was primarily agricultural, with as many as 85 percent of the people living on farms. Per capita, nonfarm incomes were low. In the Central Plain, the average of per capita farm incomes was above that of the north and northeast but below that of the rubber producing areas of the south. The farms were rather uniformly small.

Annual rates of population growth were in the neighborhood of 3 percent per annum. This rate of growth implied that as many as half a million new workers would be available each year for nonfarm employment. As a rough guess, perhaps 200,000 additional workers would have had to be absorbed each year into manufacturing and 300,000 into other urban occupations if sound economic growth were to occur. Some of the requirements for this growth were capital, entrepreneurial and managerial ability, and vocational skills.

Another requirement was the creation of a total atmosphere congenial to the development of enterprise, both domestic and foreign. Promising manufacturing industries included the processing of farm products, the manufacturing and distribution of farm supplies and equipment, and the manufacturing of light consumer goods. A scarcity of mineral products seemed to preclude major emphasis on heavy industry. It was anticipated that industrial development would have to be based on a myriad of small enterprises rather than on a few large ones.

Thailand's Problems and a Recommended Overall Pattern of U.S. Effort

The team determined that Thailand had serious problems in the areas of national security, natural resources, health, forestry, and fishing, but that the key obstacle to the country's development was the high growth rate of the population, especially of the rural population which constituted 85 percent of the total. Off-farm migration without off-farm employment opportunities led to urban poverty, slums, and degradation. The question of whether it was better for surplus people to remain on the land near families and food supplies rather than become part of an uprooted urban rabble was discussed seriously.

It was pointed out that some movement of people to the cities is desirable even in advance of industrial development, because the existence of an available labor supply already adjusted to urban life is itself favorable to industrial development. It was also pointed out repeatedly that the accumulation of surplus labor on small farms is an undesirable development from the standpoint of agricultural efficiency and productivity.

Although the team felt some preference for keeping people on farms in the absence of urban employment opportunities, it was pointed out that disguised rural unemployment and underemployment are not attractive prospects. They involve fragmentation of land holdings, deepening rural poverty, and political instability. The team's full realization of the badness of the existence of unemployed urban dwellers and underemployed rural dwellers pointed up the urgency of population control and the development of nonfarm employment opportunities.

These concepts of badness and goodness appeared to have as much objectivity—in terms of consistency, clarity (interpersonal transmittability), and workability in producing solutions—as concepts about present or future conditions in Thailand. The same line of thinking also pointed up the importance of education to increase the productivity of the surplus of people who will become available from Thai agriculture. The possibilities for birth control were discussed repeatedly. Since there are no religious inhibitions in Thai society regarding birth control, it was thought that the government might advantageously encourage voluntary family limitation.

Whatever the rate of population growth might turn out to be, the team determined that the solution of the employment problem would involve a judicious, *planned* combination of measures to achieve an orderly flow of people from rural to urban areas with steadily increasing urban employment opportunities. Among the needed measures would be encouragement of industrial development and education, especially business and vocational education.

Thus, it was concluded that U.S. efforts should be directed primarily toward the development of agriculture, industry, education, and economic planning in order to attain a balance between agricultural and industrial development and population growth. These four areas were regarded as the important keys to the future development of Thailand. Transportation, irrigation, and community development were regarded as closely related to and as part of agricultural development. This emphasis did not mean that power, natural resources, health, forestry, and fishing were not significant and should be overlooked. Instead, it was concluded that in the interest of consolidating the program the U.S. effort should be confined largely to the above-mentioned four areas.

The team produced specific recommendations pertaining to the problems that they perceived to be in the way of Thailand's development. These problems and the team's response to them are detailed in the following paragraphs.

The problem of decreasing the
threat to national security posed by
the communism of Laos and North Viet Nam

While the military recommendations for preserving the security of Thailand must remain classified as secret, it is worthwhile noting that military security increases with public and private investments in roads, dams, and education of people. It is also noteworthy that full-scale examination of the developmental problems of a country points up the overall shortage of resources for military and nonmilitary use.

The problem of inadequate
public resources for development

The team studied in detail the problem of inadequate public resources for development. Part of the solution to this problem was to be found in the Thai government's increased self-help efforts which took the form of increased taxation and increased revenue from state-owned enterprises.

The team also concluded that the government could obtain additional funds by borrowing from privately saved funds and from the central bank. They suggested that the inclusion of state enterprises within the regular government budget and the subjection of these budgets to regular procedures of audit and control would increase further the potential resources available for economic development within the country. It was recognized that increased taxation is not a clear gain in money available for economic development, because, obviously, the removal of funds from private hands by taxation does reduce the amount available for private investments in economic development.

Other self-help sources of developmental resources included (1) the facilitation of entry of foreign business and foreign capital, (2) the encouragement of private domestic investment, and (3) the removal of restraints on free enterprise and competition.

It was recognized that Thailand and the United States were joined in a partnership and that the shared objectives of this partnership were sustained economic development and military security for the people of Thailand. It was concluded that attaining these objectives was primarily the responsibility of the Thais, but that the United States could assist on a relatively small scale by providing moral support, technical assistance, and limited funds. It was pointed out that the executive branch of the U.S. government must account to Congress and the American people for expenditures on aid to Thailand and other countries and that it must seek a maximum return in economic development and military security for each dollar spent. It was recommended that U.S. aid be based on two additional conditions: sound conception and efficient execution of projects, both individually and as a part of a comprehensive long-range plan, and a significant financial and administrative effort by the Thai government, within reasonable limits of its capacity, for economic and social development. While it was not possible to reduce these conditions to measurable terms or to rigid formulas, it was judged appropriate and prudent for the U.S. government to urge that the Thai government make progress from year to year in removing obstacles to development and in providing positive conditions for development.

The problem of Thailand's low per capita income

The problem of low per capita incomes was attacked on a broad front with recommendations for U.S. aid and support in agriculture, in developing employment opportunities, in geographic redistribution of public investments, and in education—all of which are discussed under other headings herein. The problems arising out of the relationships between population growth and poverty, to be discussed in the next section, were not handled objectively by the team and, hence, not effectively.

The problem of a rate of population growth
in excess of Thailand's capacity to
provide remunerative employment

The problems created by a rate of population growth that exceeded the existing capacity to provide employment at socially acceptable rates of pay are the core of Thailand's general problem of economic development. The specific problems involved a projected tendency for unneeded people to accumulate on farms and a similar tendency for people to accumulate in cities as part of a poorly trained urban mass. Both tendencies are undesirable, leading, as they do, to projections of political instability, privation, and waste. Measures for handling such accumulation are presented in connection with agriculture, industrialization, and education (see the next three sections).

The obvious solution, population control, is not discussed elsewhere and must be discussed here. It seems fair to assert that members of the Thai study team failed to investigate objectively the normative and non-normative aspects of this possible solution to the problem. As used here, lack of objectivity on the part of team members means an unwillingness to subject either existing or alternative concepts to common tests to determine whether they should be rejected. Obviously, a lack of objectivity on the part of team members implies that the concepts (both normative and non-normative) which they did use may have been less objective than possible and desirable.

In general, team members felt that limitations on the birth rate would be instrumentally good as a means of reducing pressure for industrialization and increasing per capita income and average levels of vocational and academic attainment. However, team members did not emphasize these conclusions and thereby, unconsciously perhaps, avoided conflicts between these conclusions and the value then commonly held by many in the United States that birth control was bad, the evident high value which many Thai people place on large families and children, and the conviction held by some Thais that Thailand had to expand her population greatly to become a great Asiatic nation.

Had the team pressed their conclusions further, various non-normative concepts could have been examined in view of experiences elsewhere in the world. One of these is the belief, widely prevelant in Thailand, that there are ample land resources to support a greatly expanded population. Rejection of this belief would have raised the question of whether an expanded population would accept a still lower level of living, aggressively seek more land, or be able to succeed at industrialization and commercialization rapidly enough to take care of the expanding population. As it was, the team stuck to its own concepts, did not subject them to examination, and mildly expressed its conclusions.

Had the various non-normative and normative concepts relating to the advisability of birth control been subjected to careful examination, concepts, either old or new, might have emerged which could have been advanced boldly. These concepts might have acquired such standing through tests against experience for logical consistency, meaningfulness, and workability that they would have been widely acceptable. Such widespread acceptability would have greatly increased the relevance of the team's report.

The problem of Thailand's small, technologically retarded, inadequately serviced farms

The problem of Thailand's small, inadequate farms was attacked with a variety of recommendations having to do with developing new technology, new kinds and scale of farms, education, irrigation, roads, credit, and off-farm migration. Agriculture was recognized as a mainstay of the Thai economy for the foreseeable future and a principal source of income for the majority of the people.

Agricultural and industrial development were conceived of as being interdependent, with gains for one often accompanied by gains in the other. The team perceived that agricultural development would result in the provision of raw materials and skilled labor (skilled labor being dependent on proper education) for industry and that agricultural areas would, in turn, be a market for industrial products. It was accepted as factually true that agriculture could produce more food to supply the rapidly growing population for a number of generations, that it could produce more products for export, that it could produce raw materials for Thailand's expanding light industry, and that it could send to the cities a stream of trained, educated human beings to man the few factories and shops.

To achieve these goals, the team concluded that aid would be required from the United States and other sources and that even more self-help would be required on the part of the Thais, including additional private and public investments and the removal of institutional barriers to agricultural growth. It was recommended that the United States' efforts be directed to encouragement of (1) private investment in agriculture; (2) public investment in roads, irrigation, research, education, and other public services; and (3) the orderly transfer of people out of agriculture in synchronization with the rise in nonfarm employment opportunities.

The team felt that public investments and other efforts should be relatively greater in the northeast than in the other areas. This was in frank recognition of the military and political situation existing along the Laos border, of the unusually high rate of poverty among the rural people of this area, and of the need to decentralize public investment away from Bangkok.

The following means of encouraging private investment in agriculture were recommended: the reduction of price premiums and other export premiums and the substitution of charges for the use of irrigation water; the provision of better credit facilities; the reduction of marketing costs through improved transportation; the creation of better marketing institutions, possibly including cooperatives and the elimination of any monopoly or corruption that might exist; and the strengthening and improving of agricultural extension.

The team noted that research on farm management and reorganization, although urgently needed, was neglected by both Thais and the U.S. aid programs. Overall diversification of agricultural production was recommended. In selecting new products for expansion, attention was given to the need to earn and save foreign exchange, the need for industrial raw products, and the need for better incomes for farmers. The commodities recommended for the expansion of output included rice, rubber, corn, cassava, livestock (particularly eggs, poultry, and swine), cotton, sugar, jute, and kenaf.

The Thais were keenly aware of needs for irrigation and had a capable Royal Irrigation Department well staffed with engineers and technicians. It was recommended that foreign aid for irrigation be restricted to loans for large projects beyond Thailand's financial or technical capabilities. Irrigation water distribution facilities were so inadequate that full use of existing water supplies was prevented. The team noted a need for coordination of irrigation and road building. A serious need existed for research, both fundamental and applied, on farm business organizations and the appropriate use of agricultural land, particularly land in new settlement and irrigation projects.

Much more agricultural and general education was judged to be required for the development of efficient farmers and for converting the excess of farmers into productive workers for nonfarm employment.

It was recognized that transportation should have high priority in the development of the Thai farm economy. Inadequacies in transportation prevent the development of a specialized commercial agriculture by lowering prices received by farmers, raising prices paid by farmers, and blocking the communication of ideas. Secondary feeder roads were of particular importance in addition to an emphasis on main highways.

Little was known about the inland waterways system in Thailand, which transported about 80 percent of the nation's rice crop and moved a substantial amount of its timber products, as well as fruits, vegetables, building materials, and so forth, in the central plains area. The upland regions of the north, northeast, and the south were not served by inland waterways. The southern peninsula, however, was served by both ocean and rail transport.

The team members were convinced that rural people should share in the fruits of the economic development so avidly sought by both the Thai and United States' governments. They also reached the judgment that Thai farmers would have to move toward large, more commercial, and more technically advanced farm business to share in the fruits of such progress.

The problem of Thailand's low level of industrialization and lack of urban employment opportunities

The problems created by Thailand's low level of industrialization (only 15 percent of the people were urban) were regarded as crucial. The low level and rate of industrialization, together with the pressure of population on land, the rural poverty, and the high rate of population growth, required rapid acceleration of industrial growth. Industrial growth, as pointed out previously, has to be coordinated with agricultural growth and with the training and release of the people from agriculture for use in industry. Much was needed to promote private investment in industry in addition to public investments in transportation and power. The team made several recommendations toward this end:

1. The Thai government should make a clear and precise statement of policy as to their intentions regarding the future of state-owned enterprises.

2. A clear and precise statement should also be issued at the highest governmental levels to remove the existing doubts about what fields are open to future private investment.

3. Foreign investment benefits and procedures for granting aid should be increased in order to put Thailand on a competitive basis with Malaya and the Philippines.

4. The procedures, staff, and leadership of the institutions relating to industrial development—including business, education, training facilities, the Board of Investment, and the Industrial Finance Corporation—should be strengthened.

5. The long-deferred measures for increasing the rate of private domestic savings and capital promotion should be adopted.

6. A governmentally controlled industrial development

corporation, which would conduct feasibility surveys of possible areas for private investments and would encourage the investment of private capital in industries of promise, should be created.

The team felt that the implementation of these recommendations would need to be matched by a stepped-up program for foreign assistance that would include:

1. Reappraisal and reorganization of existing technical and vocational education programs to more fully meet the country's existing and future needs for skilled labor

2. Inauguration of an executive training program for management in private and public enterprises

3. Development, at one of the Bangkok universities, of an academic program in business administration tailored to Thailand's industrial and commercial structure

4. Strengthening of advisory assistance and staff training for the Industrial Finance Corporation

5. Provision of advisory assistance and staff training for the Board of Investment

6. Examination of the need for an industrial research center

7. Study of the problems and requirements of establishing industrial parks

8. Serious consideration, with the Thai government, of the creation of a private industrial development corporation that would conduct investment to encourage private capital to develop such sectors

The problem of inadequate educational facilities

The problem of inadequate educational facilities was examined directly, as well as in connection with the problems of low income, agricultural development, and industrialization already mentioned. The long-run objectives of the educational effort were to:

1. Raise the minimum number of years of schooling from four to seven by 1970 and to ten by 1980

2. Extend and improve both farm and nonfarm vocational education

3. Extend and improve teachers' training, including in-service and supplemental training for active teachers

4. Improve substantially the quality of the universities and establish one or more new universities in the provinces, particularly in the northeast

5. Conduct massive efforts in adult education, with special emphasis on the educational use of mass communications media

6. Conduct manpower studies and include projections to guide the planning of the educational programs

High priority was given to the training of teachers and to higher education. The study team rejected the assertion often made by certain Thai leaders that there was a surplus of educated people in Thailand and that these educated people would be a source of political instability.

The problem of an unsatisfactory environment
for private investment in industry and agriculture,
including, especially, rice and rubber production

The problem of an unsatisfactory environment for private investment was discussed separately but attacked mainly with recommendations pertaining to other problems. Conditions not conducive to the private investment required for economic growth exist in industry, commerce, and rice and rubber production. Several recommendations were made in connection with other problems which would serve to improve the environment for private investors: To increase such investment in agriculture, it was suggested, as we have already seen, that the premiums on rice and other exports be reduced; that the monopolies and corruption that existed in marketing be eliminated; that better public credit facilities be instituted; and that marketing costs be reduced through improved roads, farm consolidation, and market organization. To increase investment in industry it was suggested that (see the preceding two sections) Thai policies on state enterprises be clearly stated; that public facilities be strengthened with further private investment, domestic savings, and capital promotion; and that executive development and business training programs in higher education be improved.

The recommendations of the team for increased tax revenues might be construed as unfavorable to private investment. However, the importance to private investors of the facilities listed in a following section must be considered. The report recommended that these facilities be obtained with funds derived from taxation and foreign aid, the taxation being a prerequisite for aid from the United States.

The problems arising from having the government centralized in Bangkok

The problem of a centralized government in Bangkok was partially met with recommendations for decentralization of public investment from Bangkok to the outlying areas, particularly those in the northeast. The study team recognized that the most vulnerable part of Thailand was in the northeast because it borders on Laos, many of the people there are not fully assimilated into Thai culture and nationality, and per capita income is significantly lower than in other parts of the country. The prime minister repeatedly emphasized the government's concern about the northeast, and the National Economic Development Board (NEDB), an appointed inter-ministry agency, had developed a special plan for that area.

The problem of decentralizing the government itself was not attacked. It involved a constellation of values that would be relevant in discussions involving dictatorships, monarchies, and democracies, as well as questions of the goodness of freedom, political stability, enlightened dictatorships, absence of corruption, and so forth. No recommendations were made on these matters except to suggest that a hands-off policy be maintained in a governmental situation which looked fairly good when compared with those in many other undeveloped countries and which could be made much worse by actions that might threaten the position of the current prime minister, nullify the moderating but prominent influence of the king and queen, and be inconsistent with the U.S. policies of not interfering in internal affairs and of not supporting governments which interfere in the internal affairs of other countries.

The problem of a shortage of suitable planning
facilities, both governmental and private, to provide for the
planned growth of industry, public facilities, and agriculture

The shortage of planning facilities in Thailand presented a restraint on development. With no major business organizations, Thailand was without the extensive private planning and organizing resources of West Germany and England, which permitted them to make such effective use of Marshall Plan aid. Nor did Thailand possess highly developed governmental units to perform this function, the Royal Irrigation Department in the Ministry of Agriculture being a specialized exception. Although the government of Thailand operated many state enterprises (including breweries and slaughter houses), the only overall planning agency was the recently created National Economic Development Board (NEDB), which had to spend about as much of its meager resources developing itself as it did directing the development of the country. Several recommendations of the team were directed toward the development of planning and organizing facilities. These recommendations suggested:

1. Endorsement of a proposed advisory team from the International Bank for Reconstruction and Development to work with the Thai National Economic Development Board (NEDB)

2. Various proposals to increase the efficiency of the NEDB and strengthen its position in the Thai government

3. More educational facilities at Bangkok universities for executive development and training in business administration, strengthening of advisory assistance and staff training for the Industrial Finance Corporation, examination of the need for an industrial research center, the study of industrial parks, and consideration of establishing a private industrial development corporation

4. A much higher level of general, as well as vocational, education

The problem of inadequate development of the
Thai fishing industry

Inadequate development of the Thai fishing industry, both inland and marine, was examined briefly and hurriedly. Fish is the second most important component of the Thai diet. The United States conducted a fisheries project in Thailand from 1951 to 1957. Recently a marine survey was conducted under the Thai-German Agreement of Technical and Economic Cooperation. It was recommended that aid to Thai fisheries be left to other countries that could specialize in such aid while United States' resources were used in other ways.

The problem of maintaining and
managing Thailand's large forest industry

Maintaining and managing Thailand's large forest industry, much of which is part of the public domain, is a substantial problem. Here, as in the case of fisheries, it was concluded that the United States should stay out of the picture in order to leave a large and worthwhile area in which the Food and Agriculture Organization (FAO) or one of the Scandinavian countries could contribute technical skills and resources.

Summary

Team members worked with both normative and non-normative concepts, some of which were taken as given while others were developed during the study. Many of the given concepts remained unchanged throughout the processes of evaluation and recommendations. Others changed, revealing that there is some, but not a universal, pragmatic interdependence between non–normative and normative concepts.

There appeared to be two kinds of dependencies between normative and non-normative concepts, one of which was almost always encountered but which was not a real dependency. The common case occurred when conclusions about what it was right to do changed with changes in non-normative concepts; thus, the conclusion that it would be right to establish larger-scale farms with competitive earnings for labor and capital depends on whether it is predicted that industrial employment will or will not exist for the displaced farm people. This, however, is a sort of pseudodependency between normative and non-normative concepts, because the goodness of larger-scale farms with competitive returns to labor and capital is not modified by the existence or nonexistence of employment. Nor are the predictions of off-farm employment levels dependent on the goodness of such farms. Instead, what it is right to do depends on *both* the relevant normative and non-normative information.

In some instances, however, true dependency did appear to exist between non-normative and normative concepts. Thus, the goodness of local initiative and local tax resources became more and more apparent as members of the team developed and completed their non-normative pictures of Thai taxation and decision-making procedures with respect to public investments. Team members went beyond the conclusion that more of something which possessed unchanging good in their eyes should be obtained to concluding that a given amount of that something represented more good than they had originally concluded. Normative concepts of good and bad per se changed as a result of changing non-normative concepts.

With respect to procedures and institutional arrangements for making decisions, both non-normative and normative questions arose. In some instances, team members were interested in how decisions were made. In other instances, they were interested in the goodness or badness of existing and alternative procedures and institutions for making decisions.

The difficulty of developing concepts did not appear to be closely related to the degree of normativism involved or to whether or not decision-making procedures were involved. Thus, *some of both* normative and non-normative concepts not involving the process of making decisions were obvious and easy to acquire or develop, were moderately difficult to acquire and develop, or were beyond the capacity of team members. On the other hand, *some* concepts of the decision-making process were obvious and easy to acquire or develop, were moderately difficult to acquire or develop, or were beyond the capacity of team members.

Team members experienced much difficulty in using non-normative, normative, and decision-making concepts to reach evaluative conclusions and recommendations. It was seldom that clear cases were encountered for applying the abstract economizing principles of static neoclassical economics to determine what action should have been or should be taken by the United States. Macroeconomic theories of more recent vintage were revealed to be of more value for deducing theoretical effects than for indicating right actions. Consideration of principles of military and political strategy were of some limited value in indicating what should have been or should be done. Uncertainty about both the factual and normative future often left the team in doubt about whether to maximize the average value (present or future) of alternative courses of action, maximize the least good of alternative courses of action, maximize the greatest good of alternative courses of action, or seek some other basis for choice.

Developmental Problems in Western Kentucky

With Special Emphasis on the Activities of B. W. "Cap" Edmonds

An Overview

In the Great Depression, there were many problems in the southeastern states of the United States. These problems involved (1) the Muscle Shoals World War I nitrogen fixation plant; (2) the Tennessee River, which alternately subjected towns and cities along its course, the lower Ohio River, and the lower Mississippi River to disastrous floods and then became too low for commercial navigation; (3) undeveloped phosphate and coal resources; and (4) disadvantaged people with meager know-how, little capital, and obsolete technology who lived primarily on poor, small farms and had no off-farm work. It was part of a national setting characterized by extreme economic disorganization, low productivity, and depression.

The goods to be sought or utilized included the existing nitrogen plant, flood protection, employment opportunities, navigational facilities, farm technology, and electricity. Some of these goods were competitive; others were complementary. The non-normative concepts that were needed to solve the problems were available from many disciplines: engineering, physics, meteorology, hydrology, agronomy, economic and political science, and sociology. The creation of the Tennessee Valley Authority (TVA) was one attempt to attack these problems.

AUTHORS' NOTE: This chapter has benefited greatly from critical reviews by C. O. Bondurant, Murray, Kentucky; A. J. Brown and Wendell Binkley, Department of Agricultural Economics, University of Kentucky; and S. C. Bohannan, University of Kentucky Extension Service.

When the TVA experience is reviewed in the broad sweep of time, it is evident that several different philosophies were useful in attacking the problem. In some instances, non-normative information was adequate, and the facts sometimes spoke for themselves. For example, description of the floods, the available plant, the coal, and the phosphate ore virtually indicated what should be done. Thus, we have an instance in which a form of positivism made a clear contribution in the solution of practical problems. It was worthwhile acquiring the non-normative facts, not because a specific problem required them for its solution, but because the facts were useful in general—almost for their own sake. Thus, failure to specify problems was of little consequence in such instances and the avoidance of purpose did not materially affect ability to solve problems. Purpose was so clearly evident that concepts of goodness and badness did not have to be formulated to guide the development and use of non-normative concepts in solving the practical problems.

In other instances, problems could only be posed and solved in terms of tentative normative concepts which had to be clarified and in some instances developed, but which were *not* subject to substantial change as a result of the process of defining and solving the problem. The perceived goodness or badness of a situation, condition, or item did not appear to change, in all instances, as a result of defining the problem. The goodness of more electricity for the World War II effort is a case in point. After its goodness came to be clearly perceived, the solution turned on non-normative estimates of the consequences of alternative actions. How much electricity and how many related goods could be attained (or related bads avoided) at the margin were open questions, but not the goodness of electricity.

Among future developments not clearly envisioned as good, or even thought about in this connection, were the secondary businesses and primary users of TVA's electricity (the Atomic Energy Commission and Union Carbide), which were to grow up around Kentucky Lake. Although the possibilities for and the goodnesses of secondary industries, such as the resort, homebuilding, and motel industries, were not fully appreciated in the early 1940s, their goodness does not seem to have been dependent on the value of the means expended or to be expended in bringing them into being.

This is also quite different from saying that new normative concepts of what always had had value were produced in solving the problem.

There were also instances in which the values appeared to be dependent on or functions of the problem-solving experience of society in John Dewey's sense that *"the value of an objective as an attained end is a value of something which in being an end, an outcome, stands in relation to the means of which it is the consequence"* (italics added).[1] Examples include the value of being identified with TVA as a national effort. This value, commonly observed to be held by TVA employees and the people in the area, did not exist before the TVA.

Another example of the interrelationship between values and problem solving involved the ethics of using different decision-making techniques. Major normative questions arose involving the goodness and badness of governmental versus private control over investment decisions. To attempt to answer such normative questions was to change the importance (value) which various groups and individuals attach to each of the two means of reaching decisions.

In these days, anyone not familiar with TVA is struck, almost at once, by the lack of controversy within the TVA area about the role government has played in making investment decisions. Although the rest of the nation argues about the goodness or badness of such decision-making arrangements, most of the people in TVA and in the area immediately affected are inclined to accept such a method of making decisions as having value. This acceptance in turn enables them to get on with the process of deciding what investments should or should not be made.

Although it is sometimes claimed that receivers do not argue or look gift horses in the mouth, not all residents in the TVA area are receivers. More important than the distinction between giver and receiver, however, is the distinction between receiver and producer. In recent years the TVA area has become a vast producer of electricity, manufactured and

---

1 John Dewey, "The Continuum of Ends-Means," reprinted in *Ethical Theories*, ed. by A. I. Melden (New York: Prentice-Hall, Inc., 1950), p. 361. Originally published in *International Encyclopedia of Unified Science* (Chicago: University of Chicago Press, 1939).

agricultural goods, flood protection, and navigational services. In the face of this productivity and participation, the question of giving or receiving is not so crucial and the decision processes which have been involved in attaining such productivity are likely to be acceptable.

Developmental Problems and Their Solutions in Western Kentucky

Included in the Tennessee Valley are seven counties of western Kentucky. The land in these counties is of medium to poor quality. In the 1930s and 1940s it was badly in need of liming, fertilizing, and other advanced practices. Adequate marketing and road, credit, and other institutional facilities did not exist to supply the area with the services required for the needed improvements in the region's agriculture.

For instance, limestone quarrying and distribution facilities were meager. One quarry in Livingston County crushed lime with an antique steam engine. There was also a quarry in Calloway County. After the start of World War II in 1941, shortages of labor and repair parts closed down the quarries.

At the time the TVA dam, which impounded the present 100-mile long Kentucky Lake, was built, much limestone was quarried. This limestone was graded, with large pieces retained for use in constructing the dam and the screenings rejected and left to pile up on the bottom of the future lake. B. W. "Cap" Edmonds, other farm leaders,[2] and personnel from the University of Kentucky and TVA knew that these screenings would satisfy the need for limestone in Kentucky's Valley Counties. They also knew the values of more supporting services for agriculture and more technical training. The screenings were available for the hauling, but $60,000 worth of equipment was needed, and it was obvious to the local agricultural leaders and their advisers that a guaranteed market for the limestone would simplify the acquisition of $60,000.

Edmonds was on the state Production and Marketing Administration Committee (PMA), which was making payments

---

[2] T. F. Maddox and Rudy Hendon were among the prominent farm leaders who acted with Edmonds.

at that time to offset partially the cost of applying limestone. He arranged for PMA to issue purchase orders for the limestone. However, as U.S. purchase orders were not recognized legal instruments in west Kentucky at that time, Edmonds had to go one step further and arrange bank financing. Valuable advice and assistance about such arrangements, as well as in other later connections involving office procedures, legal questions, and related matters, were obtained from E. L. Johnson, Otis L. Weaver, John L. McKitrick, Wendell Binkley, and L. A. Vennes. The county cooperatives, which were organized under Edmonds' leadership to haul and spread screenings, distributed over 175,000 tons of limestone in three years.

The leaders also realized that capital was needed for development. Thus, Edmonds and others arranged for the cooperatives to receive 50 cents a ton for each load of screenings. The resultant accumulation of capital became the base for the cooperatives in each of the seven valley cooperatives.

Farm leaders are often as much a product of developments as they are determiners of developments. Cap Edmonds was one of the leaders who was a product of developments in western Kentucky agriculture at this time. He was keenly interested in agriculture. He farmed a place small enough to leave him time for leadership activities, had a real ability to express himself, and was receptive to ideas of others, especially individuals from the University of Kentucky Extension Service, the TVA, and other local leaders.

When Kentucky Dam was finished and the lake filled, the supply of TVA limestone was cut off. The cooperatives, working together, then sought contracts for limestone from quarries. They were unable, however, to arrange satisfactory terms for the large volume of limestone then moving because the quarry operators regarded the cooperatives as competitors. The Valley Counties Cooperative then took an option on fifty acres of limestone-bearing land and started to prepare to quarry its own limestone. As a result, commercial contracts quickly became available to the cooperative and it was never necessary to open the quarry.

Private quarry operators moved larger volumes of limestone via the cooperative than ever before. Efforts of cooperative leaders, both to improve the technical education of farmers and to create institutional arrangements favoring the use of limestone, greatly expanded the demand for limestone from farmers. This ultimately benefited the quarry operators, while the cooperative served as a retailing and educational agency.

The initial conflict between commercial and cooperative interests involved lack of both non-normative and normative knowledge. Neither the farmers nor the quarrymen realized, in a non-normative sense, how much limestone would be purchased in the area when farmers became fully aware of the goodness (normatively) of the limestone. Still further on the normative side, the quarrymen did not know about the instrumental goodness of having a cooperative that provided educational services and represented west Kentucky farmers before governmental agencies. This good was capable of more than offsetting some of the bads which the quarrymen conceived to be associated with competition from a cooperative. It appears that all parties involved learned about the non-normative and normative relationships involved during the processes of encountering, defining, and solving the problem.

While both non-normative and normative concepts were formed and extended during these experiences, there is little evidence that normative and non-normative concepts were necessarily interdependent. There is evidence that the amount of certain bads which the quarrymen would tolerate depended on how much good they could obtain or how many other bads they could avoid in exchange. They valued goods in terms of the sacrifice of other goods or in terms of exchanging values at the margins. This use of the opportunity cost principle, however, is quite different from interdependence between the values of ends and means.

The task of educating farmers about fertilizer other than lime was substantial. TVA made fertilizers available for demonstrational use at the cost of transportation from TVA plants to west Kentucky. The fertilizer was delivered in carload lots only. Initially, the shipping charges were 13.5 cents per hundred. Edmonds and another west Kentucky farm leader, Kelly Cromwell, spent ten days in 1935 convincing fourteen farmers to accept twenty tons on these terms. Four of these fourteen eventually cancelled their orders because they were afraid the new high-analysis fertilizers would burn up their crops. One field of winter wheat planted after corn was slow to germinate because of dry weather. The high-analysis phosphate fertilizer was blamed. However, when rain eventually came, the wheat did germinate and yielded well.

The first TVA Test-Demonstration Area was established in western Kentucky. Organizations were established in each of Kentucky's seven valley counties. A few years later, an over-all organization for the seven counties was formed. (This became the cooperative which negotiated with the quarry-men for limestone after the completion of Kentucky Dam.)

TVA required warehouse facilities and accountability. These were provided by the emerging Valley Counties Coop-erative whose position was strengthened as farmers learned from the demonstrations to use more and more fertilizer. Out of the Test-Demonstration effort and the leadership of Cap Edmonds and others, farmers obtained more knowledge of responses to fertilizers and the effects of an improved cooper-ative system. In one instance, they gained access to non-normative knowledge. In the other instance, a new or im-proved institutional arrangement was created in the image of human ideas of a nonexistent reality.

When interviewed, Edmonds and others stressed another important result of the experience. They argued that farmers "learned to work together" during their experience with the cooperative. Further questioning indiciated that they thought farmers had learned from experience that working together was good—instrumentally because it was a means of obtaining other goods, and intrinsically because working together was good in and of itself.

The cooperative needed a larger volume of business to spread its overhead costs. The expanding livestock industry required seeds, drugs, insecticides, and machinery services for such things as terracing pastures and building stock ponds, fencing, and waterers. The emerging cooperative was not large enough to negotiate for the production and delivery of these items. The solution was to investigate the possibility of further cooperation between the small Valley Counties Coop-erative (as the west Kentucky organization was called) and the much larger Southern States Cooperative, a regional co-operative with established arrangements for doing business with suppliers. Thus, solving the problems involved bringing into existence this additional, previously nonexistent, institu-tional arrangement patterned on a human concept of how reality could be modified. The ends or values to be attained were rather obvious and could be accepted as given. Although some non-normative concepts were required concerning the availability of supplies and the nature of the two cooperatives, the solution was found primarily in a human conception of a nonexistent institutional arrangement rather than in either non-normative or normative concepts of what was, is, will be, or ever had been.

Another interesting problem grew up at Murray, the county seat, in the early 1950s after the cooperative was fairly well established. The available commercial feed-grinding and -mixing facilities were antiquated and unadapted to the new agricultural system emerging for the area. Among other things, cooperative members were demanding feeds sweetened with molasses. Vitamins and antibiotic supplements were being used increasingly and the dairy and beef herds of the area were being modernized.

Again, the problem of cooperative versus commercial interests arose. The cooperative leaders were aware of the opportunity which the problem offered to them, but were also aware of the interests of the commercial operators and the importance of public relations. Any action taken by the cooperatives to provide additional feed-mixing services would benefit farmers and the cooperative leadership at the expense of existing commercial interests.

In this instance, the problem was presented directly to the commercial interests. Although agreement was quickly reached that there was, indeed, a demand for services, the commercial interests indicated that they were not in a position to attempt to finance the expansion in feed-mixing facilities. They reached this conclusion knowing that the cooperative would move if they did not and that the consequence would mean losses for them. As a result, the cooperative invested in feed-mixing facilities, the farmers got the expanded services they wanted, and the commercial interests lost business, absolutely as well as proportionally. The instance is an interesting example of how near unanimity was reached with respect to a non-Pareto-better adjustment[3] by

---

[3] A non-Pareto-better adjustment damages one or more persons in order to benefit one or more other persons. Pareto-better adjustments are discussed under conditional normativism in chapter 1.

persons who placed value on seeing others benefit. Such altruism and empathy seem to be necessary ingredients for solving many such problems.

The Valley Counties Cooperative, local leaders, and the University of Kentucky (U.K.) Agricultural Extension Service also took advantage of the TVA legislative mandate to educate farmers about fertilizer use. From 1935 to about 1948, each of the valley counties under a budget provided by TVA and U.K. was assigned a soils specialist from TVA and the U.K. Extension—with financial support from TVA. Later, two specialists were assigned to the valley counties, a specialist in agronomy and a farm management expert.

The valley counties now had two institutional arrangements—the cooperative and the associate agents—both concerned with fertilizer, land, and farm management problems. As the cooperative grew to provide a wider range of services, and as the educational efforts of the associate county agents became effective, several of the initial problems of the area were solved.

Philosophic Conclusions

The group of people in west Kentucky faced tough problematic situations. For the most part, the problems were attacked without special regard for any of the five philosophic positions described in chapter 1, this being especially true of the work of Edmonds and other farm leaders in western Kentucky.

As far as can be observed, the philosophic approach was conditionally normative at times while at other times it was both positivistic and normative. Edmonds' formal training was hardly the equivalent of that represented by a medium-quality high school diploma of his generation. When he and the people working with him were interviewed, they indicated that they did not consciously adhere to any philosophy of science, value, or inquiry to the exclusion of others. It appears that they either accepted various concepts of good and bad as obvious or deduced them from other accepted values and experiences. The same was true of their non-normative concepts. There is little evidence that they regarded normative and non-normative concepts to be inextricably interdependent.

Edmonds and the others simply found or assumed answers to both non-normative and normative questions in trying to see what actions were appropriate. Common sense insisted that people who talk about either non-normative or normative matters know what they are talking about—in short, their normative and non-normative concepts had to be clear and understandable. Further, their concepts had to hold together—to be logically consistent. When concepts did not lead to workable conclusions, they had to be overhauled. As far as existentialism is concerned, it is almost impossible for the indigenous midsoutherner not to relate to people as entities. Cap Edmonds was no exception; yet his indigenous existentialism was tempered with a knowledge of the importance of establishing group unity and identity. And he seldom, if ever, made the mistake of regarding knowledge or logic as constraints on either individual or group identities.

IV | Solving Credit Problems of Farmers

Past solutions of farm credit problems illustrate nicely how values have been handled by society and agricultural economists. Interesting aspects of these solutions involve (1) the study by economists of the normative as well as the nonnormative in finding these solutions and (2) the high proportion of acceptable solutions obtained.

Land credit issues became important at the end of the last century. The Federal Farm Loan Board was partly an outgrowth of the work of the County Life Commission. The Agricultural Credit Act was passed in 1923. In the Great Depression, the Farm Credit Act established the Farm Credit Administration (FCA) to extend production credit as well as land credit. By 1939, the Farm Security Administration (FSA) had evolved. The FSA and its predecessor agencies were designed to solve credit and resource problems of farmers who were not serviced by other credit agencies. Since then, miscellaneous public credit institutions have been created to solve financial problems associated with such disasters as droughts, floods, and so forth. Special facilities to service farm cooperatives were established in 1933. Since then, the public storage of surplus farm products has been financed in a variety of ways.

AUTHORS' NOTE: This chapter is based on Glenn L. Johnson and Lewis K. Zerby, "Values in the Solution of Credit Problems," *Capital and Credit Needs in a Changing Agriculture*, ed. by E. L. Baum, H. G. Diesslin, and E. O. Heady (Ames, Iowa: Iowa State University Press, 1961).

Credit Problems Solved by "Getting the Facts"

Two subtypes of credit problems fall under the rubric of getting the facts. First, there are problems of obtaining that which is valued and avoiding that which is valued negatively (i.e., that which is bad). Second, there are problems of determining what or which values best describe present or future non-normative reality. While many agricultural economists advocate that their work should be restricted to answering questions of these two types, examples of such restriction in solving actual problems are difficult to find in the history of farm credit. Those which are found are often of minor importance, involving the operation of credit institutions to attain previously agreed on goals or to carry out an action previously determined to be right.

Most everyone has had experience with the techniques that credit institutions use in formulating non-normative concepts about loans on real estate and durables. The beliefs that a credit manager formulates about the conditions of one's security, net worth, character (that is, one's system of values), earnings, and expenditures do not solve his problem of whether or not to make the loan. Between such decisions and decisions on major policy questions is a continuum of problems ranging from operational—that is, those problems solved almost exclusively by obtaining answers to non-normative questions—through those involving answers to questions of policy in the initial absence of generally accepted answers to normative questions. Thus, the examples of farm credit problems solved by getting facts are mainly semioperational and do not involve major policy issues.

In recent years a farm credit problem arose from the Production Credit Association (PCA) and various cooperatives selling supplies and equipment to farmers. A substantial amount of production credit used by farmers was extended by farm supply houses. Overextensions of credit often impaired PCA loans and produced financial troubles for farmers and farmers' supply cooperatives.

It was agreed by those working with credit problems of farmers that it would be good to coordinate the extension of such credit and PCA loans. It is important to notice the objective nature of this normative conclusion. The agreement did not simply amount to a group of people sharing the same attitude toward the world. The agreement was about the value of a world in which credit extension was coordinated with PCA loans, and the reality of such knowledge required no special value intuition. The problem could be solved with predictions of the outcome of various methods of bringing about the coordination.

In 1961, at least two production credit districts had programs in effect for providing this coordination. One of these was known as the reserve program, the other as the guarantee program. In one instance, both the farmer and the cooperative provided a reserve against bad loans. In the other case, the cooperative guaranteed the loan by cosignature. The first program was used most extensively in Michigan and proved only moderately workable. Consideration was given to shifting to the guarantee program to increase workability. Whether either program solved the problem depended on the accuracy of the program designers' non-normative predictions and not on the truth or falsity of the concept that coordination is good.

Credit Problems Involving Concepts about What Has Value and What Is or Can Be

Some credit problems involve differences between partially developed concepts about what has value and what is or can be in a non-normative sense. These examples are of two types: those involving independent ends and means and those involving interdependent ends or means. Both types involve the process of forming beliefs about both the normative and non-normative; however, interdependent values and ends—interdependent in the sense that they are traded off against each other—do not necessarily involve interdependent normative and non-normative concepts.

In writing about the federal land bank system in 1955, Murray Benedict wrote,

> The individual lender cannot afford to buy a mortgage on a farm halfway across a continent, which he probably has never seen and whose owner he does not know. Even where he does know the farmer and his security, the risk of going wrong on a single farm is too great. As a consequence, loan funds have often been very

inadequate in many rural, capital-deficit areas, even when savings accumulated in other sections of the country were seeking an outlet. It was to overcome this difficulty, and to provide an orderly and safe channel for the transfer of such funds, that the federal land bank system was created.[1]

If Benedict's statements were considered out of context, one might conclude that here was a simple case of solving a problem with non-normative concepts. Under this supposition, the necessary belief concepts would involve predictions about how the federal land bank system would serve to channel credit from lenders to borrowers. Actually, however, both normative concepts about the value of such a system and non-normative concepts about its nature had to be created and clarified over the fifteen to twenty years involved in setting up the system. Once developed, these normative and non-normative concepts became the basis for the compromise represented by the Federal Farm Act of 1916 between the goods and bads involved in view of what was possible.

While normative and non-normative concepts were developed and systematized simultaneously, there is little direct evidence that the values of the ends and means were interrelated. In some instances the bads consisted of giving up some goods, as dictated by the nature of reality revealed by non-normative beliefs. While this process of giving up one good to attain another within available means does establish an exchange value between the two goods, this is quite different from interdependence between normative and non-normative concepts.

The history of farm credit involves several studies of the non-normative conducted with the hope of helping to find the best means of attaining a previously agreed on set of values. One such study was entitled "Risk Problems of the Production Credit Associations."[2] It was authorized by the members of the District Farm Credit Boards in 1950 and carried out by a committee of agricultural economists, economists, and a research director, and included four heads of

---

[1] Murray R. Benedict, *Can We Solve the Farm Problem? An Analysis of Federal Aid to Agriculture* (New York: Twentieth Century Fund, 1955), p. 124.

[2] F. F. Hill, *et al.* (preliminary draft for discussion purposes, subject to revision, Dec. 31, 1950).

agricultural economics departments of land grant colleges. The committee was to review and appraise. It reviewed, but limited its appraisal to "presenting for discussion and consideration certain methods of improving the ability of the PCA's to meet the risk inevitable in agricultural lending."

The five methods included: (1) strengthening PCA finances, (2) setting up a mutual loan insurance reserve, (3) setting up a group reserve for contingencies, (4) consolidating production credit agencies of lending and discount, and (5) consolidating the production (chattel) and mortgage (real estate) credit units of the Farm Credit Administration. This effort was discussed and supplemented with much informal study of the importance of spreading risks. Partially developed normative concepts were also involved which had to be completed and clarified. These included the goodness of a self-supporting, independent link between borrowers and lenders.

Congress passed the Farm Credit Act of 1956 at the recommendation of the Federal Farm Credit Boards. This act put method 4 into effect by providing for the merging of the Production Credit Corporation into the Federal Intermediate Credit Bank of each district. Numerous smaller steps were taken to put method 1 into effect.

It is difficult to illustrate the second type of problem involving interdependence between normative and non-normative concepts. The institutionalists who derived their ideas from John R. Commons hold that such problems are the type most generally encountered. Commons, in turn, based his ideas on the pragmatism of John Dewey and C. S. Peirce.[3] Consultation with members of the Department of Agricultural Economics at Michigan State University who have worked on credit problems failed to produce a clear-cut example of such a problem. Similarly, an examination of a

3 Kenneth H. Parsons, "The Value Problem in Agricultural Policy," *Agricultural Adjustment Problems in a Growing Economy*, ed. by E. O. Heady, *et al.* (Ames, Iowa: Iowa State College Press, 1958). Some of the connections between pragmatism and institutionalism are found in J. R. Commons: "We therefore . . . follow more closely the pragmatism of Dewey," and, "Herein it is Dewey's psychology that most nearly fits the case." *Institutional Economics—Its Place in Political Economy* (London: Macmillan & Co., Ltd., 1934), pp. 154-55 and 647 respectively.

number of historical accounts dealing with agricultural credit problems and policies failed to produce clear-cut examples.

The inability to illustrate the case which the institutionalists feel is most frequently encountered certainly raises questions about the generality of that case. However, failure to find a clear-cut example of the kind of problem representative of that case should not indicate that the institutional point of view is without merit. For one thing, credit problems are not detailed enough to reveal the interdependence of normative and non-normative which the Dewey pragmatists held to be general. Or the difficulty may be that the simultaneous experience of both kinds of concepts makes it seem that they cannot be separated conceptually. The simultaneous occurrence of normative and non-normative concepts, however, does not necessitate the interdependence of normative and non-normative concepts any more than the simultaneous development of concepts of shapes and colors makes it impossible to distinguish them intellectually.

Credit Problems Involving Conflicting Normative Concepts in the History of Farm Credit Policy

Examples of problems involving conflicting normative concepts come largely from the history of the Farmers Home Administration (FHA) and its predecessor agencies, although there is at least one important problem of this nature in the history of the Farm Credit Administration, proper.

The second governor of the FCA, F. F. Hill, in carrying out the policies of his administrative predecessor, W. I. Meyers, felt that the Farm Credit Administration "ought to serve the credit needs of farmers" and "ought not to be used as a means of furthering other governmental programs." Henry Wallace, Secretary of Agriculture, did not agree, and the FCA was placed in the U.S. Department of Agriculture. Hill and Wallace continued to disagree over what ought to be. Hill was forced to resign in 1939 and A. G. Black was appointed to replace him. The FCA, however, was never really used as a tool in the crop adjustment programs of the late 1930s and early 1940s, largely because the major farm organization had enough power to back up the value system of those favoring a more independent credit agency. Given the distribution of political, bureaucratic, and lobby powers, Wallace's value system was less workable than Hill's. Hill's system stood the pragmatic test.[4]

As indicated above, the Farm Security (later Farmers Home) Administration has encountered repeated problems involving competing normative concepts.[5] The predecessor agency to the Farm Security Administration was the Resettlement Administration, which had grown up, in turn, out of the rural rehabilitation work of the Federal Emergency Relief Administration. This group of agencies had handled a whole series of problems defined by the dynamic, almost everchanging chain of normative and non-normative concepts concerning rural poverty held through the Great Depression, World War II, and the Korean and postwar periods. These agencies had been experimental and had often been deeply involved in systems of normative concepts which have failed to meet the criteria of consistency and clarity.[6]

---

4 Benedict, *Can We Solve the Farm Problem?* pp. 39f.

5 *Ibid.*, pp. 356-64.

6 *Ibid.*, p. 363. "The activities carried on under the Farm Security Administration attracted wide attention and were a subject of controversy throughout the years preceding World War II. The new program constituted a sharp break with tradition and there were wide differences between the personal philosophies of those who administered it and some of the more conservative groups in agriculture.

"The organization was heavily weighted with people dedicated to humanitarian and reform philosophies. In the selection of personnel the acceptance of these points of view tended to be given more weight than experience, training and hard-headed business qualities. The result was that the organization tended to be somewhat loosely administered and operated on a basis of high emotional fervor. Probably the abilities and inclinations of these disadvantaged groups to respond to improved opportunities were somewhat overestimated.

"In addition, the organization had much difficulty in recruiting a competent field staff. The task of appraising, supervising and building up these less successful farmers and farm workers was more difficult than that of aiding better-educated and more successful farmers. The best qualified field workers preferred to align themselves with the older, better-established agencies, and thus usually were not available to the Farm Security Administration.

"Both the quality of the field personnel and the success of the program were somewhat uneven over the country. In some areas very good results were obtained. In others the organization, though performing a necessary and useful function, never achieved popularity. The hard-headed farmer-directors of many farm loan associations, produc-

The rehabilitation programs of these agencies have been criticized sharply for being too paternalistic and soft and for interfering with the freedom of individual farmers. Others have praised these programs for providing low-interest credit to those whose incomes were unacceptably low, along with enough supervision and managerial know-how to raise incomes and ensure repayment. Over the years, persons and agencies have come to attach less negative value to the increments of paternalism, subsidy, and restrictions on freedom in such credit programs. They have come, in turn, to attach more positive value to the increases in income and economic independence produced by such programs, while at the same time insisting that such programs be confined *only* to those needing substantial aid. It now appears that such programs will remain part of our governmental credit policy about as long as we have rural poverty arising from a lack of control over enough resources to produce an acceptable standard of living.

Other value conflicts encountered by this chain of agencies have been settled by complete or partial abandonment of the values the agencies pursued. Agricultural fundamentalists and others attached great value to farms, farmers, and farm life. At first these values led to resettlement activities designed to establish landless farmers and wage workers in permanent homes on the land. These efforts were often corporate, collective, and/or cooperative in nature. Soon, such resettlement became inconsistent with such widely held values as efficiency (which called for the transfer of people out of agriculture), the desirability of technological advance, the desire on the part of the individuals involved to own and control their land and machinery, and a desire for freedom from group and governmental controls. With the passage of time, these competing values won out over the values attached to farms, farmers, and farm life as attainable through FSA resettlement activities. In 1946 the Farm Security Administration was replaced by the Farmers Home Administration, which eliminated all community projects.

tion credit associations and other regular credit agencies tended to be somewhat scornful of the 'soft' credit and 'unbusinesslike' methods of FSA. In the West farm employers were dubious of the FSA camps for migrants, feeling that they might become hotbeds of radicalism, and places for pampering the lazy and improvident.''

In the case of FSA resettlement activities, farmers' desire for more freedom to conduct their individual affairs prevailed in conflict with some of the values subsumed under agricultural fundamentalism and with the other values. In the case of supervised, subsidized credit for low-income farmers, this same desire for freedom to conduct individual affairs failed to prevail in competition with the value of income increments derivable from supervised and subsidized public credit.

In both cases, it is clear that compromises among the goods and bads were involved in determining the eventual course of action. Furthermore, it is clear that not *all* of freedom, *all* of the values of agricultural fundamentalism, or *all* income were balanced against each other. Instead, only the incremental changes involved in going from one course of action to another were weighed against each other.

This balancing of incremental attainments and losses against each other in view of what is possible does not necessarily imply that the goods and the bads are interdependent, as Dewey argues. To so argue would be the same as arguing that *because* iso-value product lines (the structure of goods) and iso-cost lines (the structure of bads or means) jointly determine the high profit point (which, incidentally, defines a profit-maximizing right action) and establish the marginal value productivities of the two inputs as their values, the iso-value product lines are dependent on the iso-cost lines and vice versa. Alfred Marshall saw this much more clearly than did John Dewey.[7]

The Rural Electrification Administration (REA) encountered conflicts between two widely held and strongly backed sets of values. On the one hand, many people held that farmers should have access to electric power facilities. Included among people who agreed on this matter, however, were those who did not want the government to be involved in the extension of subsidized credit to cooperatives for the purpose of constructing facilities for distributing electricity

---

7 Compare for instance, John Dewey, "The Continuum of Ends-Means," reprinted in *Ethical Theories*, ed. by A. I. Melden (New York: Prentice-Hall, Inc. 1950), pp. 305f, with Alfred Marshall, *Principles of Economics* (8th ed.; London: Macmillan & Co., Ltd.), p. 348. Although Marshall deals with supply and demand functions instead of value-product and cost functions, the comparison yields the same conclusions.

to rural areas. Thus a complex of values was involved that included the values of income to private owners of electrical distribution facilities, of free enterprise, of subsidies, and of justice. In the end, the conflict among these values led to the decision that a right action would involve the provision of subsidized credit to farmer-owned cooperatives for the purpose of providing electrical services to farmers. Such value conflicts as these and their resolution seem clearly to indicate that it is possible for value concepts to be objective. Both the subject matter that was being discussed and the method of discussion were objective.

Social Scientists' Role in Studying Values as a Basis for Right Actions

The list of men trained in agricultural economics who have dealt with the values involved in credit problems is long and respectable. Of the seven FCA governors to date, at least six are or were primarily agricultural economists. The list includes W. I. Meyers, F. F. Hill, A. G. Black, C. R. Arnold, I. W. Duggan, and R. B. Tootell.[8] Besides providing governors of the FCA, the discipline of agricultural economics has provided the FCA with subordinate administrators, researchers, and appraisers. The same is true for other governmental credit agencies.

When one considers private agencies providing credit services to agriculture, agricultural economics is well represented. One president of the Bank of America was an agricultural economist. Other agricultural economists serve in responsible positions in private credit institutions. Several agricultural economics departments regularly sponsor clinics for bankers with the express purpose of helping private banks service and see opportunities for servicing farmers. In the early 1960s the Agricultural Commission of the American Banker's Association had five advisers, at least four of whom were academic agricultural economists or farm management men. Within the Federal Reserve System, most, if not all, of the district banks have competent agricultural economists on

---

8 Marie Puhr, *Years of Progress with the Cooperative Land Bank System* (Washington, D.C.: Farm Credit Administration, Circulate E-43, Jan. 1957), p. 41.

their staff. Still further, agricultural economists from land grant colleges and private universities serve as consultants to both private and public credit institutions. Members of Congress contemplating new farm credit legislation have been served repeatedly by agricultural economists from both state and privately endowed universities and colleges.

It is instructive to look at the *Journal of Farm Economics* for the 1931-36 period when credit problems were numerous and U.S. credit institutions were in a state of flux. In this six-year period, 29 articles concerning farm credit, debt, mortgages, and related matters appeared in the *Journal.* These articles included (1) reports on the operation of the Federal Intermediate Credit Banks, the Federal Land Banks, and Agricultural Credit Corporation, and (2) empirical information on mortgage debt, foreclosures, and farm debt adjustment.

W. I. Meyers, in reporting on the new Farm Credit Administration in 1933,[9] reported on the need for FCA, FCA's organization to fill those needs, and its accomplishments in its first nine months. Meyer's paper was followed by a discussion in which W. E. Grimes dealt with desirable characteristics for the new agencies.[10] Murray Benedict followed with a major paper in which he did more than raise problems.[11] He stressed some important links between farm borrowers and the money markets: (1) attention to farmer interest, (2) nonpartisan administration of FCA, (3) decentralization of authority, (4) regional differentials for risk charges, and (5) strangely in conflict with (1) and (3) above, coordination of the FCA with the Agricultural Adjustment Administration's production control programs.

In this period, the profession of agricultural economics produced many articles that provided administrative guidance and gave little attention to the restrictions of positivism. Non-Pareto-better adjustments were not avoided and the lack of interpersonally valid welfare measures was not mentioned. Agricultural economists were too busy amassing facts, devel-

---

9 W. I. Meyers, "The Program of the Farm Credit Administration," *Journal of Farm Economics*, XVI (Jan. 1934), p. 30f.

10 W. E. Grimes, "Discussion," *Journal of Farm Economics*, XVI (Jan. 1934), pp. 40f.

11 Murray R. Benedict, "Some Credit Problems in a Federal Credit Program," *Journal of Farm Economics*, XVI (Jan. 1934), pp. 45f.

oping value concepts, defining problems, making projections about the consequences of alternative possible credit programs, ascertaining right actions, and executing those actions to let such philosophic restrictions limit the range of their attack on the major credit issues of their day.[12]

The Lack of Explosive Situations

While it is accurate to state that relatively few explosive situations have developed around agricultural economists working with the value aspects of credit problems, tensions and conflict have often been high in connection with operations of the FSA (now FHA) and the REA and when the purposes of FCA have been questioned. In a few instances, agricultural economists have stood up to be counted and have then been beaten on value questions. The Hill-Wallace disagreement is a case in point. However, the history of credit agencies is characterized by farm leaders, legislators, administrators (many of whom are agricultural economists), legal advisers, and agricultural economists doing an immense amount of homework on normative and non-normative concepts as a basis for decisions as to right actions. The evidence in recorded history is that they often succeeded in developing both normative and non-normative concepts which were consistent and understandable. In those instances in which tensions and conflicts built up to critical levels, there is evidence of inconsistent belief structures, i.e., vague, inconsistent, and unworkable normative and non-normative concepts. In many instances, the inconsistencies, vagueness, and inapplicabilities were worked out before strong positions were developed. After these difficulties were eliminated, the strong positions which had been developed usually led to solutions that have produced acceptable (right) actions rather than explosions.

Policy Decisions and the Criteria for Objectivity

A high proportion of the policy decisions reached on credit problems have been satisfactory and have met the

---

12 The actions of these early, fruitful workers' time were inconsistent with the positivistic restrictions that present-day agriculture economists often impose on themselves.

criteria of objectivity, consistency, clarity, and workability. Past work on problems has been productive in the sense that applicable, understandable, and moderately consistent actions have been recommended and adopted. The solutions have been expressed in terms of institutional arrangements which have, in turn, accomplished what public decision-making units have intended to accomplish. This record of success cannot be ignored by those who face the farm credit and capital problems of U.S. agriculture in the future. Because the general procedures followed in the past have accomplished results that speak well for the procedures, those procedures are worth summarizing:

1. Both non-normative and normative belief structures have been studied and developed by those persons (including agricultural economists) working on credit policies and programs for American agriculture.

2. Right actions have been ascertained as a compromise among the goods and bads within value structures in view of what was possible as revealed by non-normative beliefs about the nature of present and future reality.

3. Workers seem to have been able to avoid what Jeremy Bentham feared when he wrote that attempts to work with values consist "in so many contrivances for avoiding the obligation of appealing to any external standard, and for prevailing upon" another to accept one's "sentiment or opinion as a reason for itself."[13]

4. On many occasions, workers have had grave doubts about the reliability of their non-normative beliefs concerning the nature of present and future reality. Similarly, they seem to have doubted the clearness and consistency of value concepts or beliefs about the nature of normative reality. These doubts have led to humility, which has led, in turn, to flexibility of opinion concerning the rightness or wrongness of different possible actions. There has been a willingness to experiment, reexamine, and reformulate. This flexibility and willingness—this recognition of a hu-

---

[13] *Principles of Morals and Legislation,* ed. by L. J. LaFleur (New York: Hafner Publishing Co., 1948), p. 17.

man tendency to err with respect to *both* non-normative and normative beliefs—has probably served to keep individuals from taking positions not changeable except by sociopolitical explosion.

5. Workers from the social disciplines, particularly agricultural economics, have participated in all of the procedures described so far rather than confining their activities to particular areas such as those prescribed by (1) positivism, (2) conditional normativisn (including modern welfare economics), and (3) pure normativism. There is little evidence that those who worked with values have suffered more professionally or have been less productive than those who have avoided the study of values. Rather, the reverse seems to be true.

6. Increments and decrements in the degree to which valued situations are or would be attained have been frequently considered; complete attainment or abandonment of a value or set of values has seldom occurred.

7. Public actions have often been determined by roughly maximizing the difference between goods and bads or the ratio between goods and bads. Thus, these actions would tend to be right as the term is used herein. This meaning of right is consistent with what the economist generally means by efficient, so long as the concept of efficiency is left general and not restricted to mean the maximization of only money or even of utility in the narrow, Benthamic sense.

8. Non-Pareto-better adjustments have been agreed on and carried out repeatedly.[14]

9. Despite the difficulties encountered by many in attaining or finding a "common denominator of ability to attain more basic values which is neutral with respect to those more basic values," choices have

---

[14] An interesting connection between Immanuel Kant's categorical imperative and modern welfare economics is pointed out by G. I. Trant, "Ethical Systems and Agricultural Policy," *Canadian Journal of Agricultural Economics*, VII, 1 (1959), pp. 75f.

been made repeatedly among alternative courses of action involving such divergent values as income, security, freedom from governmental control, equality of property ownership, equality in access to credit, and the rights of private property.

10. There seems to be little evidence that the problem of selecting a basis for choice has ever been treated specifically as a disciplinary subproblem of a practical credit problem. Obviously, the practical problem of devising voting rules on the basis of which decisions are reached has been faced repeatedly. Because objectivity would lead to consensus, in a certain sense, the need to vote for such weighting rules arises out of a failure to attain objectivity in answers to the normative and/or non-normative.

11. Agricultural economists and other academicians have entered into and been a part of the total investigative and decision-making process. As such, they have participated with public decision makers in envisioning (projecting or simulating) the future. In this process of mutual interaction, problems of non-Pareto optimality, lack of common denominators among values, and lack of agreement on the basis for choice to use have been settled in various ways, including the establishment of voting rules and of informal covenants by which to abide the outcome of such voting rules.

V | Establishing a National Recreation Area in Michigan

In 1961 Senator Philip A. Hart (Michigan) sponsored a bill in the U.S. Senate to create in the northwest section of Michigan's lower peninsula a national recreation area. The controversy which this bill aroused is an instructive one for those who are concerned with the interaction of normative and non-normative considerations in public decision making. Before Senator Hart introduced this bill (No. S. 2153) in the spring of 1961, the feasibility of the proposed national recreation area was studied. These studies were uniformly enthusiastic about the project, and yet the groups of people who would be most intimately affected by the bill strongly opposed the project. It is interesting, then, to ask why there was this disagreement.

The problem of this chapter is complex. On the one hand is the practical problem of whether or not the citizens should have encouraged Congress to pass or to defeat a bill which was before the U.S. Senate. Each citizen had an individual decision to make relative to this problem. Since the problem was practical, it had to be solved, and inaction was one solution to it. The senators each had to decide to act for or against the bill. The parks department of the government had the problem of working out a technique to win support for a project that had a very specific locality.

All of these decisions, ideally, would be made on the basis of knowledge. Such knowledge prepares one to answer such questions as: Would it be better to have or not to have the proposed national recreation area? Is it morally justifiable to modify land resources for any purpose opposed by the owners of the land? Can a democratic government justify a nondemocratic *means* of achieving an end which seems demo-

cratically justified? In an effort to answer these questions, let us consider some of the arguments that were presented for and against the proposal.

Arguments against S. 2153—
the First Sleeping Bear Dunes Bill

Ove Jensen, representing a group called the Citizens' Council of the Sleeping Bear Dunes Area, presented these arguments against the bill:

1. No one knows where he stands with respect to property rights.

2. If this becomes a national park and we decide we don't want to

live in it, we have no assurance of getting fair market value if we sell to the park service.

3. Under the piecemeal condemnation permitted in this bill a property owner could be forced to give up some or all of his property at any time or he could be kept dangling for years.

4. In Leelanau and Benzie Counties we have five new consolidated high schools in Honor and Glen Lake. If these two districts lose this big chunk of tax base, they are going to be in serious trouble for operating expenses and to pay off their borrowings.

5. If the bill becomes law, people living in the park will have to okay zoning restrictions that border on the ridiculous.

6. As everyone who has visited this area knows, we have plenty of facilities to take care of vacationists now and for years to come without federal intervention.[1]

The *Detroit Free Press* columnist, Judd Arnett, opposed the proposal in these terms:

What is involved is the "right" of bureaucracy to invade private property under the terms of an outrageous Act that contains 80 percent gibberish and 20 percent brute strength under the old "might makes right" philosophy. . . . if the Act goes unchallenged and thereby establishes a precedent, then the federal government will be able to move into any developed area, at any time, and usurp what it wants "for the people."

. . . there is no "greater good for the greatest number" than the protection of individual rights. That is what freedom is all about. . . . this is encroachment of the most flagrant nature, and if there aren't enough people who care, then National Socialism is not a threat—it has arrived.[2]

In an editorial of October 2, 1961, the *Detroit Free Press* asserted:

Hart introduced the bill into Congress, has praised it highly, and now agrees that he doesn't understand it. He said, in fact, that it would take a "Philadelphia lawyer" to make any sense out of it.

If Senator Hart does not understand the bill, the residents of the area and the citizens of the State do. They understand enough, at

---

[1] The Citizens' Council of the Sleeping Bear Dunes Area, "The Bear is Asleep . . . But the People are Awake," Glen Arbor, Mich., 1961.

[2] *Detroit Free Press*, Oct. 2, 1961.

least, to know that the bill would allow their property to be bought, with the Secretary of the Interior serving as sole appraiser.

They know that the proposal to convert the land, part of which is already a state park, to national purposes has destroyed the building market and real estate values, and promises to do damage to the retail businessmen of the area.

They know that an imaginary figure of $10.8 million in income doesn't begin to balance the real loss in business and property rights, nor go anywhere to meet the real costs of some $50 million to acquire the land.

In order to discuss these objections it is useful to divide them into four categories: (1) political and moral, (2) monetary, (3) legal, and (4) logical.

Political and moral objections to the bill

Under political and moral objections would certainly be included the assertions about rights. The philosophy of Judd Arnett is familiar to any student of political history. Arnett speaks of the " 'right' of a bureaucracy to invade private property." Each word here deserves examination. The quotation marks around *right* clearly indicate that Arnett believes that there really is no such right, but merely something which has been called a right. His use of the word *bureaucracy* instead of *government, park service, Senate,* or words designating other social groups serves to discredit those attempting to establish the national seashore. The word *invade* is, of course, a military word. The citizens are viewed as being at war with the bureaucrats, and private property is used as a kind of personification of Americanism. What is behind Arnett's statement, then, is John Locke's philosophy of the natural law and inalienable rights. It has frequently been pointed out that of the three natural rights—life, liberty, and property—Locke seems chiefly concerned with property. The political argument against the bill is, then, that the landholders in the controversial area have a right to their land, and the bureaucrats have no right to seize or grasp it from them. There is the further argument that if such a law were to be passed in the Senate, it would have baleful consequences: it would establish a precedent which would make it possible for the federal government to be able to move into any developed area, at any time, and usurp what it wanted "for the people." In answer to the utilitarian argument that the sea-shore area was to be for "the greatest good of the greatest number"—an argument that was eventually abandoned—Arnett asserts, with no supporting argument, that "there is no greater good for the greatest number than the protection of individual rights." In the absence of such protection, he says, "National Socialism is not a threat—it has arrived."

Making allowances for the emotionalism of these arguments, the basic point of view from which they are made is that of rugged individualism. According to this philosophy of government, the individual citizen has rights that have a metaphysical reality. The grammar of *having* rights suggests, of course, that a man has rights very much as he has arms or legs and that these rights are not to be taken away from him by any bureaucratic government. Actually the term *right* has meaning only in the context of a social order, be it a political or a moral order. To say that X has a right to be given Y by Z means that X and Z live in a society in which there are social norms implementing X's demand to be given Y. If, for example, Smith owes Jones $10.00, the social order of which they are both a part will recognize Jones' demand and compel Smith to give him $10.00. Or, to say that a citizen has a right in a property that he has purchased means that the law of the land will prevent this right in property from being taken from him. The distinctive thing about the theory of property being considered here is that the right to hold property is taken to be natural, inalienable, and regarded as above *any* legal or moral claim rather than as a legal and/or moral matter.

It should be pointed out that, in justifying the institution of private property, philosophers have used two sorts of arguments. The first is that private property is necessary to fulfill or express one's personality. A man without rights to enjoy possessions is impoverished as a person, whereas a man with possessions is more fully a man. The second argument is that if a government takes from a citizen his property, the citizen's expectations are frustrated, and he loses his faith in and respect for his government.

In the Sleeping Bear controversy, those who opposed the creation of the recreation area were arguing primarily from the second point of view. Not one of them was in danger of having *all* his property rights taken away from him or, indeed, of having *any* property rights taken away without compensation. They were only in danger of having their expectations frustrated and losing faith in their government. As we shall see, Senator Hart took this matter very seriously, and as he formulated the bill in its second form he minimized the necessary frustrations of the property owners. One of the speakers (John C. Beukema) at the Traverse City hearings had the following to say about rights of property:

It is our contention that the bill should be re-written, but only after full consultation with local interests, so as to protect these basic human and property rights. If our democracy is to be preserved, it must be preserved on the hearthstone. A new approach, in which these values are carefully weighed, will not only create a national park of which we can all be proud and which will preserve the natural beauties and other characteristics of this region, but it will assure the good will of those who have built this country and made it what it is. In the long run, local cooperation is far more important to the Government and to the Park Service than any arbitrary fiat, however well intentioned.

Gentlemen of the Senate, I am sure you propose to do the right thing by the people of Leelanau and Benzie Counties. If I might briefly add a little anecdote, as Senator Hart well knows, I was one of the original pioneers in advocating the St. Lawrence Seaway. President Eisenhower appointed me to the Seaway Advisory Board, and we had the pleasure of building the Seaway. We had problems of land acquisition. So did our Canadian cousins.

One of the problems in Canada was the problem of St. Regis Island Indians who lived on a reservation there. Much of that land was needed for channel improvement. Some [Indians] sold; others wouldn't sell.

One day an Indian left his home, and the house was tractor-bulldozed into the river. That was too much for Louie Diablo, one of those Indians. He sat in front of his house with a shotgun month after month while his wife, 68 years of age, walked two miles every day to get water and groceries for the family.

Finally they went to Louie—they had offered him four times what the land was worth according to appraisal—and they said, "what will you take?" He said, "I'll take $70,000. This is no Manhattan Island deal. You folks trimmed us Indians at that time, but now we're going to get our money."

Wait a minute. There is another thing he said. "I want Lionel

Chevrier"—head of the Canadian Seaway Corporation—"to pay me that check in person."

And one day Mr. Chevrier in person, through a line of cheering Indians, saw Louie Diablo and paid that check for $70,000.

Now, that has its humorous aspects, but the point I am trying to make is that our Canadian cousins have the same democratic traditions, the same Anglo-Saxon background that we have, and they were scrupulous in seeing to it that human and property rights were preserved.

I certainly hope, gentlemen of the Senate and of the House here represented, that we may have the same regard for these people in this area.[3]

Monetary objections to the bill

For the time being, further examination of the political and moral arguments will be postponed to discuss the monetary arguments. Essentially, monetary issues concerned three distinct groups of people: (1) the local residents, (2) the state of Michigan, (3) the U.S. government. Those who opposed the bill argued that the local residents could not afford to lose the tax revenue from the lands that were to be made public. They were particularly concerned about paying for new schools. Thousands of visiters, they argued, would not provide the kind of development the region needed. Perhaps the bitterest criticism was directed not at changes to occur in the future but at the destruction of the building and real estate market which had already occurred at the time of the controversy.

The opponents of S. 2153 looked with great skepticism at the predictions of the National Park Service: "Five years after the establishment of the proposed area an additional 1.2 million people could be expected to visit the region each year," and, "Over 20 million people live within an easy day's drive of the area."

The criticism of Ove Jensen regarding these projections is

---

[3] U.S., Congress, Senate, Committee on Interior and Insular Affairs, *Sleeping Bear Dunes National Recreation Area, Hearings,* before Senator Frank E. Moss, in Traverse City, Nov. 13, 1961, 81st Cong., 1st sess., 1961, pp. 97-98.

worth examining. He writes the following in a tract called, "The Bear is Asleep . . . But the People are Awake":[4]

> This [the predictions] set us to wondering. We wondered first why 1.2 million people would visit the proposed Sleeping Bear Dunes National Recreation Area, since this is more people than visited either the Grand Canyon or Yosemite during 1960. Then we remembered predictions made for Isle Royale National Park in Michigan. We remembered that the late Congressman Louis Rabout of Detroit, in attempting to justify a planned additional federal investment of more than a million dollars there for a new boat said for the Congressional Record of January 30, 1957 (p. 1181), "A uniquely situated park, Isle Royale is accessible to 35 million people." Now, even with a million-dollar boat to take them there, only about six or seven thousand persons a year visit Isle Royale. Boat service is available only from June 18 through September 7, and rates for food and lodging are comparably higher than in our area, where free enterprise still prevails. In short, if the estimates of the tourist traffic to the proposed park area are not realistic, and we believe they are not, then the supposed advantages to the state in increased tourism must be discounted.

This is an interesting criticism in that it uses inconsistency with past experience as a reason for doubting the projection made by the National Park Service. Jensen felt that a credibility gap existed because a congressman had made a projection about Isle Royale which proved to be wrong. The fact that the National Park Service was something quite different from Congressman Rabout makes Jensen's argument a classic example of the fallacy of the undistributed middle: Congressman Rabout, who was associated with the government, made a prediction that was false; the National Park Service, associated with the government, also made a prediction; therefore, the prediction made by the National Park Service was also judged false. Jensen's identification of the park service with Congressman Rabout can be explained by his general hostility to government.

The board of education of both the Glen Lake Community Schools and the Honor Public School opposed Bill S. 2153. The Glen Lake Community School District takes in

---

4 The Citizens' Council of the Sleeping Bear Dunes Area, "The Bear is Asleep . . . But the People are Awake," Glen Arbor, Mich., 1961. This pamphlet will be mentioned several times throughout this chapter and will be referred to hereafter as the "tract."

most of the southwestern half of Leelanau County. Its board of education argued that 55.17 percent of the district's $10,348,643 valuation was included in the proposed park area and that one-third of its 635 students lived in that area. The board testified before the Senate subcommittee that "passage of S. 2153 would work a severe hardship upon continued operation of our district."[5] According to the board's projections, taxpayers still had 20 years to go on the 26-year, $500,000 bond issue that built the school. Senator Philip A. Hart indicated that he might ask for federal funds to help the school with operating costs, but there were no known federal funds which could be used to help pay off the bonded indebtedness.

In the tract, Jensen wrote the following:

> The Honor Public School objects to S. 2153 because in the words of the Board of Education, "It would seem eventually to remove approximately 2/3 to 3/4 of the tax valuation base of the present school district, a base which is already a minimum one in providing the educational opportunity which is felt necessary for the children of this area." The Board points out that "To sacrifice support for education for the purpose of establishing recreational facilities does not seem consistent in considering our local, state and national welfare." The State of Michigan already holds title to 35,000 acres of land within this district for which it pays 15 cents an acre in lieu of taxes. Total valuation within the district is only $3,620,000. There are 427 pupils. The building, erected in four stages from 1949 to 1955, costs $341,000. It will not be paid for until 1963.

Another of the tract's economic arguments leveled against the bill was directed at the influence which a national park would have on the area.

> Leelanau and Benzie are unlike most resort areas in that their income from summer business is based mainly upon the people from Michigan and other states who own houses on lakes here and return to them each season.

> These people, many of whom would leave if their homes were taken into a national recreation area, don't spend money just for food and gasoline. They build, repair and furnish homes. In many townships they pay more than half of the property taxes that support schools and county government. They come in early spring and remain until late fall.

---

5 *Ibid.*

Both counties do all they can to attract transient tourist business which comes in a rush during July and August. Most of the hotels, motels, and restaurants then close for the remainder of the year. A national recreation area would be adding to this problem rather than solving it.

Sleeping Bear Dunes are famed throughout the nation, yet at no time during the summer of 1961 were the state parks on either side of the dunes filled. There is no admission fee for either of these parks. There are adequate public accesses to nearby lakes and streams, many county, township and village parks.

Economy of the two-county area is based mainly on resort business and cherry growing, both of which are expanding. Leelanau is the third greatest cherry producing county in the nation. Thousands of itinerant workers pour into the area every summer to help with the harvest. Their earnings are pumped back into the economy through stores and service stations.

What Leelanau and Benzie need are small, year-around industries—not a big government-owned playground that would choke off property tax revenues, jam more business into the already profitable two months of summer, and force vacationists to pay higher (park concession) prices.

On the state level, the opposition pointed out that Michigan was then (in 1961) nationally famous for its fiscal plight and that making state-taxed property into a federal park was no help in solving Michigan's economic problems. Representative Robert P. Griffin argued on a federal level that the government was broke and should not consider nonessential measures. Others took the same sort of approach.

Legal arguments against the bill

The legal arguments were perhaps best represented by the lawyer for the Citizens' Council, Kenneth Thompson from Traverse City. The following is a quote from his statement at the hearings at Traverse City on November 13, 1961:

In all our opinion the text of S. 2153 raises questions of real concern to all property owners. The bill authorizes the Secretary of the Interior to acquire all the land and other property and improvements comprising the area depicted on the boundary map, incorporated by reference in the bill. Property acquisition may be by condemnation among other methods, through the exercise of the government's power of eminent domain. Other provisions of the bill state that the Secretary's right to exercise the authority to condemn private residential property shall be suspended under certain conditions and that lands of the State of Michigan or local governmental bodies may be acquired only by their concurrence.

However, we understand the power of eminent domain to be inalienable and no legislative body can bind itself or its successors not to exercise this power when public interest and convenience require it. A statutory provision that the power of eminent domain is delegated, cannot by agreement, restrict their right to exercise the power.[6]

This particular legal argument seems to have no answer. Certainly no act of Congress could pledge that future governmental officials would give up the right of eminent domain. Thus, the local residents were safeguarded by the good will and honesty of future park officials but not by law. Because of this, the reputation of these officials became very important and, as it changed, the attitude toward the bill changed.

Logical arguments against the bill

The logical arguments rested on semantical considerations as well as alleged inconsistencies. Certainly the wording of Senator Hart's bill was anything but a model of clarity and explicitness; certainly it was changed a number of times. Perhaps the logical inconsistency which most concerned local property owners was that which had to do with the government's right to buy private land. The original bill stated quite clearly that "the Secretary may exclude from the land so designated any beach or waters on Lake Michigan together with so much of the land adjoining any such beach or waters as the Secretary may deem necessary for public access thereto." In a letter of explanation sent to residents of the region, Senator Hart wrote:

My position is, and the Bill (S. 2153) provides that the National Park Service would be prohibited from condemning or "confiscating" private homes or cottages built prior to July 1, 1961.[7]

---

[6] *Sleeping Bear Dunes . . . Hearings,* pp. 80-81.

[7] Letter from Senator Philip Hart, U.S. Senator, to property owners in the boundary of proposed Sleeping Bear Dunes. The text of the letter is included in *Sleeping Bear Dunes . . . Hearings,* p. 28.

With reference to this language, Kenneth Thompson pointed out,

> Owners are not clearly protected under S. 2153 against future policy changes by the Park Service. Section 5(a) on page 6 of the bill provides that the Secretary may issue amended zoning standards "whenever he shall consider such amended regulations to be desirable due to changed or unforeseen conditions." Section 5(d) on page 8 provides that if the use of any property "fails to conform to or is inconsistent with any applicable standard contained in regulations issued pursuant to this section and in effect at the time of passage of such by-law, the Secretary may, at his discretion, terminate the suspension of his authority to acquire such improved property by condemnation."[8]

When inconsistencies and vaguenesses in the bill's wording were pointed out, Senator Hart answered that the bill was not in final form and would be changed after hearings were held. The Senator's response, then, was to say that any inconsistencies, ambiguities, and vaguenesses were bad and should be removed in later forms of the bill.

Arguments in Defense of S. 2153

Whereas the criticisms of this proposal were couched in terms of natural rights, monetary interest, logic, and law, the defense of the bill was largely in utilitarian terms. It was pointed out a number of times that only citizens alive 50 to 75 years from the time the bill was enacted would be in a position to judge the wisdom of the bill.

The arguments in favor of Senate Bill S. 2153 tended to reflect a substantially different view of government, of ethics, and of law. It should be noticed that those who were working for the passage of this bill based their actions upon a considerable amount of research. Much of this research was the sort discussed in the introduction when projections were described. Notice the concern for the future in the arguments below, where it is pointed out that 10, 40, or 50 years would bring changes that would be of great importance for the decisions then being made. Senator Hart pointed to the

---

8 *Sleeping Bear Dunes . . . Hearings*, p. 82.

following facts and projections in his statement defending the bill:

1. Sleeping Bear Dunes and adjoining lands were singled out in the 1958 Great Lakes survey for national preservation.

2. In 10 years it may be completely impossible to consider acquisition of an area along this part of the Michigan shore whose size and beauty would be of national significance.
   a) Further development would make the cost prohibitive.
   b) Change would result in the loss of natural and scientific features detracting from its national significance.

3. By 1975 the population of the U.S. will increase by 50 million.

4. In 40 years the population of the U.S. will double.

5. Forty years ago people had 40 percent less leisure time.

6. In 40 years, visits to our National and State Parks have jumped from 50 million visits a year to more than 331 million visits.

7. In the North Central states live 29 percent of the population but only 14 percent of the recreation area. This includes the land and water areas managed by park, forest, fish and wildlife and water agencies at all levels of government.

8. In the Western area which has only 15 percent of the population one finds 71 percent of the recreation area.

9. Tourism ranks along with manufacturing and agriculture as leading sources of revenue in Michigan, which ranks fourth in the nation in dollars spent by tourists.

10. Direct impact of tourists' business accounts for 100,000 jobs and $650 million a year. Most recent studies, including indirect benefits, raised this figure to 200,000 jobs and income of 2.6 billion.

11. On the basis of the MSU study of the economic feasibility it is estimated that $10.8 million of new tourist income from 1.2 million annual visitors could be expected in the Grand Traverse region within 5 years.[9]

It should be noted that none of these facts were presented as opposing the right of the property owner to private ownership of his land. Hart was, in effect, suggesting that the right of the community to public use of the land for recreational purposes is a more urgent right than the usual rights of property; he was also suggesting that, in terms of economic

---

9 *Ibid.*

advantage, the people of the area would benefit, whether they recognized it or not, from the creation of the national lakeshore area. It will be pointed out later that part of the complexity of this problem centered around who owned the land involved. Much of the region affected was owned by people who lived in other parts of the country during the winter. For them, the arguments regarding the economic benefits to Leelanau and Benzie counties were not persuasive.

At the beginning of this chapter it was pointed out that the problem of the Sleeping Bear recreation area was a complex one. We have seen some of the arguments for and against the bill. We now turn to some of the procedural aspects of the problem.

Procedural Problems

Bill S. 2153, which was to affect profoundly the lives of the residents of northwestern Michigan, was not discussed with them before it was introduced into the Senate. This fact alone accounted for much of the bitterness that local citizens felt. The National Park Service had, at one time, planned to have an office in Traverse City during the summer of 1961 for advising and informing people about the nature and consequence of this legislation. Such an office was never established. Hearings were held in Glen Arbor at which Conrad Wirth of the park service spoke, but his attitude and approach to the questions of local residents turned people even more forcefully against the bill.

The bitterness felt toward Mr. Wirth was expressively described in the following excerpt from Mr. William F. Meinhard's testimony at the Traverse City hearings:

> On August 30, Senator Hart, not being able to be present, sent a group of National Park Service men, headed by Conrad L. Wirth, Director, to address a meeting of 2,000 people at the Glen Lake Community High School. . . . After a lengthy and favorable introduction by our Mr. Jensen, Mr. Wirth exclaimed, "You have made a good showing but we are going to vote you down" and then proceeded for a quarter hour to list the achievements of the National Park Service and confirm his own importance as the third generation of the Wirth family in this bureau. After referring to our chairman as a fertilizer salesman, he told the overflowing house, most of whom

were hoping for light on their future status, not heat, "They call me a bureaucrat and I'm proud of it."

It should not be difficult to understand how boos and hisses escaped from such a large group of people composed of those who want to protect their homes and livelihood or investments in property for retirement or summer homes from the ruthless obsession of their employee, Mr. Wirth.[10]

The people of the area organized citizens' councils to oppose the legislation and, under the leadership of Ove Jensen, wrote many letters informing property owners of the developments related to the bill. They also published a 24-page brochure called "The Bear is Asleep . . . But the People are Awake," which contained quotations from Congressman Robert P. Griffin, Secretary of the Interior Stewart Udall, Conrad Wirth, Robert Belcher, *Life* magazine, and a number of newspapers throughout the country. Among other pieces of information in this publication were indications that Senator Hart and the park service had been less than completely ingenuous in their arguments in favor of the bill. For example, in a television interview with Secretary Udall and Senator Hart, the latter said of federally owned acreage in Michigan: "They are just small chunks. . . . You have to have a helicopter and a parachute to get into it, and most of it nobody would want to get [to] . . . if they had the parachute and helicopter."[11] In view of the fact that there are five national forests in Michigan which cover 2,543,000 acres, Hart's quip seems inappropriate. Furthermore, the brochure entitled, "A Proposed Sleeping Bear National Seashore"[12] contained two pictures of scenic vistas meant to be taken as privately owned beaches and dunes that were supposed to be preserved for posterity. It turned out that both of these regions belonged to the state of Michigan. Jensen's brochure commented, "Most of the pictures in it [the "Sleeping Bear National Seashore"] were taken either of, or from state owned lands," yet not one of them was identified as such.

Another cause for concern among the opponents of the bill stemmed from Senator Hart's assurances that families

---

10 *Ibid.*, p. 120.

11 "The Bear is Asleep" tract.

12 Natural History Report of the U.S. Department of Interior and the National Park Service, 1961.

would be able to continue living in their homes within the proposed national recreation area. The assurance seemed less than convincing when the director of the National Park Service, Conrad L. Wirth, wrote in the May 1959 issue of the *National Geographic*, "Another thing I'd like to see accomplished is the elimination of private ownership inside park boundaries."

The residents of the affected region were, at the outset, almost 100 percent opposed to the sort of change that a national recreation area would bring to northwestern Michigan. They argued that the bill's supporters misunderstood the economic needs of the community and that the bill jeopardized the orderly functioning of the school systems, would destroy the way of life which the residents had selected for themselves, and would alienate the summer people who contributed substantial economic support to the region.

Many of the arguments against the idea of a recreation area were not generally known, but nevertheless explain the bitterness and depth of local emotions. The property owners of Leelanau and Benzie Counties were descendants of pioneer settlers in the region; some of their deeds went back to the time of Van Buren and Abraham Lincoln. They regarded the land as theirs by virtue of the labor and care which they had put into it. Furthermore many cherished the land as a way of life, having tried city life with its steady income and chosen to return to their splendid isolation. Like many other regions of this sort, the dominant political philosophy was conservative, Republican, and individualistic. From this philosophy came great distaste for governmental interference, particularly if the government was a federal "bureaucratic" one. Part of this political philosophy placed great stress upon industry, thrift, and sobriety. To these people, the thought of turning their homes and homeland into a playground for "shiftless, lazy, and indigent city trash" was anathema. Their objections contain numerous references to "playground," "property rights," "self-seeking bureaucrats," and "loss of freedom." The Secretary of the Interior became a "veritable dictator." They objected to "this whimsical move on the part of the federal government," and, in a literary metaphor of great expressiveness, they said, "Under the 'old concept,' a man's home is his castle, but under the 'new concept' advocated by Interior Secretary Udall, a man's home can become his neighbor's sand castle."

The early actions of both the National Park Service and the sponsors of S. 2153 in the Senate showed lack of concern for the human beings most intimately affected by the legislation. Two of the most telling sentences in Jensen's tract were: "As residents of the area, we had not been consulted at any time by representatives of the National Park Service. Even our Congressman was not consulted."

The lesson for democracy to be learned from this poor initial solution to an admittedly important national problem was that public support for parks is lessened if they are instituted at the expense of people. As a Pareto-better economic solution, this bill could never pass. The residents of Leelanau and Benzie Counties who felt they would be hurt deserved to have a voice in the disposition of the land resources which they had done so much to develop. Unless these residents could, by democratic persuasion, be converted to the National Park Service's point of view, there was serious question whether any future advantage could justify the Sleeping Bear National Recreation Area. Even if the need for future recreation land was very great, even if ". . . the only persons who will be able to know for certain what actions should be taken are those very young children who will be alive 50 to 75 years from now,"[13] a democratic decision could not be based on the supposition that people were merely means to an end. Whether or not the residents of Leelanau and Benzie Counties had justifiable reasons for their opposition to a federal seashore area, their interests deserved hearing and respect. They were not things with essences but human beings with identities and existences, to put the matter in existentialist terms. However justifiable the end, the procedure undertaken was clearly open to criticism.

Justification in Normative Matters

In ethics there are two sorts of justification. One is a justification in terms of an accepted ethical or legal system. To justify the action of a policeman who arrests a man driving his car 80 miles an hour in a 65 mile an hour speed zone, one need only call attention to the speed law which has been violated. But to justify the man's speeding one would

---

[13] *Sleeping Bear Dunes . . . Hearings.*

need to appeal to a value taken by the social order as higher than the speed law. If the man was rushing a dying child to a hospital, the arresting officer would probably accept his reason and escort him the remainder of the trip. If, however, he was rushing to reach a cocktail party on time, he would probably be found guilty.

But sometimes the question involves a change in the structure of the social order itself. To justify this, one obviously needs to establish the rightness of the change by showing that the new order better satisfies the normative purposes of its members than the old one. This is never an easy thing to do, although sometimes social engineers treat it as if it were.

The Sleeping Bear controversy is a crucial one precisely because it represents a proposal to change, and to change fundamentally, the social order with respect to land ownership. The proposed fundamental change was to establish a means of taking land which neither the owners nor their congressional representatives wanted to have taken. This was *not* justifiable in terms of an immediate public emergency, and the argument as to its necessity was not consistently, clearly, and pragmatically developed.

In the tradition of American law, private property rights have been regarded almost as fundamental as the rights of life and liberty. The colonists included in the Bill of Rights for the Constitution the famous fifth amendment, which ends, ". . . nor shall private property be taken for public use without just compensation." In later years the courts put an important reservation on the right of the government to take private land for public use. This reservation was that the power to take private property must not be used except in the public interest. It is on the question of whether or not the recreation area was in the public interest that the disagreement reported in this chapter rests. Constitutionally, the court has declared that it is for Congress to decide what type of "taking" is in the public's interest. Thus, on a purely legal basis, the opponents of Senate Bill S. 2153 seem to have a rather weak case.

Whether Congress decided what was in the public interest on the basis of all relevant knowledge or on the basis of political expediency determined to a large degree the success of the democratic enterprise. A report in 1962 suggested that President John Kennedy had not taken seriously the hearings about this bill. His arguments, it will be noted, are substantially the same as those made the previous year by Senator Hart and the park service. However, it should also be noticed that a compromise is suggested, and it was indeed the compromise which later became the basis of a reformulation of the bill. A press release read:

President Kennedy asked Congress today to include Michigan's Sleeping Bear Dunes in an expanded federal park system which would help meet obligations to "numberless generations."

Meanwhile, Interior Secretary Stewart L. Udall told United Press International he was "much more hopeful" than before about prospects for passage of the controversial Sleeping Bear proposal.

"I think I am beginning to see the ingredients of a compromise," he said, adding that he planned to visit the area sometime this year.

Udall, who earlier suggested a Sleeping Bear area of more than 90,000 acres, said he was "always willing to compromise to size."

The Citizens' Council of Glen Arbor, leader of opposition to the proposal, said it was not surprised Kennedy mentioned Sleeping Bear.

"We believe the Hart-McNamara bill is not in the best interests of the state and nation and that when all of the facts have been brought out in further hearings, it will be defeated."

Kennedy noted that there were 341 million visitors to federal land and water areas in 1960 and that the projection was expected to double by 1970 and increase five-fold by the end of the century.

"The need for an aggressive program of recreational development is both real and immediate," Kennedy said.

The President proposed spending $500 million over the next eight years to acquire land for recreational purposes. Money would come from:

A user fee to be charged visitors to federal recreational areas.

An annual charge placed on recreational boats.

Receipts from the sale of surplus non-military lands.

Diversion from the highway fund of refundable, but unclaimed, taxes paid on gasoline used in motor boats.

"With each passing year prime areas of outdoor recreation and fish and wildlife are pre-empted for suburban growth, industrial development or other uses," the President said.

He said the nation was compelled "to consider and meet our obligations to our children and the numberless generations that will follow."

Kennedy also asked more money to buy recreation sites in cities and legislation to preserve national wilderness areas. He asked for measures to conserve the nation's water supply.

The President also asked Congress to approve an increase of $50 million in the program designed to help state and local governments purchase land for recreational facilities.[14]

This press release shows how normative and logical issues enter into decisions concerning land uses. The Sleeping Bear controversy is representative of the difficulties encountered in many public choices. Men of good will on each side of the question were reasoning together in a conscientious effort to take a right action. To take such an action they tried to discover what action maximized human interests and purposes as indicated by the value concepts involved. The extended hearings, the investigation by social scientists at Michigan State University, the park service, congressmen, the Citizens' Council, interested residents and others, the many letters written to newspapers, and editorials—all contributed to a better understanding of what the right action was. The authors believe that any disinterested person critically examining the first part of this chapter will agree that it offers substantial evidence that:

1. Values can be known and such knowledge exists.

2. Values can be arranged in systematic structures.

3. Knowledge of values is not essentially different from non-normative knowledge.

Because of the existence of this knowledge and its development in the present controversy, Senator Hart and other supporters of S. 2153 were convinced that the bill was unsatisfactory. Thus, they discarded it and formulated an alternative bill. The second part of this chapter will examine this second bill and show ways in which it was superior to the first.

---

14 "President Kennedy Gives Sleeping Bear Top Priority," *State Journal*, March 1, 1962.

The Second Sleeping Bear Dunes Bill

After almost a year of hearings, discussions, letters, and committee reports, Senator Hart replaced Bill S. 2153 with Bill S. 3528. In introducing the new bill, Senator Hart said:

> Since introducing a year ago the original bill proposing the preservation of the Michigan shoreline at Sleeping Bear Dunes, it is my good fortune to be able to report today that much progress has been made toward resolving some of the difficult questions posed by that first bill.

> Mr. President, there have been numerous public and private meetings, much thoughtful correspondence, a public hearing by the Subcommittee of Public Lands of the Senate Interior Committee, and immeasurable effort on the part of many groups and individuals. To those who have written, met, and talked goes much of the credit for bringing this new bill into being.

Certainly many of the criticisms of Bill S. 2153 were not applicable to Bill S. 3528. The arguments against the former had been taken seriously, and an attempt had been made to modify the original bill in such a way as to meet squarely the objections contained in them.

The argument that the proposed national lakeshore would violate property rights was answered by specifying "inland lakeshore residential area" within which residents' property would be "permanently protected from condemnation." Since almost all of the property owners who had objected to the original bill held land within these areas, the arguments of many citizens were answered. Furthermore, within the park the following commercial land uses were to be permitted: "marinas, commercial farms, orchards, rental cottages, camps, crafts and art studies, and Christmas tree farms." Senator Hart says, after listing these uses, "As far as we know, all businesses currently within the proposed park fall into one of these categories."

The object of the new bill was obviously to preserve traditional private property rights while creating a recreation area to preserve "this unique corner of creation." Thus, the political and moral objections discussed earlier were met by agreeing with those who hold that the right of property is a fundamental right. The only people who were not protected were those who had purchased undeveloped land holdings for the purpose of land speculation. These people were not to be forced to sell their property at a loss, but were prevented from realizing the profits they had anticipated. Against the argument that "the bill would allow their property to be bought, with the Secretary of the Interior serving as the sole appraiser," S. 3528 provided that "the Secretary shall make every reasonable effort to acquire property through negotiation and purchase. Where agreement is not reached and condemnation proceedings are filed, the owner of such property shall be paid the fair market value thereof as determined in said judicial process." Whether such a formulation would satisfy all of those who believe that the "natural" right of property was endangered remained to be seen, but certainly the revised bill went a long way in the direction of appeasing the followers of John Locke.

The new bill protected the financial interests of individuals largely by allowing existing commercial land uses within the park areas to continue and by pointing out that "this lakeshore will bring to the area and to the state of Michigan economic benefits in terms of increased transit revenues equivalent to the establishment of 10 average-sized Michigan industries."

In answer to the concern of local school boards and administrators, Senator Hart explained that until private property was transferred to the Secretary of the Interior, it would remain on the tax rolls. If advantage was taken of the act's provision for 25-year estate (section 10), section 7 authorized the property to be taxed for local purposes. (Section 7 said, "Nothing in this Act shall be construed as prohibiting any governmental jurisdiction in the state of Michigan from assessing taxes upon any interest in real estate retained under the provisions of section 10 of this Act to the owner of such interest.") "This provision has been included because of the expressed desire of local school and county officials to minimize the tax loss in the period when undeveloped land would be acquired and before new development brought into the counties as a result of the lakeshore would raise the overall property evaluation throughout the area."[15]

There was no attempt, obviously, to meet the objection that the federal government was broke and should not be

---

15 *Sleeping Bear Dunes . . . Hearings.*

considering nonessential measures at that time. However, Representative Griffin, who had made this argument, proposed an alternative park scheme. Thus, he was apparently persuaded that national parks were essential and that the federal government was not as broke as he had originally argued.

Although Kenneth Thompson's legal arguments still had some force, they were made less relevant by the creation of inland lakeshore residential areas which would be "permanently protected from condemnation." While Thompson was correct in asserting that "the power of eminent domain is inalienable" and that "no legislative body can bind itself or its successors not to exercise this power when public interest or convenience require it," the record of the park service seemed to give assurance that this right would not be abused. Those who were students of law recognized that there was considerable difference between laws as words in statute books and laws as social realities. If one thought of the park service as a social reality, the past conduct of this body became relevant in predicting its future behavior. Those men who had strongly opposed the earlier creation of a somewhat similar park at Cape Hatteras, North Carolina, were apparently now persuaded that the national seashore was a good thing. One of the Dare County (North Carolina) commissioners, Lawrence L. Swain, who originally opposed the project, now said, "Ninety-eight percent of the people were against the proposal. I felt that it was my duty as their elected representative to do everything I could to stop it."

But later Swain agreed with David Stick, who was an early backer of the project, that the national seashore had been beneficial to their country. Most others apparently agreed.

"I don't say that there's no opposition to the park," Stick said "but the bulk of it has evaporated."

But in the beginning, he had said, "there was a national aversion to the park. The people felt that despite safeguards on their hunting and fishing they would never be able to pursue either one.

"However, they've found that they can hunt and commercial fish as much as they want," he said.

Stick added that the park has been "a very beneficial and helpful addition to the community in many ways."

"For one thing," he said, "we've gotten publicity we couldn't have gotten without the help of the Park Service. The Park Service does a better job of selling us as a resort than we could do ourselves."

The service's conservation efforts have impressed Swain.

"They've taken over an extensive area of our coastline and made an extreme effort to stabilize it," he said, "We should never have been able to do this without them."

The Park Service had built mounds of sand between the ocean and the rest of the land and planted it with grass in order to stablize the coastline. The value of this was proved during a storm which destroyed much property along the Atlantic Coast.

"If development had gone on, if the coast had been developed commercially like some wanted to do, I don't think there would have been a building left after this storm," Stick added.[16]

Publicity such as this unquestionably helped the park service's cause in Michigan. When these favorable comments on the activities of the park service are compared with such comments as the following, the importance of understanding in the effective operations of governmental agencies becomes apparent.

What is at issue is the fact that if the government can force the sale of private property merely to satisfy its greedy ambitions, is there, then, any limitation to what the government can or cannot do? Or can the entire democratic process be trampled underfoot by self-seeking bureaucrats?[17]

By June 30, 1963, the *Detroit Free Press* was carrying editorials indicating that the showdown was coming in what it called "the war of the Dunes." Those opposing the park still argued that the park was a "federal land grab" that would violate basic property rights guaranteed in the Constitution. They also argued,

Michigan already has one of the best state park systems in the country as well as nearly 700 public fishing sites and 6.3 million acres of State-Federally owned lands. Why, they ask, should the Federal Government encroach on an area containing 1,600 improved properties?

What were the results of this debate? All concerned seem to agree that the firm stand taken by the opposition had

---

16 *Topeka Capital Journal*, Apr. 15, 1962.
17 *The Arizona Republic*, Dec. 6, 1961, p. 6.

resulted in needed safeguards being written into the bill and the substitution of specific provisions for vague generalities. This suggests that the debate resulted in a clarification along logical lines, which would not have occurred without the debate. It is worth noting, furthermore, that the opponents conceded that the park campaign resulted in long overdue zoning ordinances. The results, then, included right actions which would not have occurred had there not been intensive interaction among decision makers and investigators.

It was not until the 1970 legislative session of Congress that the bill passed to establish the Sleeping Bear Dunes National Lakeshore in the state of Michigan. The delay of nine years increased the cost of acquiring the land from $12,200,000 to $19,800,000, but won support from many of the early critics. There were still many vocal opponents, and some of the citizens threatened to tie up the development of a national lakeshore for years by judicial action. Nevertheless, the fundamental formulation of the second bill remained intact in the bill which was finally passed. An obvious attempt was made to assure land owners in the affected area that they could continue to use their land as they wished as long as the owner used his property "in a manner consistent with the applicable standard set forth in subsection d of this section, and such prohibition against condemnation shall remain in effect for so long as such property is so used." Subsection d reads:

> Any zoning bylaw or amendment thereto submitted to the Secretary for approval for the purposes of this Act shall be approved by him if such bylaw or amendment contains provisions which:
>
> 1. Contribute to the effect of prohibiting the commercial and industrial use (other than a use for a commercial purpose as authorized under section 13 of this Act) [Section 13 of the Acts reads: "In any case not otherwise provided for in this Act the Secretary shall be prohibited from condemning any commercial property used for commercial purposes in existence on December 31, 1964, so long as such use does not impair the usefulness and attractiveness of the area designated for inclusion in the lakeshore. The following uses, among others, shall be considered to be uses compatible with the purposes of this Act: Commercial farms, orchards, motels, rental cottages, camps, craft and art studies, marinas, medical, legal, architec-

tural, and other such professional offices, and tree farms.[18]] of all property within the boundaries of such area which is situated within the county or township adopting such bylaw or amendment;

2. are consistent with the objectives and purposes of this Act so that, to the extent possible under Michigan law, the scenic and scientific values of the lakeshore area will be protected;

3. are designed to preserve the lakeshore character of the property by appropriate restrictions upon the burning of cover, cutting of timber (except tracts managed for sustained yield), removal of sand or gravel, and dumping, storage or piling of refuse and other unsightly objects or other uses which would detract from the natural or traditional lakeshore scene;

4. provide that no construction, reconstruction, moving, alteration, or enlargement would afford less than fifty-foot setback from all streets measured at a right angle with the street line, and a twenty-five foot distance from an abutters' property lines. Any owner or zoning authority may request the Secretary of the Interior to determine whether a proposed move, alteration, construction, reconstruction, or enlargement of any property would subject such property to acquisition by condemnation, and the Secretary, within sixty days of the receipt of such request, shall advise the owner or zoning authority in writing whether the intended use will subject the property to acquisition by condemnation; and

5. have the effect of providing that the Secretary shall receive notice of any variance granted under and of exception made to the application of such bylaw or amendment.

Thus, the bill which was finally passed had gone a great distance to answer the early charge that the zoning standards "go far beyond accepted standards of zoning."

Conclusion

A right action was defined earlier as one determined to be best in view of the non-normative and normative beliefs involved, where *best* means that which maximizes human interests and purposes as indicated by the value concepts

---

18 It is interesting to observe that motels, medical, legal, architectural, and other such professional offices have been added to the second Sleeping Bear Bill, and that Christmas tree farms have become tree farms.

involved. In view of this definition, it is appropriate to ask at the end of this chapter whether the passage of the bill to establish the Sleeping Bear Dunes National Lakeshore was a right action.

Before answering this categorically, it should be pointed out that almost everyone would agree that the bill as passed was an improvement over S. 2153. This improvement was possible because of the care which Senator Hart and the subcommittee on public lands of the U.S. Senate Committee on Interior and Insular Affairs took to hear from so many of the people intimately interested in the legislation. As a matter of fact, when Senator Hart made his initial remarks at the Traverse City hearings, he said:

> Since Senator McNamara and I introduced the initial legislative proposal, a number of property owners and other interested individuals concerned with specific details of the bill have raised useful and helpful questions. Each of these questions has been pursued and analyzed. I would suggest, Mr. Chairman, as the subcomittee considers this legislation, that a number of amendments should be adopted which would strengthen and clarify the bill for the benefit of both the Government and those who might own property within the final boundaries.

The bill which was finally passed reflected the results of the suggestions, questions, and analyses mentioned in this passage. Thus, we can say with some assurance that it comes closer to being a right action than did S. 2153. The important issue is whether the authors of the bill did everything reasonable within their power to understand the normative concepts relevant to their proposed legislation.

Certainly Senator Hart paid careful attention to a number of individuals and agencies who were in a position to advise him expertly. He took into account the results of a study made by the Institute for Community Development at Michigan State University,[19] and he was in correspondence with numerous conservation and recreation associations. He care-

---

[19] During the discussion of this bill, Michigan State University was accused of being partisan in its report to the National Park Service. President Hannah of that university, after defending the integrity of Dr. Charles R. Adrian, director of the institute, pointed out that "Michigan State University has not taken sides in this controversial issue but has tried to be of service in the interest of making possible an informed final decision on a matter of public policy."

fully considered the counsel of numerous private citizens, some interested and some disinterested. Senator Hart then had to solve the practical problem of framing a Senate bill which would best satisfy the conflicting interests represented. He became quite willing to admit the mistakes which were made in the course of the bill's history. The people of the region should have been consulted earlier and kept better informed of the progress of the legislative thinking; Conrad Wirth's unsympathetic approach undoubtedly alienated and exaggerated misunderstanding; and the information upon which decisions were made was frequently too little and too late.

Senator Hart, in reflecting on the long struggle, came to much the same conclusions that we have come to in this chapter. He commented in a letter that the early handling of community relations in regard to the proposal was very poor and that it would have been desirable to have had more consultation with local leaders prior to the introduction of the bill. He closes his letter with this statement:

> One of the interesting observations I have made since working on this project is that the National Park Service—possibly because its sole early history involved working with Federally-owned lands where private ownership was minimal, if existent—has not, to date, developed a sensitivity to public relations in the more populated areas where they are sometimes now working. In contrast, the Department of Agriculture—which has, of course, operated north, east, south, and west for many years—is much more attentive to an early information program in the affected area.[20]

If, however, the thesis of this book is correct, and one can make objective value judgments on the basis of experience and logic, it seems to the authors that Senator Hart's decision was a right one and that his action was a right one, although it could not in the nature of things be Pareto-better. The legislative process, as Senator Frank E. Moss pointed out, is essentially a matter of accommodating various conflicting interests; where there is a genuine conflict of interest there can hardly be a decision which some do not oppose. In a democracy, however, decisions made on the basis of the best possible knowledge aim to minimize the frustration of citizens' interests. Whether the bill which was finally passed does this

---

20 Letter from Senator Hart to Lewis Zerby, May 1, 1969.

may not be known for certain by this generation. Senator Hart, in his opening statement at the hearings, said:

> In my heart I think the only persons who will be able to know for certain what action should be taken are those very young children who will be alive 50 or 75 years from now. Only they will be able to see and to know whether we in the 1960's have acted in a way that will preserve a unique corner of creation.[21]

Senator Hart shows by these words that he is aware of the near impossibility of making adequate projections into the future to determine what action should be taken now. Such projections would make it unnecessary to wait for the very young children of today to judge today's actions. However, even inadequate projections are helpful. They can be provided, at least in part, by already existing formal and informal techniques. Such techniques are obviously valuable tools for legislative decision makers. Senator Hart seems to have felt the lack of a common denominator of values between the present generation and future generations. This book suggests that such a lack can be overcome, at least partially, by interactions between investigators using imaginative, accurate simulation models and decision makers such as Senator Hart, particularly if there is empathy for succeeding generations (see chapter 9).

If this statement is meaningful, then neither a positivistic nor even a conditionally normative approach would have been able to handle this problem, for such approaches assume that normative investigation is cognitively meaningless and that only positivistic knowledge is acceptable.

In this case, we saw that normative knowledge, while deficient, could be acquired. We also saw that the nature of man, both as an individual and as a part of a social community, had to be considered. The existentialist argument was of value but not entirely sufficient because group as well as individual identities were involved.

---

21 *Sleeping Bear Dunes . . . Hearings.*

VI | Some Problems of Michigan's Pickle Producing Industry

In 1957 several groups became concerned about the relatively low earnings of Mexican Nationals being brought to Michigan to pick pickles. These groups included the U.S. Department of State (USDS), which had responsibility for negotiating with the Mexican government in matters concerning employment of Mexican Nationals in the United States; the U.S. Department of Labor (USDL), whose interest in the earnings of Mexican Nationals grew out of the pressure exerted on it by labor unions to avoid competition for domestic employment; and the pickle processors, who desired to preserve the ability of farmers to deliver pickles. Pickle producers also had a keen interest in importing and paying wages to Mexican Nationals. Last, and probably least insofar as having power to influence the situation, was the Mexican National himself.

As a result of pressure from these various groups, representatives of the National Pickle Packers Association (NPPA) and the National Pickle Growers Association (NPGA) produced a formula for paying Mexican Nationals for picking the 1958 crop of pickles. It was generally recognized in designing this formula that earnings for Mexican Nationals were low on fields with poor yields. The new formula provided that Mexican Nationals who worked in fields producing more than 120 bushels per acre would be paid one-half of the value of the crop. The proportion of the value of the crop going to the Mexican Nationals who picked in fields yielding less than 120 bushels was increased.

Involvement of Michigan State University's
Department of Agricultural Economics

The Agricultural Economics Department of Michigan State University (MSU) was asked in the spring of 1958 to evaluate the operation of the new formula in the summer of 1958. The request came from the NPPA and the NPGA. *Objective* evaluation was sought in view of tensions resulting from the problem.

Initially, representatives of the U.S. Department of Labor refused to furnish MSU researchers with lists of farmers employing Mexican Nationals. Apparently, there was some conviction that the MSU researchers working on the problem were selling out to the National Pickle Growers and National Pickle Packers Associations.

Some farmers were equally suspicious of the MSU research. A new grower organization, the Michigan Pickling Cucumber Growers Association (MPCGA), was created to take over some of the functions of the NPGA, which some people regarded as a captive organization of the NPPA. One county agent, helping in the organization of the Michigan Pickling Cucumber Growers Association, was referred to as a "tax paid rabble rouser" by at least one processor.

In the correspondence involved in setting up the project, the head of the Agricultural Economics Department wrote:

> It was my understanding that during the summer of 1958, we would try to accomplish two things: (1) the evaluation of hourly earnings of laborers picking pickles in the State of Michigan, and (2) the evaluation of the formula which the USDL has agreed to allow the pickle industry to try this year in the reimbursement of farm labor. A second step to the evaluation of the formula will be to attempt to create a more workable formula or correct any deficiencies which may be apparent after the summer's work. . . . We at Michigan State are looking forward to this project with you and other representatives of the pickle interests of this state and nation. We genuinely appreciate the importance of the problem which needs immediate attention and will of necessity rely heavily upon members of your organization for guidance and help throughout the entire course of the project.[1]

---

[1] Letter dated June 19, 1958, from L. L. Boger to W. E. Dailey, Jr., President, Dailey Pickle Company.

In reply to this letter, the administrative head of the NPPA wrote:

> Thank you very much for your concise letter of June 19th covering the pickle project. Believe you have covered our objectives and understanding adequately. Would like to point out two things, however. First, "the evaluation of hourly earnings," "evaluation of the formula" should give particular attention to workers earning less than 70c an hour so that if and where they occur we will know the reasons why. Further, some evaluation of the ratio or percent of unwilling, incapable to capable workers.[2]

The legal minimum rate was 70 cents per hour. The Gift and Grant statement transferring funds from the NPPA to Michigan State University stated:

> Brief statement of objective of grant: (1) to determine hourly earnings of migrant labor in pickle harvesting and (2) to evaluate USDL approved formula for reimbursement of farm labor in pickle harvesting.

The Michigan Agricultural Experiment Station's project outline stated,

> Objectives: (1) to ascertain the hourly earnings of pickle harvest labor for Michigan in 1958, and (2) to evaluate the adequacy of the USDL approved formula in insuring minimum hourly wages for pickle harvest labor.

Clearly, MSU researchers were obligated to reach *evaluative* conclusions. In a preliminary report dated December 2, 1958, MSU researchers summarized their objectives as follows:

> The broad objective of the study as visualized by the Department of Agricultural Economics is to evaluate the effect of the Worker Yield Return Formula [WYRF] upon the pickle industry in Michigan. Subobjectives include (1) the impact of the formula upon the earnings of pickers and farmers, (2) factors accounting for the individual variations in pickers' earnings, (3) the effect of the formula upon the size distribution of pickles delivered to receiving stations, (4) the attitudes of farmers and pickers toward the formula, (5) the potential effects of the formula upon the future supply of pickles to processors and consumers, and (6) possible alternative wage formulas and arrangements that might be considered to achieve the objectives of the interested parties.

---

2 Letter dated June 30, 1960, from W. E. Dailey to L. L. Boger.

In their final report, the researchers stated:

> In requesting this research, the executives of the associations . . . indicated that they wanted an *objective evaluation* of the Worker Yield Return Formula. This was interpreted to mean (1) unbiased estimates of what went on in the industry in 1958 and (2) suggestions for changes in the formula and its administration consistent with accepted and/or new, clear, consistent, applicable objectives of interested parties such as pickers, growers, packers, responsible government agencies and pickle consumers.
>
> The study reported herein had as its objectives (1) the estimation of the average hourly earnings received by Mexican Nationals picking pickles in Southern Michigan and (2) the evaluation of the Worker Yield Return Formula . . . generally followed by the industry and accepted by the U.S. Department of Labor in determining the rate of reimbursement for Mexican Nationals picking pickles in Michigan in the summer of 1958. In connection with the first of these objectives, particular attention has been given to Nationals receiving a season average wage of less than 70 cents an hour. More particularly, both the situations under which they worked and the personal characteristics of the workers receiving low wages have been studied. In connection with the second objective, that of evaluating the formula, particular attention has been given to ways of correcting apparent deficiencies in the operation of the formula. Possible improvements considered include educational and research programs as well as changes in the WYRF itself. [Italics added.]

Procedures and Results of the Investigation

The approach of the MSU researchers was twofold. An attempt was made to describe the situation existing in 1958 and to predict what the future would hold both with and without various alternative, industry-wide actions. In addition, as a partial basis for determining a set of right goals as a solution to the problem, much time was spent trying to sort out, understand, clarify, and make consistent the various values that motivated interested parties to take the positions which they took.

Contracting arrangements and cultural conditions vary in different areas of the state. Therefore, it was necessary to work with a random sample of pickle producers if the results were to be considered applicable on a probability basis to the universe of pickle growers. That portion of the state where pickles are produced and picked by Mexican Nationals was divided into small areas, and a sample of these areas was drawn on a random basis. Within a selected sample area all farms that employed Mexican Nationals to pick pickles were included as sample farms.

The sample included 81 farmers, 76 of whom furnished useable data. The farmers furnishing useful data employed over 1,100 Mexican Nationals and sold pickles to 15 companies through 25 receiving stations. Had the USDL been willing to furnish lists of farmers certified to employ Nationals to pick pickles, such lists could have been sampled at random, thereby substantially reducing surveying costs.

Each farmer in the sample was asked to provide information regarding the cultural practices used in producing pickles, certain costs of production, his knowledge and attitude regarding the Worker Yield Return Formula, and his general attitude and practices regarding the use of labor in picking pickles. In addition, the farmers were asked to keep detailed records of the hours spent by their workers in various activities.

The workers were interviewed (in Spanish) regarding their reasons for entering the pickle picking labor force, their understanding and knowledge of the WYRF, their attitude toward picking pickles, and certain personal characteristics that might possibly influence their earnings.

Daily receipt and weight slips for each field were microfilmed in the offices of the pickle companies. The earnings statements of all workers were also microfilmed.

The data from all of these sources were transferred to International Business Machine cards for tabulation and analysis. Cross-referencing permitted reconciliation of data produced by other organizations, such as the USDL, with data from the study. Where inconsistencies appeared, further investigation was carried on to determine which set of data (non-normative concepts) was most reliable in terms of being consistent with other and accepted concepts as well as with current experience and observations.

Other, more normative investigations were less formal. In the course of the study, MSU researchers had repeated meetings with executives of the NPG and NPP Associations to ascertain and understand the values held by these two organizations. In addition, all meetings held with growers, whether by the NPGA or by the new Michigan Pickling Cucumber

Growers Association, were attended by at least one MSU researcher. At these meetings, the experienced goodness and badness of different conditions were often discussed.

As the work of the researchers progressed through the summer, accounts of normative experiences accumulated and the normative picture was further clarified by discussions, some quite logical. Normative and non-normative concepts were interrelated and conclusions began to emerge about what was wrong with the 1958 formula and what would be right to do about the situation.

The processes used in reaching tentative decisions about what was right to do were vague, complex, and hard to understand. At times many people tended to make decisions on the basis of what was best in the long run. In doing so, they seemed to be trying to maximize the present net value of average expected net returns. At other times, some people wanted to play it safe by adopting a course of action that would ensure that the worst which could happen would be good enough to guarantee certain minima. Some were unwilling to follow courses of action that would hurt themselves for the benefit of others; others with more empathy were willing to do so. This compassion for others was often encountered in interviews with farmers who had had first-hand experiences with the plights of the Mexican Nationals.

At about this point in the process of approximating what was right, MSU researchers decided that their normative and non-normative concepts and consequent evaluations should be checked by various interested groups for omission of important concepts and for such things as inconsistencies, misunderstandings, and vagueness. Consequently, the following abridged, tentative statement was prepared as a basis for discussions with members of interested groups.

Tentative general impressions and observations. These tentative comments will deal with growers, climatic conditions, diseases, marketing, laborers, the operation of the worker yield return formula and, finally, some of the directions which later recommendations may take. As our empirical analysis is incomplete, this tentative presentation does not deal with all objectives of the study.

I. *Growers*

    A. Grower dissatisfaction was prevalent throughout the state during the summer.

1. Industry-wide dissatisfaction primarily involved the price received by growers for pickles. Though price complaints are traditional with farmers, the price received for pickles together with high (labor) costs apparently make it difficult for other than efficient growers with better than average land and production practices to make satisfactory incomes. As better growers, however, can easily turn to competing crops the price range which discourages the less efficient producer while encouraging the efficient producer may be fairly narrow.

2. Dissatisfactions which appear to vary from company to company involve:

   a. Some resentment of the 6 percent labor association charge on the grower's share of receipts (3 percent of total). There was little objection to a flat fee per worker.

   b. The operation and management of some receiving stations.

   c. The supervision and allocation of workers by the labor associations in some areas. The late arrival of workers, their early withdrawal and non-uniformity of grower treatment were frequent causes of complaint.

   d. Uncertainty, during the pre-planting period, as to the availability of picking labor.

   e. The way the worker yield return formula operated. Though many farmers resented the paper work the formula required, the farmers with small acreages and/or those who were not doing well in general seemed to resent it the most. Where grower dissatisfaction with companies existed, this was sometimes associated with a tendency to blame the company for the creation of the formula. Many conceived the formula as protection for workers (in principle, at least) at the cost of shifting more of the impact of low yields due to poor weather to farmers. Others felt the formula to be an encroachment on the freedom of farmers. A significant number of farmers understood the formula well enough to know how to manipulate it to their advantage and some of them did so. Some means of manipulation do and/or might include:

(1) Using production from unreported fields to boost production in reported fields

(2) "Borrowing" pickles from neighbors or from fields with yields in excess of 120 bushels per acre and reporting them as coming from fields which yielded less than 120 bushels per acre

(3) Forcing pickers to harvest and take to receiving stations overripe, damaged and deformed pickles which were obviously worthless but which served to increase reported per acre yields

B. Most growers want to see pickers earn a "decent" wage in their fields. Growers with low yields tend to indicate that they will either quit growing pickles or increase yields. They say, however, that paying more than 53 percent (50 percent to pickers plus 3 percent to the labor association) of the crop to get it harvested would make them unwilling to continue production regardless of yield per acre.

C. Growers regard the available domestic laborers as distinctly inferior to the Mexican Nationals as pickle pickers. It is our impression that most growers are satisfied with the Mexican Nationals as laborers.

D. It is our impression that net returns to growers vary widely from company to company and that the WYRF has not influenced them materially. Low net returns for individual growers appear to be due to poor performance on the part of companies, labor associations and the growers themselves more than to poor performance on the part of Mexican Nationals.

II. *Climatic Conditions* . . .

Though this year's particular weather pattern had its influence on the operation of the WYRF and on the success of labor procurement programs, this year was probably not unusually abnormal. Variations in weather of similar magnitude but of different natures and, hence, with different impacts are to be expected.

III. *Diseases*

Some growers in the sample who planted SR-6 pickleseed were troubled with mosaic. All cases of abandonment noted to date because of mosaic were in fields planted to this variety.

IV. *Marketing*

Grower-company relations appear to depend importantly on (1) the personality and skill of the receiving station operator and (2) the efficiency with which the receiving station is operated. Where the receiving station operator is also the labor association field man, another possible cause exists for poor grower-company relations. There appears to be considerable variation in the skill and efficiency with which receiving stations are operated. This varies from company to company as well as from station to station for individual companies.

A. Following are some causes for poor grower-company relations which involve the operation of receiving stations:

    1. Long waiting periods at the receiving station

    2. Slow unloading caused by

        a. Small capacity graders

        b. Mechanical breakdowns

        c. Inadequate numbers and quality of receiving station laborers

    3. Unclean, unoiled, inaccurate grading machines which are said to carry small pickles over into the next larger grade thereby reducing the earnings of both growers and pickers

    4. Low capacity, inaccurate scales

    5. The feeling on the part of some growers that the associations (grower) (a) overcharge the Nationals for food and other items furnished and (b) furnish inappropriate items

B. Several instances were observed or reported to interviewers of receiving station policies which, with and without the cooperation of growers, tend to prevent accurate evaluation of the influence of the WYRF on average hourly earnings of Mexican Nationals. These include estimating hours worked from amount picked, recording hours worked in company records which differ from those reported by the farmer and adjusting hours reported in company records to increase earnings per hour. Such actions interfere with the effective evaluation of the formula by making it extremely difficult to produce accurate estimates of actual hourly earnings. The final estimates in our study will be based on hourly data from what we regard as the best combination of data from the following three sources:

    1. Detailed records kept by farmers

2. Less detailed "estimates" from farmers who would not keep records

3. Company records

V. *The pickle picker—his attitudes and the associations*

A. The present impression is that the Mexican National does not understand the operation of the WYRF well enough to manipulate it to his own advantage. Whether or not crew or natural leaders among the Mexican Nationals do or do not understand it well enough to manipulate is unknown. In any event, no obvious attempts of workers to manipulate the working of the formula were noted.

B. The WYRF tended to destroy a common interest of grower and picker in maximizing the value of the crop when yields were low enough to place the sliding scale in effect. Under these conditions the grower has become more interested in the share he receives and less interested in the total value of the crop.

C. We anticipate that season average hourly earnings of many Mexican Nationals will run below 70 cents per hour when based on the "best available" data on hours worked. Conversely, we expect that many Mexican Nationals will average over 70 cents per hour. We anticipate that these differences will be related to dollar returns per acre. We also feel that the relation of average hourly earnings to bushel yields per acre may be quite different this year than last.

D. It is difficult to see, at this point in our analysis, how the WYRF could have substantially increased average hourly earnings of Mexican Nationals as it was administered in 1958. Out of 24 farmers, only one has made wage formula adjustment payments.

E. Growers felt that a number of labor associations delayed placement of workers at the start of the season for the following reasons:

1. To get a large first pick to boost the per acre bushel yield

2. To eliminate low picker earnings before the plants come into full bearing

3. To move the 35th day nearer the end of the season to include more of the peak yielding days in the period from which the official yield is computed

F. Farmers who obtained Mexican Nationals from associations which recontracted sugar beet workers had a more adequate supply of labor throughout the season than those who received Mexican Nationals from associations which contracted directly for Mexican Nationals.

G. Delayed placement of laborers resulted in a high proportion of large pickles in the first pickings which, in turn, damaged vines and:

1. Increased the bushel yield per acre.
2. Lowered gross dollar returns per acre (this grower opinion has not been checked) to lower the total season earnings of farmers and, perhaps, of individual pickers. Farmers seldom expressed opinions about the influence of delayed labor placement and the high proportion of large pickles in the first picking on the hourly earnings of pickers.

VI. *Some directions which our final recommendations may take*

A. The possibility, among other things, of putting the WYRF on a value per acre basis instead of a bushel per acre basis will be considered.

B. Ways of minimizing paper work on the part of growers, receiving stations and processing companies will be considered.

C. Recommendations will be developed for companies and labor associations to follow in contracting acreage and administering Mexican Nationals. These recommendations would not have formal status, of course, but might improve the organization of the industry, stabilize and increase net earnings of growers, increase picker earnings, and stabilize the supply of pickles at no more than a modest increase in pickle prices. The range in earnings from grower to grower and company to company includes good earnings to both growers and pickers. The good earnings within the range indicate that substantial improvements in the overall situation are possible. Among other things, these recommendations will deal with the optimum number of workers to be certified per acre, timing of arrival of workers, housing, education of both pickers and growers, selection of growers and acres of production, possible hourly guarantees, etc.

D. Revisions of the WYRF should attempt to restore and further develop a community of interest—

    1. educating, supervising and helping inefficient producers,

    2. or replacing inefficient producers with efficient ones.

E. Development of the mechanical picker should be pressed. The problematic labor situation can be expected to get worse in future years as Mexico's industrial development progresses.

The Nature of Dissatisfactions with the Tentative Report

The tentative report was not received with great enthusiasm. Interested persons and organizations were uneasy about certain non-normative and normative concepts assumed or presented in it. Still further, there were dissatisfactions with some of the tentative conclusions and recommendations arising in part from the procedures used to reach conclusions about what should be done, given the facts and normative concepts used.

Following are some of the non-normative concepts in the report which caused dissatisfaction:

1. Research data on hourly earnings of Mexican Nationals were viewed with suspicion. At least one company president found the study data inconsistent with data he had on the earnings of Nationals working for farmers selling pickles to his plant.

2. Details about how earnings per hour were related to hours worked per season, characteristics of farms, characteristics of Mexican Nationals when employed during season, and so forth were not sufficient.

3. Information about the earnings of farmers producing pickles, including, particularly, the relationship between farmers' earnings and the earnings of Mexican Nationals, was not sufficient.

4. Information about the influences on earnings and on the industry of the WYRF developed by the industry and placed in effect by the U.S. Department of Labor for the 1958 crop was not sufficient.

Dissatisfactions with values or normative concepts in the report were also expressed. More specifically:

1. Companies and farmer groups were concerned about their independence. Perhaps they feared that researchers placed less value on their independence than they themselves did and would therefore make recommendations for stronger governmental control of the industry.

2. There are conflicting ideas about the value of higher pickle prices. Growers wanted higher prices. Processors wanted an unchanging or higher processing margin without the reduction in volume of sales which would result from higher retail prices. The USDL wanted the minimum hourly earnings of Mexican Nationals increased to reflect both the State Department's interests in negotiating with the Mexican government and the concern of labor organizations with both quantitative and price competition from Mexican Nationals for Michigan jobs. As a result, the USDL was not opposed to increases in pickle prices.

3. The survival of pickle producers was held in high regard by pickle producers, processors, county agents, and local authorities. There was much concern over the fate of small producers encountering financial problems. Some interested groups feared that MSU researchers might not value survival of pickle producers highly enough.

4. There was strong preference for education (to teach farmers how to increase the earnings of Nationals) and voluntary adjustment as opposed to controls involving coercion. Although there was little fear that the MSU research group undervalued education, there was some fear that they might underrate the badness of control through coercion.

The third target of dissatisfaction involved the methods used by researchers in interrelating non-normative and normative concepts to arrive at conclusions about what ought to be done. For example:

1. At one point, a company representative complained that the researchers had been asked to carry out what he termed an "objective evaluation," by which he meant non-normative as opposed to normative evaluation. To him, *evaluate* meant to determine a quantity, as when

the mathematics student is asked to evaluate $Y = 5 + 4X + 2X^2$ for $X = 2$. Determination of the average hourly earnings of Mexican Nationals in Michigan was another example of what evaluation meant to him. He was uncertain about how an investigation could lead to conclusions about what action to take without considering values or normative concepts.

2. Among the researchers, those trained in modern welfare economics had a preference for Pareto-better solutions, i.e., solutions which make at least one person better off without making anyone worse off. These same researchers would also have accepted solutions that provided for the compensation of those made worse off by those made better off. The difficulty, however, was that fundamental aspects of the problem involved a dissatisfaction with the status quo—the problem being, in part, one of making certain persons worse off in order to make others better off.

Remedying the Non-normative and Normative Deficiencies of the Tentative Report

The several kinds of non-normative and normative concepts found to be deficient were investigated further by the researchers. New concepts were developed from experiences recorded as data in the various survey efforts and while working with interested groups in the industry. Inconsistencies among concepts and with experience were also reduced. Researchers focused their attention on the workability of recommendations that would follow from certain concepts. The presence of unworkability frequently revealed a need for further effort to eliminate previously undetected inconsistencies among concepts. Some of the results of these further investigations are presented below.

As a result of the study, it was estimated that the average hourly earnings of Nationals was 78 cents per hour for the summer of 1958. This average was weighted according to the numbers of hours worked by each individual worker. The hourly data used in computing average hourly earnings were the "best" hourly data.[3] Statistically, the average of 78 cents per hour is significantly different from 70 cents an hour.[4]

Despite the fact that average hourly earnings received by all Nationals exceeded the level of 70 cents per hour, many of them failed to reach that level. Of the 852 workers whose earnings were studied in detail, 286 worked on the farms in the sample for less than 50 hours during the season. Such workers were brought in from nonsample farms for short periods. Because they worked only a few hours on the sample farms, their average hourly earnings for the season varied more than the season's averages for workers employed for more hours. One of these men, for instance, earned an average of $2.70 an hour for the few hours recorded on sample farms, and 14 averaged more per hour than any worker working over 50 hours.

Conversely, average hourly earnings for the group with less than 50 hours on sample farms *also* varied downward more than for workers who were employed for over 50 hours. For instance, 11 received an average of less than 35 cents an hour, which was the lowest average paid to a worker who worked more than 50 hours. In view of this variance in the data for workers working on the sample farms less than 50 hours, it was decided that estimates of the percentage of Nationals averaging less than 70 cents per hour, for all hours worked during the season, should be based on the distribution of earnings for men working at least 50 hours. On this basis, it was estimated that *no more than 30.2 percent of workers received less than 70 cents per hour on an average basis per season.* This estimate would have been decreased somewhat if, say, 100 hours rather than 50 hours had been selected as the minimum.

Essentially, the same picture emerged when the average weekly earnings for those Nationals who worked a 65- to 70-hour week (6 to 7 full days) was $47.56. Of the 78 such

---

3 Because the "best" (thought, for various reasons, to be most accurate) hourly data from grower, worker, and company records were used, this estimate may vary substantially from estimates based on either company or grower records alone. The above figure of 78 cents per hour should be regarded as more accurate than an average based solely on either company or grower hours.

4 The difference between 78 and 70 cents is more than 11 standard deviations of the differences between arithmetic means.

weeks worked by the Nationals in the sample, earnings of 44 of those weeks or 56 percent were less than $46, or about 70 cents an hour. In the case of 55- to 60-hour weeks (5 to 6 full days), 154 such weeks produced an average weekly earnings figure of $42.66, with 44 weeks or 29 percent producing earnings of less than $40 or about 70 cents an hour. There were also 513 45- to 50-hour weeks (4 to 5 full days) worked at an average weekly wage of $38.55, with 151 weeks or 29 percent falling below $33 a week or about 70 cents an hour. Those working a 35- to 40-hour week (3 to 4 full days) put in 588 weeks at an average weekly wage of $31.55 with 191 or 32 percent falling below $26 or about 70 cents an hour.

Many weeks were worked in which less than 35 hours were recorded because of the transfer of workers to and from sample farms, partially worked weeks at the beginning and end of the season, rain, illness, loafing, and so forth. Weekly earnings figures showed much more variation than season averages. Hence, the percentage of weekly earnings falling below the equivalent of 70 cents an hour should exceed the 30.2 percent of the workers who received less than 70 cents an hour on an average basis for the season.

Whether hourly or weekly earnings were examined, it was clear that about 30 percent of the workers received the equivalent of less than 70 cents an hour for the season as a whole.

The fact that only 2 of the 70 growers involved actually made adjustments because of the WYRF was very significant. The 1958 yield of pickles per acre in Michigan, as estimated by the crop-reporting service, was 147 bushels, the highest then on record—20 bushels above the 1957 figure and 85 bushels above the 1944-53 average. Apparently, the existence of the WYRF caused many contractors to follow contracting policies and many growers to follow production practices that increased the average yields per acre.

Of the 79 farmers in the study, 43 reported their yields for the last year they grew pickles. Their 1958 average yield was 10.7 bushels per acre per farm higher than their yield the previous year in which they grew pickles. Of the 79, 47 indicated that they made a definite attempt to increase their yields. When asked their reasons, 40 percent indicated that they attempted to raise their yields "to meet the 120 standard of the WYRF," while 96 percent indicated they did so "to increase income from the pickel enterprise." The following tabulation shows the number of farmers who indicated that they employed each of several practices to increase yields in 1958:

Practice Employed	Number of Farmers Using Practice
Decreased row width	12
Decreased distance between plants in the row	12
Planted on more productive land	3
Planted earlier in the season	3
Increased amount of fertilizer applied	36
Increased number of fertilizer applications	19
Practiced better weed control	6
Used irrigation	5
Increased use of insecticides and fungicides	8
Other	10

The resultant higher yields reported above in turn increased average hourly earnings of Nationals even though the WYRF adjustments went into effect on only two of the sample farms. Many members of the industry and many growers made a substantial effort to increase both yields and the earnings of Nationals in 1958. This favorable effect was not permitted to obscure the fact that both companies and growers sometimes participated in practices which tended to prevent WYRF adjustments from going into effect.

MSU researchers also studied conditions associated with both low picker earnings and low earnings by farmers at the farm level. The important factors associated with low average hourly earnings for Mexican Nationals were determined to be:

—Low yields per acre

—Low value per bushel picked

—Proportionally too few 1s and 2s (size grades)

—Poor association and/or grower supervision of Nationals

—Off-farm employment

—Improper supplies of labor at different times during the picking season

Most of these factors were *also* associated with low net returns to growers to cover the use of their land and risk. Of these factors, low yield per acre was the most important.

The study revealed that the problems that the Nationals create for growers *were not* an important cause of low hourly earnings. Furthermore, yields of between 120 and almost 200 bushels per acre sometimes produced average earnings of less than 70 cents an hour. The latter fact was due to companies which permitted growers to market very large pickles in order to meet the 120 bushel WYRF minimum. At least one station received large, unuseable pickles, used them in figuring the grower's average yield, and then dumped them in a field. Such actions were regarded as bad—as wasteful and dishonest—and became the basis for demands to change the system to remove temptation to engage in such actions.

The growers whose yields averaged between 120 and 200 bushels per acre, and who sold to companies which bought number 4s, produced an average of 15.6 percent 4s; several growers exceeded 25 percent. On the other hand, growers whose yields averaged over 200 bushels per acre, and who sold to companies buying 4s, averaged only 12.3 percent 4s. Some growers whose yields, if picked with normal size distribution, would have been so low as to cause the WYRF to increase the portion of the crop going to the pickers, prevented this from happening by consciously increasing the proportion of large sizes picked.

Yields determined, in large part, both the average hourly earnings of Nationals and the net earnings of growers per acre. Yields were associated positively with:

—Pounds of elemental N, P, and K applied up to 300 pounds per acre

—Plant population per acre up to about 17,000 plants per acre (farmer count)

—Number of sprayings and dustings up to three

—Years of experience at growing pickles

Yields were associated negatively with:

—Proportion of time spent in off-farm employment

—Number of companies to which the grower has sold

—Elemental N, P, and K in excess of 300 pounds per acre (farmer count)

Loams or loamy soils seemed to outyield the heavier soils. Farmers with plantings under 25 acres averaged lower yields than those with plantings in excess of 25 acres. Farmers specializing in pickle production had the lowest average yields (144 bushels per acre), while 8 truck farmers had an average of 264 bushels per acre and one fruit farmer had a yield of 280.

It was also clear that high yields were not the result of just one thing. Instead, several factors—soil variety, fertilization, spraying and dusting, picker supervision, plant population—all contributed to high yields. Growers with high yields carry out many good practices; growers with low yields carry out fewer good practices.

At the packer-processor level, several conditions were associated with low earnings of Nationals. Although the sample on which the study was based was not designed to produce reliable data for each packer involved, quite reliable data were secured on a portion of the 15 packers buying pickles from the growers included in the sample. These data are supplemented by information gleaned in interviews with more than 80 growers over a period of three months and from conferences with members of the industry.

These sources of information indicated that there were important differences in average hourly earnings from packer to packer. For instance, the average hourly earnings of 41 Nationals working for 15 growers, all selling to one company, were only 59 cents per hour. By contrast, 32 Nationals working for 5 growers who sold to another company averaged 97 cents an hour. These differences were associated with differences between the companies in average yield per acre for contracting farms, proportions of 1s and 2s picked, buying policies, supervision of laborers, and failure of screening procedures to eliminate growers who employed poor production practices and secured poor yields.

Still further, serious questions were raised by some growers about differences among companies in the accuracy of grading machines. Dirty grading machines caused 1s to be graded as 2s, 2s as 3s, and so on. There was also evidence that some companies aided farmers to obtain a yield per acre above 120 bushels by buying very large pickles which were not used.

Some responsibility for low earnings must be assumed by the packing industry because of the poor performance on the part of those packers who violated either the intent or specifications of the WYRF or, in some cases, both. Still further, variations in supervision, in contracting policies, and in operation of receiving stations from company to company account for some low earnings for which the packers bear responsibility.

Empirical analysis of survey data revealed that several characteristics and conditions were associated with low earnings of Nationals. Some worker characteristics are related to average hourly earnings. For instance, Nationals of questionable agricultural background, over 35 years of age, and over 5 feet 8 inches tall had low hourly earnings. On the other hand, why a worker sought work in the United States—that is, his motivation—was not associated with average hourly earnings.

Many growers as well as Nationals received low earnings. A grower seemed to expect to receive a minimum of $20 per acre for the use of land and for assuming the other risks involved in laying out over $60 per acre (exclusive of picking costs). Yet almost 40 percent (37.8) of the growers covered in this study failed to net $20 an acre.

These low earnings were due primarily to low yields. Some causes of low yields, such as failure to fertilize adequately, failure to spray and dust, and planting on poor land, were the responsibility of the farmer. Other causes of low yields, such as floods, wind damage, hail, the late arrival of laborers, and frosts, were beyond the control of farmers and constitute the risks for which he expects to be compensated.

During the 1958 season, the suggestion was often made that the basis of the WYRF should be changed to a value of crop per acre rather than physical yield. Another suggestion was that the basis of WYRF be changed to miles of row per acre instead of acre to allow for (1) the extra walking involved per acre for pickers when growers space their rows closer together to increase per acre yields, and (2) to encourage growers to space rows correctly on soils of different fertility and water-holding capacity regardless of yield per acre.

Incentive payment plans appeared extremely important in

obtaining production, care of vines, and clean pickings. Two sources of low earnings under the existing incentive payment plan were the overhiring of workers and the retaining of workers in the fields too late in the season. Of the workers interviewed in Spanish, 8 percent complained that they lacked work because there were too many workers in the fields. At the same time, 12 farmers complained that workers were withdrawn too early in the season. The statistical study indicated that pickers working for the complaining farmers received higher average earnings for the season than did those working for farmers who did not make this complaint. The incentive plan in operation penalized pickers but not growers for the overhiring of workers and for retaining workers in the fields too late in the season, making it necessary for place-ment agencies to restrict the number of pickers assigned to each grower and to withdraw the pickers before it was in the farmers' interest to have them withdrawn.

Experience as a harvest worker of any kind in the United States seemed to have no influence on hourly earnings. The number of workers with more than one year of experience at harvesting pickles was not sufficient to reveal any relation-ship.

If kind of motivation had anything to do with a worker's performance, this study failed to measure its effect. Men with no dependents did as well as those with dependents; men with few dependents, as well as those with many. Moreover, whether a man was driven north by unemployment in Mexico or attracted by the higher wage rate did not affect his earnings.

To some extent, incentive, the stimulation of which is a justification for piece rates, was reduced by compelling work-ers to pick in groups and by failing to assign them rows. Evidence of the adverse effects of these practices was found both when the workers voiced reactions to them and in hourly earnings.

Of the workers working on individual account, 96 percent preferred to continue to do so. On the other hand, 45 percent of those who were pooling preferred not to pool. Moreover, only 2 percent of the workers working on assigned rows were dissatisfied with the arrangement, whereas 40 percent not assigned rows wanted them. Pooled workers earned an average of only 65 cents an hour in contrast to the

81 cents earned by workers picking on individual account. When assigned rows, Mexicans made an average hourly wage of 82 cents; when not assigned, only 69 cents.

MSU researchers also came to realize that certain long-run trends in farm wage rates and in farm versus nonfarm income levels were important in making recommendations for the future of pickle production. The interrelationships, through time, were examined by making projections both formally and informally concerning the effects of following different alternatives. The projections dealt with conditions, situations, and things valued positively and/or negatively by different groups of people in the industry.

In 1934, the per capita income of nonfarm people was $468 compared with $165 for farmers. In 1944, the corresponding figures were $1,328 and $696. In 1947, they were $1,392 and $822. Since then, the ratio of farm to nonfarm per capita incomes has been falling. In 1956, nonfarmers received $2,018 while farmers received $902. In the years just prior to 1959, farmers did not keep up with the rapidly rising nonfarm incomes, even relatively.

From the 1935-39 period to 1959, wages of hired farm labor increased more than 4.5 times, and rapidly advancing industrial wage rates were expected to continue to exert an upward influence on farm wages.

It was reasoned that, in the absence of technological advances in pickle production that would permit raising more pickles per man, rising nonfarm incomes would continue to increase the net returns per bushel to growers that were required to maintain pickle production. Similarly, it was reasoned that members of the pickle industry should anticipate that nonfarm wage rates would probably continue to increase the *minimum* level of hourly earnings for Nationals that would be acceptable to the governments involved and to labor organizations. A rapid rate of economic growth in Mexico would eventually increase the minimum wage for which Nationals would be willing to pick pickles in the United States.

It was clear that increasing yields per acre was one way of increasing both the average hourly earnings of Nationals and the net returns to growers. However, it was recognized that the ability of increases in yield per acre to offset the trends mentioned earlier is limited. If nonfarm incomes and nonfarm wage rates continued to advance as rapidly as they had been, either labor-saving technological advances or advances in pickle prices would be required, along with higher yields, to maintain pickle production in the face of rising wage rates and improving alternatives for farmers' time and resources. As other parts of the United States were making rapid industrial advances and were experiencing rapid increases in wage rates, shifting the center of pickle production to areas with low wage rates would probably just delay the rate at which technological advance and/or price adjustments would be required in the industry.

Four kinds of technological advances appeared worth pursuing:

1. Those which would increase the number of acres that individual growers could devote to pickle production relative to other crops

2. Those which would reduce the labor required for picking

3. Those which would reduce the labor required for processing and marketing pickles

4. Those which would make it possible to meet the consumers' demand for pickles with material requiring less picking labor per bushel

Technologies that would increase the number of acres of pickles a grower could handle involved spraying, dusting, and introducing disease free varieties and cultivation techniques, which, by and large, result from a background of research and extension, and are therefore hard to augment rapidly as a basis for increasing technological advance. Supporting applied efforts currently being used, however, would speed the rate at which such specific advances were produced.

Labor requirements in processing and harvesting could be reduced by specific study of the organization and operation of receiving stations to eliminate separate grading for individual workers or groups. Quality control techniques widely used in industry could be used to determine grades by modern sampling techniques. Reduction in labor requirements at receiving stations would result in savings which might be available to the processing industry to offset the trends mentioned earlier. Although specific knowledge was not sought in this area when conducting this study, incidental observations indicated that important possibilities existed.

The development work then being done on a pickle picking machine was a major step toward a labor-saving technological advance in picking. Successful development of this machine would have called for major reorganization of the industry to handle the size composition of the crop that would be available to process in the period of time available for processing.

Another type of technological advance making it possible to reduce the labor requirements of the pickle industry involved the use of larger pickles to satisfy consumers' demand for pickles. Labor requirements per bushel varied from less than 30 minutes a bushel when over half the pickles picked were standard 3s and 4s, to more than 45 minutes per bushel when the proportion of 3s and 4s fell below 40 percent.

Under the existing pricing schedules, laborers who picked more than 50 percent 3s and 4s got 54 to 76 cents an hour, while those who picked less than 40 percent got 63 to 87 cents an hour. Although the crudeness of the study did not permit precise recommendations on this matter, it was clear that the possibility of using more 3s and 4s, with their low labor requirements, deserved investigation. It was recommended that such an investigation should also consider the advisability of shifting the schedule of prices paid, by grades, to encourage a modification of proportions of larger pickles grown and picked. It was noted that mechanical pickers, when developed, would necessitate further examination of the schedule of prices by grades.

The industry was depending on higher yields and increased efficiency on the part of growers without increasing the price paid for pickles. Growers responded well. However, there would be a limit as to how far the growers could go, and, when the limit was reached, the question of average price level would arise. Perhaps both pickers and growers could benefit, in terms of price, from technological advances and increased efficiency in processing, marketing, and picking and from greater use of larger pickles—much as the entire industry was benefiting from increased yields and efficiency on the part of growers.

Normative concepts which emerged in the course of the study included:

1. A clearer understanding of the wrongness of regulations which encouraged wasteful manipulation of production and marketing

2. The placing of higher value on institutional arrangements that bring about adjustments through education and positive incentives as contrasted to control enforced with coercion

3. A clearer understanding of how the value of survival for a pickle producing business depends on its earnings and on available alternatives

4. A wider agreement that earnings of Mexican Nationals above 80 cents an hour are good

Several decision-making concepts emerged during the course of the study. The need for a means of making non-Pareto-better choices became increasingly clear as the absence of Pareto-better alternatives was established. No specified legal procedures were available or easily employable. The general procedure that evolved was one of developing non-normative and normative concepts among a wide range of interested people. As these concepts became clear and increasing agreement about them was reached, the nature of the problem and its detailed subproblems became apparent. Agreement on normative and non-normative concepts, in turn, permitted new Pareto-better solutions. These solutions, as well as further agreement on normative and non-normative concepts and recognition of a community of interest, lead, in turn, to agreement on non-Pareto-better solutions, even on the part of some of those who were made worse off by the solutions. In some instances, such agreement arose as a result of willingness to endorse a generally agreed on value—for example, a willingness to forego certain gains reaped from shady practice in 1958 rather than fail to endorse the goodness of honesty.

Final Evaluations and Adoption of the Recommendations

The final evaluations and recommendations reached are reported verbatim below.

The general conclusion is that while in the first year of operation of the WYRF, average hourly earnings were over 70 cents, certain deficiencies were noted. The deficiencies include—

1. about 30 percent of the Nationals averaging less than 70 cents an hour for the season as a result of conditions over which they have little control but which are at least partially controllable by industry associations, individual processors and individual growers;

2. 38 percent of the growers with net returns (including rent charges for land and risk) of less than twenty dollars per acre; and

3. a tendency for the WYRF to encourage practices on the part of both packers and growers which are contrary to the long-run interests of the pickle industry.

To correct these deficiencies, it is recommended that:

1. Consideration be given to the possibility of placing the WYRF on a dollar yield per acre basis rather than on its present bushel yield per acre basis. As the dollar value of the crop per acre reflects both yield per acre and quality, it is even more closely related to average hourly earnings than bushel yield per acre. According to this study, the average price paid per bushel of pickles was 96.3 cents. Using this price per bushel, the dollar yield which is equivalent to 120 bushels is $115 per acre. Placing the WYRF on a dollar basis would have the advantage of eliminating the inefficiency resulting from increasing per acre yields through the production and marketing of large, unusable pickles not normally classified as 4s. Where practiced, this circumvented the intent of the WYRF, thereby preventing that formula from increasing the average hourly earnings of Nationals. It is also of crucial importance in this connection, to note that pickles are not a profitable enterprise for growers with yields so low they find it necessary to engage in such activities. In addition, there have been indications that a change to a value basis would significantly reduce the bookkeeping and computations for farmers and processors not involved in computing bushel yields. This may be increasingly important if sampling methods are developed and receiving stations to determine payment rates for the crop.

2. Consideration be given to means of reducing the proportion of both Nationals receiving less than 70 cents an hour and growers netting less than $20 an acre to cover land changes and profits. It is suggested that this reduction be brought about with some combination of—

   a. educational programs and

   b. an increase in standards in the WYRF.

3. The basic materials for three educational programs have been produced in this study, in other research at the Michigan Agricultural Experiment Station, and by the industry and its associations. It is recommended that:

a. Any educational programs contemplated for growers be carried out by the industry associations operating through their representatives and cooperating with the MSU Cooperative Extension Service. Available material to use here has to do mainly with increasing yields per acre and eliminating poor labor supervision.

b. Any educational programs contemplated for packers be carried out largely by the NPPA. Available material to use in this instance would be useful in screening contractees, in formulating contracts and in guiding the operation of receiving stations.

c. The labor associations use the materials from this study which bear on recruitment of Nationals for their own enlightenment. These materials indicate the kinds of Nationals which are likely to have unproductive low earnings regardless of circumstances under which they work.

Educational programs appear to be a promising partial alternative to higher standards in the WYRF whether or not that formula is converted from bushel to dollar yields per acre as recommended above. It involves less regulation of individuals, businesses and organizations and places the responsibility for consequences on the individuals making the decisions. Raising the standard in the WYRF to 200 bushels or about $195 per acre would have eliminated almost all 1958 season average hourly earnings below 70 cents per hour for individual Nationals. Serious side effects would accompany such actions, however. As growers producing less than $200 make very meager returns without penalties, the imposition of penalties would impose severe hardships upon such growers. Still further, raising wages by regulation seems less satisfactory to all concerned than treatment of the basic causes of low earnings, namely

—Low yields and poor labor supervision on the part of some growers

—Unwise contracting, supervision and buying practices on the part of some packers

—Unwise recruitment of Mexican Nationals

Reliance should be placed on education, in preference to regulation, to the extent that the industry and public agencies can carry it out.

4. Because of the upward trends in wages and in the incomes of farmers and nonfarmers, it seems advisable for the industry and individual packers to:

   a. Encourage the development of labor-saving technology. The industry is to be commended for its forward looking support of research on the pickle-picking machine. More support (both through public appropriation and private contribution) seems highly justified.

   b. Reappraise hourly earnings and net returns of growers periodically. Depending on future rates of progress in labor saving technology in pickle production, such reappraisals at a later date may have to include an appraisal of the price structure for the raw product in order for pickles to compete with alternatives used for farmers, productive resources and the labor of Mexican Nationals.

5. For the season ahead, it appears that care to avoid overcertification, prompt withdrawal of workers at the end of the season, the educational programs mentioned above, and/or higher WYRF standards are capable of decreasing the proportion of Nationals averaging below 70 cents per hour substantially below that of the 1958 season.

   In addition, it is recommended that the industry investigate possible alternative ways of combining the incentive pay system now used with some method to create an economic inducement for the grower to avoid overhiring and retaining workers too late in the season. Such investigation should recognize that incentive plans appear to be of great importance in pickle picking. Thus, minimum hourly rates, which might be used to protect the worker in such situations, could not be as high as minimum acceptable season average hourly rates without endangering the benefits from incentive plans in pickle picking.

The above recommendations were submitted to the National Pickle Packers and the National Pickle Growers Associations. These Associations in turn presented the conclusions at hearings conducted by the USDL. As a result of these hearings, the recommendations were adopted in toto. The industry operated according to governmental regulations on the basis of these recommendations for three years—1959, 1960, and 1961. The educational programs recommended were carried out in 1959 by the Michigan State Cooperative Extension Service and by the NPPA. Pickle growing contracting policies followed by the processors were also changed to eliminate a high proportion of growers with low yields.

Although no specific studies have been made of the effects of the regulations and educational programs, the general impression exists throughout the industry that earnings of both Mexican Nationals and pickle growers improved as a result of (1) the concentration of pickle production on better land and in the hands of farmers able to carry out practices which would increase yields per acre, and (2) the tendency of the new formula for paying Mexican Nationals to discourage certain of the undesirable practices which had developed under the earlier WYRF. Certain growers unable to produce higher yields were eliminated. They have not objected strenuously, because the research and educational programs have made it factually clear to them that they had little to gain by staying in pickle production. By and large, it appears that the conclusions about what was right to do have met the test of workability and have solved the problem faced by the Michigan pickle producing industry at the time the problem was posed to MSU researchers.

Philosophical and Methodological Conclusions

The problem statement involved normative as well as non-normative elements. Solution of the problem involved:

1. Construction of new and clarification of old non-normative concepts on the basis of both experience and logic. Answering these cognitive, non-normative questions contributed greatly to the solution of the practical problem.

2. Construction of new and clarification of old normative concepts on the basis of both experience and logic. Answering the cognitive, normative questions also contributed greatly to the solution of the practical problem.

3. Use of varied (and sometimes poorly formulated) bases for choosing the right thing to do on the basis of the positive and normative concepts which were constructed and clarified.

Construction of non-normative and normative concepts was sometimes but not always interdependent. Hence, the complicated approach of pragmatism was sometimes useful but was not always required in solving practical problems.

A conditionally normative approach would have precluded the answering of the cognitive, normative questions noted to have contributed greatly to the solution of the practical problem in 2 above.

Previous WYRF regulations lead to unobjective, distorted value concepts which did not stand the tests of consistency and workability. More specifically, pickles having little or no value for processing acquired false value as a means of permitting circumvention of wage regulations by growers. Such values were inconsistent with the values of honesty and of higher wages paid to Mexican Nationals. This distortion of price structures (normative) was objectively discernible.

The solutions arrived at went beyond Pareto optimality to involve obtaining some conditions judged to be good at the cost of imposing damages on some individuals. Interpersonally valid welfare measures were not evolved for use in reaching conclusions to impose such damages. It is also clear, in retrospect, that it was not possible to reduce the various goods sought and bads avoided to a common denominator to permit maximization of the difference. Still further, it was not clear whether maximization of the average, expected differences between the goods and bads would have been an adequate basis for choice, even had interpersonally valid welfare measures of a common denominator been available.

The technique used to handle the problems noted above was one of almost continuous interaction with decision makers in an attempt to see the consequences, through time, of following various alternatives in policies and programs. In these interactions informal projections of the consequences of following various alternatives were repeatedly used.

VII

Developing a Long-Run Plan for the Department of Agricultural Economics at Michigan State University

In 1959 the Committee on the Future was appointed at Michigan State University by its president, John A. Hannah. In the spring of 1960, as a result of the report of that committee and subsequent administrative directives, the Department of Agricultural Economics at Michigan State University (MSU) found that it was expected to develop a long-run (five-year) plan for the department. This plan was, ostensibly, to be used to administer the Department of Agricultural Economics and would thus influence the work and promotions of the agricultural economists at Michigan State University and the environment in which they would operate.

Members of the department and their administrator faced a problematic situation: decisions had to be made about the various things the Department of Agricultural Economics ought to do in the following five years. This problematic situation was especially interesting for the student of philosophic value theory and agricultural economics, because, regardless of the philosophic positions of the agricultural economists involved, they were forced to participate in problem-solving activity. The most positivistic researcher in the department faced a practical problem in which he would have to bear, to some extent at least, responsibility for the decisions reached. The situation prevented department members from adhering to any philosophic position that would keep them from participating in the solution of this practical problem.

The Initial Procedure Used to Attack the Problem

Subsequent to the request of the administration (in accor-

132

dance with the report of the Committee on the Future) that individual departments prepare and submit program plans for the next five-year period, individual members of the Department of Agricultural Economics were encouraged to submit their views on any aspect of the department's program as it currently existed or as they hoped it would develop. Twenty-five such contributions were received by the department head and informally approved by members of the department. It was the duty of this committee to examine individual contributions and to prepare a set of recommendations.

The committee was chaired by the department head and consisted of: (1) the chairman of the Committee on the Future appointed earlier by President Hannah (this man was also a member of the Academic Council); (2) a member of the Graduate Steering Committee for the College of Agriculture; (3) a member of the department's Planning Committee for its previous staff conference held in 1957 and editor of an earlier statement on the long-range research program for the department; (4) a member of the department's Planning Committee for the staff conference in 1957 (also a representative for the department's off-campus educational extension program); and (5) a member of the department's Teaching Committee.

This committee began deliberations early in May 1960. It first listed the important values held by individuals or groups of individuals interested in the department's programs. It then developed a description of existing conditions affecting future programs. Within the bounds of these two statements, a set of goals was prepared. These goals were regarded as compromises between those concepts of good and bad contained in the first statement and the possibilities contained in the second statement. The set of goals was divided by the following major subheadings, which were functional:

1. Development of theory and methodology
2. Collection of general-purpose data
3. Analysis of problems
4. Teaching and counseling
5. Development and implementation of the program
6. Professional activities

This statement was submitted to the departmental faculty, criticized, reviewed, and revised. A second statement was then prepared and approved.

The Nature of Survey Results

In a number of instances, two or three department members cooperated in the preparation of their individual statements about the formation of a five-year plan for the Department of Agricultural Economics. In other instances, primarily in the extension program where the department's internal structure was more highly developed, project leaders called their staffs together to present statements concerning the five-year plan, these statments being confined largely to the areas of extension work under the supervision of the respective project leaders.

In all, 31 documents were received by the department head and transmitted to the five-year committee. Of these 31 statements, 6 came from graduate students and 25 from either individuals or groups of individuals on the staff. The 25 statements from staff members can be divided into those dealing with (1) rather general problems and needed general developments in the department, and (2) specific details. There were 12 general statements, 11 from individuals and 1 from a group. There were 13 more specific statements, 8 from individuals and 4 from groups.

A systematic rereading of the 31 statements indicates great diversity in the approaches to answering questions about what the department ought to do in the ensuing five-year period. Very few of the statements appeared to be based upon a systematic non-normative examination of the environment in which the department was operating. Similarly, there was little evidence that systematic normative investigations were carried out in reaching conclusions about what ought to be done. There was also little evidence that non-normative and normative considerations had been interrelated systematically in a formal method of analysis to determine what should be done.

The meager evidence of systematic non-normative, normative, and decision-making analysis in the reports, however, contrasts sharply with abundant recommendations about what ought to be done. Perhaps the dearth of analysis backing up these recommendations was to be expected inasmuch as the respondents were not asked, specifically, to justify their conclusions.

The five-year committee was required to produce a set of consistent, workable recommendations about what ought to be done. The need for a set was evident from the diversity of recommendations in the 31 statements and from the conflicts among the various specific statements dealing with special areas of interest. Many of the participants advocated expansion. Within the budget limitations facing the department, it was obviously not possible for the five-year committee to recommend expansion in all areas. Moreover, a number of individuals had also indicated that the long-run problem of the department was not one of expanding budget and size but of getting more output from the resources then being used in the department.

Another kind of conflict in the statements had to do with competition among the three areas of responsibility in the department—teaching, research, and extension. In a few instances, staff members expressed some concern over the competition between undergraduate and graduate teaching programs and professors. There was also some evidence of cleavage between, on one hand, practical researchers and extension workers, who tended to be multidisciplinary, and, on the other hand, more fundamental (disciplinary) researchers, who often had interests in theory and in methodology more nearly or strictly disciplinary in character.

There was not, however, complete agreement among the multidisciplinarians. Some of the practical-minded workers had multidisciplinary interest growing out of a specific focus on a selected set of practical problems, while the more intellectually oriented individuals in the department were interested in multidisciplinary research as a broad intellectual exercise that would help establish breadth in research and educational programs.

At about this point in the deliberations of the five-year program committee, it became evident that a systematic investigation was required to obtain a moderately consistent, understandable program of recommended actions which would stand the test of workability in the practical environment in which the Department of Agricultural Economics would exist and operate. The first step in this investigation was the development of two statements. First, an attempt would be made to describe the environment in which the department operated and would operate in the following five years. Second, a normative statement would be developed that would help determine what the department ought to do in the ensuing five years.

The committee gave no specific attention to such questions as: Can value statements be developed independently of factual statements? Or, can non-normative concepts be developed independently of normative concepts? Or, is it possible to produce an objective statement of values for use in such endeavors? The committee's failure to ask such questions at this time was probably a source of both strengths and weaknesses in its overall activities. Because these questions were not asked, it was possible to get on with the job of developing both normative and non-normative statements. Offsetting this advantage, however, was the fact that such questions were put off to a later date, at which time they resulted in some lost motion on the part of the committee.

The Committee's Attempt to Develop Statements of Conditions and Values Relevant to the Five-Year Plan

Conditions restricting future programs in the Department of Agricultural Economics

The committee recognized three broad sets of restrictions having to do with (1) the existing program commitments of the Department of Agricultural Economics, (2) administrative relationships at Michigan State University, and (3) other important factors such as budget. The committee also recognized that many of the conditioning forces relating to the departmental program were not explicitly specified in any policy statement, charter, or body of rules and that many of the conditioning forces had grown out of certain traditions that remained implicit in the situation.

Among the existing program commitments were those involving resident instruction, both undergraduate and graduate. In addition, the department had heavy, continuing responsibilities for teaching in the College of Agriculture Short

Course program. Certain commitments also existed to training foreign students. Finally, the department had substantial program commitments to the Agricultural Extension Service and to various farm organizations.

While the research program of the department was built primarily around individual projects and programs, there were many ongoing commitments to projects and individuals that could not be modified until after they had run their normal course.

Various administrative relationships also placed limits on the range of possible programs that could be developed for the next five years. Because MSU is a publicly supported institution with a deep sense of responsibility to the land grant philosophy, the public, with its demands for services, constituted a restriction as well as an opportunity on the kinds of programs that could be developed. It was recognized that the more structured administrative relationships with the Extension Service were somewhat more restrictive than those with the Agricultural Experiment Station. The requirement that departmental personnel serve on university and college committees was also a restriction on the time these same people could devote to programs.

Among the other forces to be considered, available budget was recognized as a very definite restriction on future programs. It would be inappropriate to publish the departmental budget here. However, the committee knew the budget as it was broken down into the three main functions of the department—extension, research, and teaching—as well as the amount of money going into miscellaneous accounts to support the department's international work and to replenish revolving accounts. The committee also had at its disposal a distribution of operating expenses by the three main functions and data on man equivalents devoted to various areas of work. The number of man equivalents was also expressible in terms of number of classified employees and number of graduate assistants assigned to the various areas of work.

Values of importance in formulating goals

The committee defined values as concepts having to do with what ought and what ought not to be. The inappropriateness of this definition did not become clear until after the committee had completed its work. The committee recognized that such concepts were held by many groups and individuals both inside and outside of the Department of Agricultural Economics and that these groups had various claims upon the department for the maximization of the various oughts and minimization of the various ought nots.

In addition, it was recognized that there was considerable variation in the power which various groups and individuals had to enforce their claims as to what ought and ought not to be within the department. It was stated that "inconsistent, vaguely conceived values rarely lead to workable goals even when used in conjunction with excellent factual statements about existing conditions and the future." The committee was also aware that consistency does not require an absence of competition among values.

In making up the statement of values relevant in formulating goals for the department during the ensuing five years, the committee initially assumed that the values and goals would be related to existing conditions and possibilities to determine, by some unspecified process, what ought to be done in the following five years.

In the value statement, values were classified according to persons holding them. Three broad categories of such persons or groups were distinguished: (1) the MSU academic community, (2) those persons directly responsible for allocation of funds to MSU and its Department of Agricultural Economics, and (3) the clientele of the Department of Agricultural Economics. Four further subgroups of values were distinguished: (1) those values which determine the character of MSU as an academic unit, (2) the general values of academic communities, (3) the professional values of agricultural economists, and (4) other values.

Among the values that identify the academic character of MSU are the values of Western civilization and democracy. The committee also noted that the university, as an academic unit, attaches much value to helping a high proportion of the general public solve individual, collective, educational, and other problems. Further, it was noted that the research programs of the university are built on the normative proposition that it is good that a large proportion of the population be served without regard to vocation, wealth, or socioeconomic position.

It was stated that the MSU administration held in very high regard administrative flexibility, orderliness and control, unity of purpose, and continued growth. Faculty control and democratic procedures within the university were also held in high regard, although they were subject to sacrifice in the name of administrative flexibility, orderliness, unity of purpose, etc., which, in turn, could be sacrificed for fuller attainment of the values of Western society and in the service of a growing society.

In surveying the general values of an academic community, the committee recognized the pursuit of truth as having paramount value. Thus, within the department, special value was placed upon acquiring an understanding of and the imparting of knowledge concerning economic phenomena. It was also recognized that teaching is valued highly when teaching is defined to include the teaching of colleagues, public officials, and the general public as well as resident students.

Certain professional values of agricultural economists were also recognized as important in determining the future of the department. The committee stated that the unifying characteristic of people working in the field of agricultural economics is an interest in knowledge about productive relationships and in the behavior of social groups and individuals having to do with the allocation of scarce resources among alternative uses in the production and distribution of farm products. This statement implied that agricultural economists highly value (1) describing the environment in which farm products are produced and distributed, including attention to the social and political institutions and the physical and human resources found in that environment; (2) refining and teaching the principles of economics as they can be applied in agricultural economics; and (3) analyzing opportunities for the fuller attainment of public and private objectives through the use of scarce resources. It was also stressed that, as economists, agricultural economists value efficiency in acquiring and imparting knowledge.

Also given special attention were the values placed upon individual teaching, research accomplishment, personal initiative, originality, and creativity despite the administrative structure of MSU which placed heavy value on centralized control and administrative flexibility, at least at that time.

The next major group of values considered were those held by persons responsible for allocating funds to MSU and to the department, including the state legislature, the U.S. Congress, several research agencies, the Economic Research Service and other divisions with the USDA, and various private institutions and foundations. It was noted that state legislators have an interest in results that solve the practical problems of the people of the state of Michigan, which implies that they value less highly liberal education, basic research (if less relevant), and adult education of less direct applicability. The committee also stated that there is a general conviction that services of publicly supported educational, research, and extension programs ought not to compete directly with similar services produced by private business firms.

National agencies supporting the departmental research programs place higher value on results that have national implications or that deal with problems cutting across state lines than on results applicable only within one state. It was noted that foundations and business firms often desire certainty in research results and hence are reluctant to finance highly speculative, experimental research. It was taken as given that many members of the state legislature place a high value upon forms of academic organizaton that identify responsibility and control over program direction within the university, and that the members of the legislature are generally suspicious of faculty committees and diffused authority. On the other hand, decentralized location of educational facilities is held in high regard by the legislature.

Another set of values consists of those held by the clientele of the department. Most students, for instance, value personal attention from and immediate access to professors and generally informal relationships between themselves and faculty. They also desire a wide selection of courses and consistency and fairness in examination and grading. In general, undergraduates value applied work with foreseeable applications leading directly to some kind of remunerative job upon graduation and a state and national reputation for the university as a whole, but they are less concerned about reputations of individual teachers.

Graduate students, on the other hand, value the reputation

of individual professors as well as the reputation of the department. They also place high value on good grades, predictable examinations, and predictable examination outcomes. In some contrast to undergraduates, they hold theoretical work, mathematics, and work in the other social sciences in high regard. Graduate students place high value on physical facilities and housing, program flexibility, and freedom to choose professors and research projects in their major field of study.

Assistantships that require a minimum of work on nonthesis matters are highly valued. Graduate students also desire flexibility in time requirements on assistantships. Generally speaking, they hold in high regard training that prepares them for research, extension, and teaching in other universities, and they subscribe to the values of science in the search for truth.

It was noted elsewhere that agricultural economists place a high value on the development of theory, reliable data, and research methods. Agricultural economists employed in private firms and farms desire individual services and information having direct and immediate application to the problems they face.

Farmers tend to place high value on having MSU in general and the College of Agriculture and its departments in particular first serve the interests of farmers and farm people, this conviction extending to undergraduate programs and research. Agricultural economics personnel employed by business firms often feel that research and information which would impair their competitive position or interfere with conduct of their business is bad.

Public decision makers also use services of the Department of Agricultural Economics. Some personnel from both governmental and farm organizations hold that information inconsistent with their normative and non-normative concepts is bad, but, nonetheless, desire information that is accurate and unbiased by those who produce the information.

Some general comments on the non-normative and normative statements

Two kinds of confusion are evident in the statements about the existing conditions and values relevant to the development of the long-run plan. Some of the statements about existing conditions had to do with the values held by various groups in a position to impose their wills. Thus, it was noted that one of the conditions determining the kinds of programs that could be devloped was the value concepts of those financing MSU.

Another type of confusion present in the statements had to do with the distinction between a value and a goal. Some of the statements about values had to do with what ought to be done rather than with what was good or bad per se. This confusion originated in the original instructions of the committee, but was not detected by those staff members responding, which indicates that the confusion was widespread and not confined to the committee. Thus, there was a tendency to skip, prematurely, the intermediate step of answering non-normative and normative questions before determining what ought to be done.

Philosophies of Inquiry

Although the committee was not dedicated to any specific philosophic position, several positions were represented. The attempt to develop a statement of existing conditions indicated a fairly strong positivistic inclination, while, of course, the attempt to produce a normative statement indicated that the committee was far from exclusively positivistic.

Because the normative statement was developed independently of the non-normative statement about the conditions restricting the kinds of programs that could be developed, it can be concluded that the committee, at least, acknowledged the possibility of carrying out normative and non-normative work independently of each other. This acknowledgment indicates that the committee was not solely pragmatic in the sense that the pragmatist believes that the processes of developing normative and non-normative concepts are necessarily interdependent. Further, the committee was not solely conditionally normative in that it was not willing to assume a set of given values and then address itself to the question of maximizing attainment of those values; instead, the committee specifically set out to develop a value statement to use in its deliberations.

It is interesting that the committee did not have a clear-cut procedure for deciding what would be right to do (as a practical matter) on the basis of its non-normative and normative investigations, which tended to be more disciplinary than practical. The general procedure apparently was one of first getting some idea about what individuals thought should be done; then developing the two statements, one non-normative and one normative; and then forging a set of recommendations that would be, in some sense or another, an appropriate compromise among the goods attainable and bads avoidable in view of what the non-normative investigation indicated was possible.

The Nature of a First Tentative Report

The first report was entitled "A Statement of Goals and Guidelines for the Program of the Department of Agricultural Economics, 1961-62 to 1966-67." This report was drafted for departmental review on June 17, 1960. It contained four main sections in addition to a foreword. The first section was an introduction. The second stated a set of departmental goals for 1961-66. In addition, the report contained two appendixes. Appendix A was entitled "Values of Importance in formulating Goals." The second was entitled "Existing Conditions of Importance in Formulating Goals."

The foreword merely stated the general procedure for developing the report and concluded with the following statement:

> The present statement reflects in substantial measure the joint thinking and contributions of the entire department. No two individuals, of course, would write such a statement in exactly the same vein; hence, the committee must accept responsibility for its present form. They do so with confidence that it accurately suggests some of the main community interests and aspirations of the department with respect to program, direction and emphasis for the next five years.

The first section of the report

The introduction to the report contained the following:

... the Committee first attempted to list some of the important values held by individuals or groups of individuals whose views influenced the design of departmental program. Next, it reviewed existing program commitments and other circumstances affecting or limiting opportunities for program development. These two steps provided a basis for setting broad goals. Examination of present activities then pointed to certain needed changes for accomplishment of the chosen goals. Finally, steps toward implementing the proposed changes were outlined.

... the goals reflect attempts to harmonize "what is" with "what ought to be." In total they review much about the department's conception of the scope and purpose of its activities.

Note again how what ought to be is used to refer to the normative instead of the right actions or goals in accord with the terms defined in chapter 1.

There then followed a statement of the department's scope and purpose. The department's central purpose was "to acquire understanding and impart knowledge." There was a discussion of the obligations of teachers as well as a statement that the unifying characteristic of all work in agricultural economics is an interest in knowledge about the behavior of social groups and individuals. This was developed into statements about the kinds of information that the department held in high regard. Service and problem-solving activities were deemed important.

Undoubtedly it can be seen that this statement of the department's scope and importance is actually a value statement indicating the things considered good in the Department of Agricultural Economics. As such, it tended to make the appendix on values redundant.

The second section of the report

The second section of the committee's report was entitled "Goals for 1961-66." It was introduced with the statement that the goals of the Department of Agricultural Economics are regarded as compromises between the many values involved and the various institutional and other forces that influence what can be. The goals were discussed in five sections having to do with (1) the development of theory and methodology, (2) the collection and analysis of general-purpose data, (3) the analysis of problems, (4) teaching and counseling, and (5) maintaining an environment for individual professional growth and achievement.

1. Goals with respect to the development of theory and methodology

   a. The maintenance of sufficient diversity within the department to foster a variety of theories, methodologies, and philosophies that develop and improve the dynamic theory of the firm

   b. The development and improvement of static and dynamic theories of consumption

   c. The development and improvement of the theory of the growth of communities and economies

   d. The development of improved statistical methodologies

   e. The development of theories of aggregation (first, static, then dynamic) with respect to both supply and demand

   f. The development of improved measurement techniques for controlled experiments

   g. The development of social and political theory relating to the institutional changes needed in solving agricultural policy problems

2. Goals with respect to the collection, development, and analysis of general-purpose data

   a. The supplementation of, not competition with, major large-scale data-gathering agencies in gathering data on non-normative matters pertinent to departmental programs

   b. The development of expanded and improved secondary estimates for agricultural and related industries

   c. The measurement of structural relationships within and among the agricultural and related industries

   d. The development of an expanded and improved body of information relating to individual farming firms, related business firms, and consumption units

3. Goals with respect to the analysis of problems

   a. The clarification of conflicts among values involved in public issues

   b. The identification of promising adjustments among the social institutions in public policies relating to agriculture's use of credit and capital

   c. The appraisal, on a continuing basis, of short- and long-run changes in the prospects for supply, demand, and price for Michigan farm inputs and outputs

   d. The evaluation of possible structural changes in Michigan agriculture

   e. The appraisal, on a continuing basis, of economic opportunities for adjusting the use of resources on Michigan farms

   f. The appraisal of economic opportunities for adjusting the use of resources by farm suppliers and marketing firms

   g. The identification of values that influence economic decisions of businessmen, managers, and consumers and that aid in formulating alternative public policies for agriculture

4. Goals with respect to teaching and counseling

   a. The improvement of general knowledge among Michigan people of the underlying values, basic economic principles, and important facts (non-normative information) that describe and influence the operations and interrelationships in the total agricultural economy

   b. The improvement of understanding among operators of Michigan farms and farm-related businesses of the use of economic principles, facts, and analysis in making operating decisions

   c. The development of leaders who can apply economic principles, facts, and analyses in guiding public and private decisions

   d. An increase in the productivity of efforts directed toward formal academic training by attracting students with high capabilities

    e. The promotion of maximum intellectual growth of students and an increase in students' excitement in the search for knowledge and the desire to continue learning

5. Goals with respect to maintaining an environment for individual professional growth and achievement

    a. The maintenance of an intellectual environment that would encourage and facilitate individual intellectual growth and achievement

    b. The maintenance of an administrative organization and environment that would stimulate intellectual growth and professional achievement

    c. The maintenance of a physical environment that would facilitate program achievement and intellectual growth

The third section of the report

Section three dealt with the department's current activities and needed changes therein. This section was broken into subsections corresponding to those in the section stating the goals of the department. The discussion of needed changes indicated that the goals in the preceding section were not clearly defined as things which ought to be done or things which were right to do in C. I. Lewis's sense—that is, as appropriate compromises among goods and bads in view of what was possible. Instead, the goals were value statements and the needed changes set forth in the third section were really compromises among the values (found in Appendix A and in Section II) that the committee regarded as appropriate in view of its recommendations about what was possible to do.

The needed changes correspond to C. I. Lewis's definition of what is right to do. The values in Appendix A cannot be clearly differentiated from the goals in Section II. The goals in Section II were obviously regarded as good but not necessarily attainable in view of the conditions that existed. Similarly, that part of Section III dealing with present activities corresponds to Appendix B, which purportedly described existing conditions.

There is a strong presumption, at least, that both Appendix A and B were rough first approximations which were later refined in Section II and part of Section III, respectively. If this is so, then the report, by its initial ambiguity, demonstrates that the committee made progress in formulating more consistent—that is, logically and with experience—and more understandable—and hence, more objective—normative as well as non-normative concepts.

Because the goals in Section II were not regarded as necessarily attainable, it was necessary in Section III to recommend specific actions as the "right things to do in the following 5-year period in view of existing conditions." Thus the following recommendations are found in the third section:

> Additional activities needed to permit achievement of the proposed goals (with respect to theory and methodology) are as follows: Increased attention should be given to the extension of fixed investment theory to consumption items. . . . The development of managerial theory needs further attention, particularly as it relates to the management of nonfarm agricultural businesses operating in an oligopolistic environment. . . . With the expansion of the core memory of MISTIC plus the anticipated refinements of our computing facilities, new programs and methods should be developed.

> Additional attention should be given to the development of improved theories of application with respect to both supply and demand.

These statements about needed changes are what the committee found it right to recommend that the department do. The statement of goals found in Section II either occupies an intermediate position between the normative statement in Appendix A and the statements of needed changes found in Section III or replaces the normative statement. The glossary in chapter 1 of this book would label what the committee termed *needed changes* as *right goals.*

The report's confusion about values and goals shows up specifically with respect to recommended needed changes in the collection, development, and analysis of general-purpose data.

> Balancing the existing program against the goals specified earlier, the following changes appear desirable: (1) the mail-in farm account project should be improved by (a) increasing the representativeness

of the sample by type of farm and summarizing the data accordingly, (b) refining the data on information obtained from respondents, particularly as related to inputs, (c) improving the accounting procedures to reflect accurately changes in investment, income, expenses and earnings, and (2) high priority should be placed upon working with primary data collecting agencies to improve measurements of agricultural inputs and outputs and the secondary estimates of economic movements in agriculture related industry, (3) work with commodity oriented departments and resource oriented departments should be increased to improve basic physical input-output relationships for economic analysis, and (4) structural analysis of demand-supply relationships by commodities for aggregative relationships in agriculture should be extended so that important problems encountered by farmers and farm oriented businesses can be analyzed.

The recommendations for needed changes in (1) teaching and counseling, including extension, (2) professional activities, and (3) environment and physical facilities all indicate that the needed changes are courses of action that the departmental committee found to be the right actions to recommend to the department. The committee either left the statement of goals suspended between the more purely normative statements in Appendix A and the statements of needed changes (right goals as defined in chapter 1 of this book) or replaced the normative statements with statements of goals.

The fourth section of the report

Section IV of the report was entitled "Implementing Needed Changes, 1961-62" and was essentially a statement of the right actions for the first of the next five years—the difference between a right action and a right goal being that between doing and proposing to do.

Presentation and Disposition of the First Tentative Report

The first report was presented to the faculty and discussed more or less section by section. Members of the committee recorded the thinking expressed in these discussions. In addition, many written suggestions were submitted to the committee. The committee was instructed to redraft the report, taking into account these various discussions and suggestions.

The suggestions varied widely. Some were addressed to the appropriateness of the normative statement. Sometimes the value statements were questioned for their consistency and at other times for their accuracy. Similar questions arose about the goals statement in Section II. The non-normative statements (Appendix B and the first part of Section III) encountered similar difficulties. A number of the comments questioned the conclusions which the commitee had reached about the "needed changes" in the departmental program. No clear-cut criticisms were directed at how the committee interrelated concepts of goodness and badness, per se, with the non-normative descriptions of the existing situation to determine what changes were needed.

The Preparation, Nature, and Acceptance of the Second Report

In preparing the second report the committee studied and discussed the criticisms and comments received on the first. The written statements submitted to the committee are of considerable interest to students of philosophic value theory because they are applicable to the determination of the right actions by the agricultural economists. Hence, a number of them will be quoted here, even though they were often submitted in rough, handwritten form.

One man stated:

I feel that _____'s impression that we appear to be primarily other-oriented and fail in our unique responsibility of social criticism is valid. The university is one of the few social institutions that can afford the luxury of backing off and viewing our society and economy broadly and with a critical look at commonly held values themselves as well as how to achieve these values more effectively.

Later, the same person wrote:

The idea of evaluating these objectives themselves could be added. The next paragraph speaks of our obligation to emphasize knowledge whose benefits will be widely shared by the public rather than favored individuals. In addition it is our obligation to address ourselves to the problems of groups who may be in the minority and are not well organized with significant political power. Such a group may be migratory workers and if we do not analyze their problems probably no one will.

Another person commented:

Two further steps would be worthwhile: (1) sorting from among the many possible goals listed the (say) 10 that we want to place highest priority on in the next five years, and (2) working out plans for implementing these 10 goals.

Later the same person wrote:

I have only two suggestions for the committee to consider before submitting the report. First, that major surgery be performed—in short, to remove the appendices except for a few nuggets that could be brought from Appendix A to the introduction and from Appendix B to Section III. I consider the material in the appendices interesting, and the committee performed a useful service in developing it as a background for committee and staff consideration. But I consider much of this material unnecessary (and some of it inappropriate) to transmit outside the Department. Second, that all of the five-year goals be rounded up, given short descriptions, and reproduced on a one to two page digest and placed near the beginning of the proposal—along with a note that further elaboration of them will be found in the body of that statement.

This person was obviously concerned with the duplication of Appendix A and the section on goals and the duplication of Appendix B and the first part of Section III. He also valued clarity rather highly as a criterion for accepting or rejecting normative concepts. In a side comment, this same person wrote:

Some of the things that the committee attributed to groups as their values are not really their values, but a compounding of values and reactions to the circumstances they face. E.g., legislators frequently have to vote and make public pronouncements which do not reflect their values if they're not going to get skinned at the next election. Also, some researchers show that students don't enter college with a high value on grades, but reflect this "value" after they have had it beaten into their heads for a few years.

Still another person wrote:

As I indicated in the departmental meeting, I feel that the list of goals on page three omits the primary goal of the department. We thus leave the impression that we have a department without academic purpose. There seems in major part to be a confusion throughout the manuscript of professional goals with academic goals. These are not the same. The discussion of goals in sections IID and IIE leave one with the impression that the highest values one may aspire to as a student or a teacher are those of a profession. If we have any aspiration for academic respectability this is most unfortunate.

The same person had the following comments on Appendix A, which dealt with values:

On page 2 of Appendix A the values of the MSU academic community are discussed. "The distinctive academic character of Michigan State" implies to me that all other values will be sacrified for the survival of Michigan State University as an organization by the expedient of remaining functional in this society. I can only remark on this as a reaction that can be obtained to what has been said in the paragraph. I am not sure this is what you meant, but I think I can subscribe to it either way. I should only like to point out that in the following section on "the general values of an economic community" that I get the implication that the value system of science is equated with academic values. I do not think this is consciously intended but it is, I think, the implication, and of course, is not so. On page 8 of Appendix A in the section of "professional values of agricultural economists," I believe that two quite highly held values are omitted. These are (1) a general dedication to the increase in the quantitative and qualitative strength of the profession and (2) a related value, the survival of the profession.

Another person wrote:

I believe that there are a number of meaningful and important academic goals which we and other departments should strive to reach. These are not vague, intangible and long-run as _____ suggests. We do need to try to make a better image of the role of the Michigan State University faculty member with respect to the kinds of jobs he will take or his interest in basic research and his unwillingness (at least for some) to prostitute. . . . for dollar goals regardless of the source and purpose.

Still later this person wrote:

With respect to the goals on pages 5 and 6 there is an inconsistency between this and other sections. This is that no data will be collected or processed with respect to international trade and the impact of agricultural exports or the operations of agriculture overseas. Elsewhere there is recognition given to expanded work in this area. There should be some reference to the need for data in this section.

Obviously, this person valued consistency rather highly in appraising concepts to be used in determining right actions. Still later, the same reviewer wrote:

> On the bottom of page 7 or the top of page 8 I would suggest inserting another goal as I read it in the meeting this morning. "8. To develop an understanding of the functions of agriculture in other countries for the information of Michigan and other citizens, students at the University and decision making officials."

Another wrote:

> In attempting to meet the purpose of this department it must be recognized that individuals vary in their beliefs as to how best to achieve the fundamental objective outlined above. These differences will arise because of conflicts in evaluating the payoff from particular activities as well as conflicts in evaluating the needs of society. Within the department, it is not only desirable but necessary that these conflicts be examined periodically and the direction of the department as a unit rather than the direction of the individual be properly oriented.

Another departmental member wrote:

> There seems to be a conflict between goals found in the statement. On pages two, seven (part six), and A-3 one would gather that we only work in the public interest. On page six part C it appears that we are "rather directly concerned with helping to solve the problems of our clientele." Though no where does it state who our clientele are, in many cases they include commercial farmers and marketing firms. Work with these often would be difficult to be categorized as being in the public interest as we generally think of it. This is particularly true of work with bargaining agencies and in policy. I think that the statement should explicitly recognize that this conflict is inevitable and that we serve our clients as they come to us and that our first one and most important one is probably commercial agriculture much as the dean has pointed out on several occasions.

Later this same critic wrote:

> It is unclear to me what is meant by a "workable goal." Does this mean attainable?

In commenting about one of the goals, still another departmental member wrote:

> Basically, this goal implies some concentration of teaching. . . . It seems to me there is a possible conflict here between the land grant

philosophy (educate all the people) and this statement which implies that some people are to be educated for leadership (the liberal arts philosophy).

Later this same reviewer wrote:

> Is it necessary to spell out all the values of key elements connected in any way with this department beyond a paragraph mentioning that values of certain groups affect us? I suggest that serious consideration be given to dropping Appendix A from the report. . . . Similarly Appendix B contains much information that is both obvious to us as a department and to the administration. Some thought might be given to dropping or reducing this section, although I believe this section to be slightly more useful than Appendix A. . . . It seems to me the report should be cut down to perhaps 15 pages. I believe this could be done if the main goal were specified more concisely and if minor points and obvious statements [were] omitted. The report need not specify something for everyone, so to speak, but it ought to present our *main* purposes and what changes need to be made to better implement our main concerns.

The second report was based on the first but varied substantially in organization. The two appendixes, one on values and the other describing existing conditions, remained. The latter, however, was renamed "factual considerations." No very substantial changes were made in the appendix on values. More substantial changes were made in the factual appendix, which incorporated some of the descriptive material from the first part of Section III in the first report. Extension was treated under a separate heading in the new report. Other sections were more fully developed.

The introduction was modified in the second report by stressing the roles which the two appendixes played in the report. The section on the department's scope and purpose was left in. The discussion of scope summarized and slightly duplicated Appendix B on factual considerations and the discussion of purpose summarized and slightly duplicated Appendix A on values. A significant addition reads:

> A dedication to the spirit of an academic community involves the *freedom*, opportunity, and obligation to examine critically the surrounding society. Because faculty members in agricultural economics hold in high regard the freedom to criticize their socioecnomic environment, particularly as it relates to their special field of interest, they accept the obligation to do so with scholarly integrity and they recognize the rights of colleagues and others to disagree.

The section on goals was maintained but was substantially modified to treat the needed changes outlined in the first report as goals. The set of goals dealing with individual professional growth and achievement was subdivided and expanded into two sections dealing with (1) academic purpose, intellectual growth, and professional achievement; and (2) physical environment and service facilities. In the second report, the section on goals occupied twelve pages compared with seven in the first report, the extra five pages coming mainly from the former Section III that dealt with needed changes.

For each set of goals there is a set of needed activities to achieve goals; hence, the confusion between values (statements of good and bad per se) and goals (right actions to be attempted) that had existed in the first report was not eliminated. Instead, the confusion was rearranged. One has difficulty knowing whether the appendix on values or the statement of goals represents the underlying set of values providing departmental purpose. This confusion was not reduced by the third discussion of purpose in the introduction. Conversely, when one examined the committee's recommendations about what should be done, he was not quite sure whether he was expected to find it under goals or activities needed. The report states:

> The goals of the Department of Agricultural Economics are regarded as compromises among the many values held by various individuals inside and outside of the department as to what "ought to be" and the various institutional and other forces that influence "what can be." Each of the individual goals is regarded as being attainable within five years; all can be attained if implementation is adequate. This will involve continuing many activities of the present program and initiating a number of new activities. These activities become goals of an instrumental nature, and are mentioned under each group of desired accomplishments.

Two sections of goals and activities needed are reproduced here for illustrative purposes.

B. *Goals with Respect to the Collection and Synthesis of General-Purpose Data*

General-purpose data have multiple uses and are commonly gathered and processed without specific reference to their use in analyzing and solving individual problems. Thus, they are to be distinguished from special-purpose data that are more narrowly oriented. General-purpose data include secondary estimates derived from data collected by others, and certain structural estimates of the economy or its parts, as well as data collected directly. Goals with respect to developing these kinds of data are as follows:

1. To encourage the major, large-scale data-gathering agencies to collect the general-purpose data needed in the department's program and to supplement their activities to the minimum degree necessary.

2. To develop expanded and improved information about individual farms, farm-related businesses and consumption units.

3. To develop expanded and improved secondary estimates describing economic activity in agriculture and related industries of the Michigan, American, and world economies.

4. To gather normative data of broad usefulness to research and teaching in the department.

Activities Needed to Achieve Goals

General-purpose data from the Bureau of the Census, the U.S. Department of Agriculture, the Bureau of Old Age and Survivor's Insurance, the nationwide 1955 household food consumption survey and the Lansing Consumer Panel will continue to provide a basis for the synthesis of secondary estimates and for further analysis. The following changes in activities are proposed:

(a) Giving high priority to working with the primary data-collection agencies for improved measurement of agricultural inputs and outputs and for improved secondary estimates of economic movements in agriculture and related industries.

(b) Adjusting the Mail-In Farm Account sample to increase its representativeness by type of farm; summarizing the data accordingly; refining the information obtained from respondents, especially in relation to input data; and improving the accounting procedures to reflect more accurately the continuing changes in investments, incomes, expenses and earnings.

C. *Goals with Respect to Analysis of Problems*

A large share of the total departmental program is rather directly related to certain problems of its clientele. Efforts are devoted to anticipating potential problems and helping to avoid them, as well as to assisting in the solution of current problems. Related functions in these efforts include both analysis and teaching, but goals with respect to the latter function are listed in a subsequent group.

Many problems can be resolved by adjustments in private or public policies and activities relating to resource use; other problems can be resolved only by detecting and reducing conflicts among inconsistent values. Analyses of both kinds of problems are needed. Agricultural economists, however, recognize the limitations of the specialist in attacking many or most significant problems without the knowledge of other specialized disciplines.

Problems may emerge unexpectedly, or they may acquire a new urgency because of changing values held by influential groups among the department's clientele. Thus, goals are stated in a way that does not preclude shifting emphasis in accordance with developing needs.

Goals for analysis of problems include the following:

1. To clarify conflicts among values involved in public issues relating to resource use, income distribution, economic growth, and stability. Some value conflicts that need clarification exist with respect to

    (a) competing claims for land and water resources,

    (b) rapid economic progress versus the welfare of farm people and perpetuation of the family farm,

    (c) the role of government in past and future economic development, and

    (d) sharing costs and benefits of public programs.

2. To identify promising adjustments in the social institutions and public policies relating to agriculture's use of credit and capital.

3. To appraise on a continuing basis the short-run and long-run changes in the demand, supply and price prospect for Michigan farm inputs and outputs.

4. To evaluate possible structural changes in Michigan agriculture, in terms of the number of economic functions of individual operating units in production and marketing.

5. To appraise on a continuing basis the economic opportunities for adjusting use of resources on Michigan farms in ways that will produce more successful results for individual farmers and the economy as a whole.

6. To appraise economic opportunities for adjusting the use of resources by farm suppliers and marketing firms, where such an appraisal can be expected to contribute to the attainment of public objectives for resource use, income distribution, and growth.

7. To identify values that influence economic decisions of business managers and consumers.

8. To clarify the performance of agriculture in other countries, in relation to the interests of Michigan citizens and students.

9. To identify and analyze alternative public policies that have the objectives of

   (a) correcting any adjudged inequities in returns to farm people,

   (b) maintaining desired progress in farm and nonfarm productivity, and

   (c) permitting American agriculture to play a suitable role in the world politic. l economy.

Activities Needed to Achieve Goals

Among activities to be continued for accomplishing the above goals are those relating to adjusting farms and farm-related business to changing conditions, interpreting legislation affecting agriculture, attempting to anticipate agricultural problems, and operating a consumer preference panel.

Increased emphasis is proposed for the following topics:

   (a) The aggregate implications of farm and nonfarm firm adjustments.

   (b) Possible changes in public institutions and policies affecting growth, income distribution and use of land, water, and credit resources.

   (c) Outlook information relating to short-range and long-range prospects in various segments of agriculture.

   (d) Economic analysis of basic physical input-output relationships developed in cooperation with commodity-oriented and resource-oriented departments.

   (e) Economic analysis of problems arising from the cost-price squeeze at all levels in the agricultural economy.

Approval of the second report, both within the committee and by the department, involved overcoming certain conflicts. Personal willingness to concede in the interest of obtaining approval overcame several conflicts. In some instances, opposition was out-maneuvered, while in others it was out-numbered, although formal votes were not taken. Where consensus developed about facts, values, and the appropriateness of the basis for choice employed, neither out-maneuvering nor out-numbering was required because conflicts were not present.

Final departmental consideration had to be completed by June 30, just eight days after the meeting to consider the first report. Hence, some decisions were rather forced, and agreement on *a* report acquired considerable value. Rules for obtaining final approval by the departmental staff were not specified. Indeed, the need for such approval was not established.

The committee chairman (who was also the department head) pointed out that no two persons would write the report in the same way and that, hence, any statement would not please anyone in its entirety. He then indicated that if there were no serious objections to the report, it would be transmitted to college and university administrators. Certain influential members of the department indicated that they could "live with it," i.e., that it was at least workable. In other instances, silence gave consent. The consent of several members was somewhat skeptical because of their misgivings about the facts, values, goals, and needed actions presented in the report. In no instance, however, were these misgivings judged important enough to prompt serious objections to the report. Thus, the report was regarded as approved and, as such, was transmitted to the higher administration.

Voting and Various Tests for Objectivity

In the process of preparing the departmental report, objectivity was never regarded as the establishment of a one-to-one relationship between concepts and reality. Serious questions always existed about both the reality of concepts having to do with the existing situation and the reality of the various value and goal concepts developed by the committee. Concepts, however, were regarded as unacceptable and, it is to be supposed, unobjective when they were found to be internally inconsistent and inconsistent with experience. Similarly, they were found to be unacceptable and presumably unobjective when they were so vaguely stated that they did not possess the characteristic of interpersonal transmissibility.

The acceptability of concepts was also judged by whether or not they led to recommendations people could live with—which is another way of saying that the concepts had to lead to workable recommendations about needed actions. All of this implies that objectivity or acceptability of concepts depended on the criteria of consistency (internal and with experience), understandability, and workability.

It is extremely interesting to note that when a recommendation was based upon normative and non-normative concepts which met these criteria and led to recommendations which people could live with, there was no need to out-maneuver and out-number the opposition; instead, virtual consensus existed. In the cases of consensus, it did not matter whether the power of individuals was weighted equally, as it is in many democratic voting processes, or unequally, as it is when strategies, administrative power, and/or the power of personal influence are used. It was clear that the need to resort to arbitrary distribution of power among individuals in making decisions grew out of a lack of objectivity with respect to the normative and non-normative concepts employed and in processing objective or nonobjective concepts to reach the conclusions that made up the five-year plan.

Transmittal, Use, and Nonuse of the Report

The report was transmitted by the head of the Department of Agricultural Economics to the dean of the College of Agriculture for transmittal to the administrative group for the university as a whole.

One test of a set of recommendations is whether or not they are ever used and, if used, whether they solve the problems which they are designed to solve. During the ten years since the transmittal of the report to the administration, it has been possible to see something of its usefulness and whether or not it has tended to solve the problems faced in the department.

Despite the fact that the report was produced at the request of the university administration, it has been used primarily within the Department of Agricultural Economics rather than at college and university levels. The report provided the structure for a departmental series of "July forums," held in the summer of 1961, which were designed to appriase progress within the department and to determine further changes needed. The department head and others also found the report of considerable value in visiting with persons about the nature of the department. In the spring of 1962, the department was required to establish a set of bylaws, for which the appendix of the report, which dealt with the existing situation in the department, proved valuable.

Probably the most important effect of the report was felt by persons familiar with the changes that were made in the department's teaching, research, and extension programs in the 1960-68 period. These changes indicate that many of the recommendations were, in fact, carried out. Still further, there was a considerable consensus in the 1960-68 period that these changes were in the correct or right direction for the 1960s. It would, however, be rather difficult to establish that the changes resulting from recommendations in the report were the best that could have been effected.

There are probably two main reasons why the recommendations were not used at college and university-wide levels. One of these reasons is the heterogeneity of the reports prepared by various departments. Some departments spent a great deal of time preparing the reports, while others left the preparation of the report up to one man (sometimes the department head), who worked on it for, perhaps, one afternoon. Many of the reports did not suggest substantial changes in the programs of the departments concerned, but instead called mainly for expansion of the existing program without attention to restrictions imposed on the colleges and university by such things as budget or previous commitments.

The second reason why the report was not used at college and university levels was the lack of provision for integration of the departmental reports at the college level. Had the deans of the colleges been required to produce a five-year plan for their colleges, the reports might have had more effect. In that case, the deans could have used them as raw material for preparing college plans, much as the departmental committee used suggestions from individual professors as raw material in the preparation of the departmental plan. However, it must be observed that the heterogeneity of the reports from the individual departments would have made the job of developing five-year plans for the colleges an extremely difficult one.

One of the uses of the five-year plan extended beyond the 1960-66 planning period. At the time the departmental by-laws referred to above were prepared, bylaws were also established for the university as a whole and for the various colleges. These bylaws provide for college-wide plans to be established five years in advance and to be revised each year by dropping the year that has just passed and adding the next year in sequence. This process will require five-year planning on the part of both colleges and the university. Thus, both the contents of the 1961-66 plan of the Department of Agricultural Economics and the experience gained in constructing it have proven to be of some value.

Some Generalizations about the Philosophic
Implications of this Experience

Philosophic positions involved

The committee adhered primarily to two philosophic positions—the positivistic and the normative. Pragmatism was not precluded and may perhaps have been used. (See the section which follows.) Conditional normativism as defined in the first chapter was not used initially in preparing the report, because those preparing the report did not assume ends as given but, instead, proceeded with the task of formulating a statement of values. In some subsequent instances, conditionally normative methods were employed once the values had been developed and accepted.

It appears that the final report was materially improved by the positivistic efforts that went into the preparation of Appendix B on facts and into other statements about existing conditions and likely outcomes of certain actions. It is clear that normative understanding improved as the committee proceeded from the first crude attempts to state relevant values through the refinement of these statements and evolution of statements about goals and changes. The next section will indicate that it would have been unwise to preclude completely pragmatic approaches and that the preclusion involved may have been damaging. At certain times in the deliberations of the committee there is no doubt that it was efficient to ask questions about how to maximize attainment of a given set of ends with the resources available, indicating the validity of conditionally normative methods in some instances at least.

Problems arising out of the existence of multiple normative and non-normative statements in the first and final reports

As previously noted, both the first and the second reports contained a number of statements having to do with values, and these statements ranged from rather pure consideration of the goodness and badness of conditions, situations, and things per se to statements about what should be done under specific circumstances. The committee seldom knew whether it was dealing with statements about goodness and badness per se or making statements about what ought to be. There was considerable evidence of an inability to distinguish between concepts of goodness and badness per se and goal concepts, such confusion being characteristic of situations thought to be universal by pragmatists.

Some analysts might interpret the existence of multiple statements about values and goals and the confusion of values with goals as evidence that the pragmatic interpretation is a valid one and that there is a means-ends continuum of values, with normative concepts being dependent upon non-normative concepts about the existing situation, which, in turn, are functions of what is valued in the situation. Other analysts might interpret the existence of multiple normative statements as evidence of the need to refine initial, crude, normative statements with subsequent analysis, perhaps independently of positivistic investigations. There was substantial evidence that members of the committee and the department were concerned with questions of consistency, clarity, and workability of the value concepts in Appendix A and also in the goals statement of both the first and second reports.

Much of their concern was independent of the positive statements in Appendix B and elsewhere in the report.

When one turns to the positivistic or non-normative statements found in Appendix B and elsewhere, similar questions
arise. One is not entirely sure whether multiple non-normative statements arose out of what was an essentially pragmatic situation or whether they arose out of the need to
make the initial non-normative statements more consistent
(internally and with experience), understandable, and workable independently of the normative investigation.

The role of criteria governing the
acceptability of concepts

Several criteria were employed in accepting and rejecting
both normative and non-normative concepts. Among these,
consistency played an important role in developing both the
non-normative and normative backgrounds for the recommendations. Questions of the internal consistency of non-
normative and normative recommendations were raised repeatedly both within the committee and by members of the
department. Questions were also raised about the consistency
of both normative and non-normative concepts with experience.

Questions of clarity were raised repeatedly with respect to
both the normative and non-normative. Although sentence
after sentence was rewritten to produce clarity, the clarity of
the final report was nonetheless seriously questioned.

Such questions about consistency and clarity indicated the
need for employing a third criterion, which was often used in
judging the concepts presented in the report—the criterion of
workability. It was impossible to obtain both perfect consistency (internal and with experience) and perfect clarity, yet
the report had to be completed and recommendations had to
be made. Long before perfect consistency and clarity were
obtained, people concluded that the report had reached a
degree of perfection in these respects that made it possible, as
they said, "to live with it." When influential members of the
department decided that the report was good enough for
them to live with, they seemed to be saying that it was

workable insofar as the recommendations affected the values they were interested in attaining or in seeing the department attain.

Methods of making choices

The methods that the committee used in making choices are largely classifiable into two categories: (1) those involving the distributions of power to enforce individual conclusions about what ought to be done and the employment of strategies to ensure that what an individual thought ought to be done would, in fact, be recommended; and (2) those which involve neither the distribution of power among the choice makers nor the employment of strategy.

In using these two broad categories of choice-making procedures, it could be observed that the need to employ power and strategies seemed to be almost inversely proportional to the degree to which the committee succeeded in producing concepts (both positivistic and normative) that met the criteria of consistency, clarity, and workability. As the important concepts involved in making a recommendation acquired the objectivity that accompanied meeting these criteria, unanimity about recommendations tended to be reached. This unanimity, in turn, made it less and less important to have distributions of power attached to the different persons holding conflicting views. Similarly, unanimity tended to reduce the usefulness of strategies used to circumvent the powers held by various persons.

Just as meeting the criteria of consistency, clarity, and workability reduced the need to employ power distributions and strategies, so the failure to meet these criteria made it imperative to employ power distributions and strategies to reach decisions in the time allowed.

Serious normative questions exist about what basis for choice should have been employed. By and large, there was a rather strong conviction that bases for choice which did not involve power distribution and strategy were preferable to those involving a distribution of power and strategy. It was recognized, however, that some bases for choice involving the distribution of power and strategies also have value and are good. Generally speaking, there was a preference for bases for choice which distributed power rather equally among groups, although some people thought that power should be distributed in relation to the competence, knowledge, and administrative rank of the persons involved.

VIII Establishing a Division of General Studies at the University of Nigeria

In the basic design of educational systems can be found the interplay of the normative and non-normative factors that must be confronted to find creative solutions to a given problem. Presenting comparative and evaluative solutions to known agricultural or development problems poses for the agricultural economists a choice of practical steps which should or may be taken.

The educator who is placed in a novel position where he must make use of both normative and non-normative data in designing new programs (as in working within a social or cultural milieu which has had no background for such programs) may initially have no measurable criteria with which to validate the new approach. He must take the practical steps according to the guidance of the normative and non-normative concepts that are at his disposal and at the disposal of his counselers and experts. Like Cap Edmonds (see chapter 3), he must often take these steps alone and wait for the rightness of his move to be demonstrated by its consequences in the future. The goodness of his educational innovation must be demonstrated by its relevance to actual intellectual or sociocultural needs of the community that the novel program serves. There is little or no chance for prior proof by quantification.

In the cases of the migrant workers (chapter 6) and the TVA (chapter 3), the locus of the problem was apparent in a need that was both *felt* and expressed by those who asked for the intervention of outside experts in helping them to solve the problem. In the case to be examined here—building the general studies program at the University of Nigeria—the need was felt by the people who were served but whose cultural

167

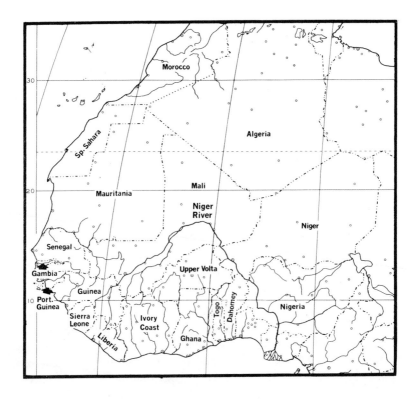

backgrounds made it impossible for them to express the need in a way that allowed the attempt at a solution to be accepted before its worth was demonstrated.

Education as a cultural expression was faced with serious problems in Nigeria, for there was little of the cultural or political cohesion necessary to support novelty. As a colony of Britain, Nigeria was founded with little attention to natural ethnic, religious, or cultural groupings. Governmental boundaries cut across tribally homogeneous peoples and included within them conflicting religious and cultural communities. While the British ruled Nigeria these diversities were preserved in the north by a system of indirect rule, which meant that the colonial officers kept their hands off local affairs. They preserved peace as best they could and insisted on certain minimal standards of natural law and justice, but, for the most part, they allowed the people to continue in traditional patterns.

The traditional pattern in the north was a feudalistic Moslem culture with strong opposition to change and strict enforcement of traditional patterns of behavior and religious observance. Christian missionaries who were welcomed in the south made little progress in the north. By contrast, the southern culture was receptive to change and welcomed the British traders and missionaries as people who could help.

In the years to follow many of the young Nigerians educated in the United States and England, among them Nigeria's president, Nnamdi Azikiwe, wanted a strong, united Nigeria with a government patterned after the Westminister model. During the struggle for independence, the north showed a strong disinclination for breaking with England for fear of domination by the south, while southern nationalists, even at the expense of dominance by the north, accepted a constitution that divided the country into three regions, of which the north was far larger than the east and west combined.

As a part of the program for independence, Nnamdi Azikiwe proposed founding a university in the east to promote nationalism. As the first chancellor of this institution, Azikiwe was one of the strongest forces in determining its character. From its inception, it was determined that the university was not to be a carbon copy of any British or American university. It was to be a uniquely Nigerian institution with advisers from both England and the United States but always under the control of the Nigerian council.

Unlike universities patterned after either U.S. or British models, the University of Nigeria was to have a strong African emphasis and include African studies. Also to be included were practical departments such as agriculture and engineering, a vigorous continuing education program, as well as a division of general studies that would contain four basic courses to be required of all students.

While the new nationalism helped find acceptance for the African studies program—and the obvious needs for agricultural transformation[1] and engineering know-how made these

---

[1] From the very first Azikiwe thought of the University of Nigeria as following the basic ideal of the American land grant universities. It was conceived of from its inception as an educational institution in

programs welcome—the idea of a general studies program was viewed with suspicion and hostility. The university opened in 1960, to coincide with the year of independence. By 1962 the students had staged a riot against the administration of the university; one of the underlying grievances was rumored to be the general studies program.

Originally the four general studies courses, use of English, social science, natural science, and humanities, were required for all students. However, when the university inaugurated a three-year program for students with higher qualification, some students were allowed to take just two of the four courses, but they had to take those two least similar to their major program. Hence, if a student was studying in one of the natural sciences, he would be required to take humanities and social science; if he was working in the humanities he was required to take natural science and social science or use of English.

The rationale for requiring all of the students to take general studies courses is important for a number of reasons. Most of these students came from backgrounds of experiential deprivation compared with those of Western students. As university graduates, they would be cast into policy-making roles. Dr. George Johnson, the first vice-chancellor of the University of Nigeria, pointed out, however:

> From its very introduction the program was extremely controversial. It had its hostile critics among faculty and students, as well as its supporters. In fact the battle for survival raged so heatedly that, had it not been for Dr. Azikiwe's belief in the basic values, the program might never have survived its birth pangs.

The students saw the general studies program as an unnecessary prolongation of their time in the university; some lec-

---

which all of the people of the nation would be served. As a majority of these people were farmers, the needs of farmers were to be given an important place. Thus, the College of Agriculture, with its work in agricultural research, its extension program, and its courses to train Nigerians in the expertise of modern farming, was not to be on the periphery of the university's program but was to be a part of its essential reality.

The story of this university's birth and early years is described in Lewis and Margaret Zerby, *If I Should Die Before I Wake—The Nsukka Dream* (East Lansing, Mich.: Institute for International Studies in Education, Michigan State University, 1971).

turers saw the time used for general studies as time robbed from their honors programs. One geologist cynically put the matter thus: "I hardly have time to make geologists out of these students. There certainly is not time to educate them as well." The students argued that if other universities required three years of honors work only, whereas they were robbed of time by general studies work, they could not possibly be as well trained in their special disciplines as students from other universities. The government officials, most of whom had been trained in the British pattern, saw general studies as a lowering of standards and as an importing of low-quality American education into Africa, which heretofore had had only higher-quality English university colleges.

Against such opposition as this the supporters of general studies offered their four courses in natural science, use of English, social science, and humanities. The adjective *general* was used to mean several different things:

1. The courses were general in the sense that they were designed for all of the students in the university. Other courses were for specialists, but each student getting a degree from the University of Nigeria was required to take the general studies courses.

2. The courses were general in that their subject matter represented *basic* topics for intellectual investigation. One course concerned the nature of man's knowledge about the natural physical world; another concerned the social world of which each man is a part; a third course directed the student's attention to the telic dimension (i.e., the dimension concerned with purpose and value) of his culture as it related to himself on the one hand and to competing cultures on the other. Such studies as these are clearly more basic than courses which fragment knowledge into numerous segments for purposes of detailed anlaysis.

3. The studies were general in that each course made use of and drew materials from a number of different academic disciplines. They were interdisciplinary fields of inquiry.

4. Most importantly, the courses of this division were concerned with the general needs of students as human beings and as effective citizens and leaders; their pur-

pose was the development of human resources as exemplified in comprehensively educated minds and responsible characters.

Such a program as this had not been practiced in any of the British university colleges in Africa. University colleges followed the traditional British pattern of limiting each student's academic work mainly to a single discipline. Because of its novelty, there were no text books for such a program. It was not possible to import syllabi from other universities since the purpose was to "Nigerianize" the material to make it relevant to the students' needs. Teachers were forced, by the nature of this assignment, to be creative.

In being creative a kind of paper-and-pencil simulation was practiced by advisers and Nigerian staff. The consequences of alternative programs were examined to determine their effect through time on the future of the students and Nigeria. It seemed obvious that the role of these students in the development of a modern nation demanded that they be given more than specialized training in one particular discipline. It was necessary that they understand the problems of Nigeria both then and in the future.

With this in mind, the teachers of social science, for example, first tried to introduce to their students such disciplines as psychology, sociology, economics, and political science. When it seemed evident that such an approach would not achieve the kind of broad understanding necessary to produce what Azikiwe called "a new breed of Nigerians," it was abandoned and the course was organized around problems of economic development, nation building, and the transformation of Nigeria from a traditional society to a modern society. The frequently asked question was, what are the likely long-term consequences for Nigeria of one program as contrasted with others? Thus, administrators and professors practiced a common-sense method of determining the consequences through time of what was known from past experience and present investigation.

On another level, both staff and students were required to imagine creative new approaches to old problems. In economic development, for example, various models were described. The relevance of various models to Nigeria's needs was constantly discussed. Another question was how models needed to be modified to fit the Nigerian scene. Needless to say, such an approach to social science met with stiff opposition from both staff and students who conceived of education as concentration on a specific discipline, often by rote learning and following authorities.

The early development of the general studies program suffered initially from a lack of teachers in the division. In its early phase, general studies courses were taught by teachers borrowed from other departments. Although they were officially given released time to do this teaching, they looked upon such work as an interruption of their "real" work, and thus they gave help grudgingly. As late as spring 1963, the University of Nigeria budget allowed for only one senior staff member, and this position was not filled until 1964.

During the 1962-63 session, the work of general studies was directed by an Agency for International Development (AID) adviser from Michigan State University (MSU) who also served as head of humanities. Other MSU/AID advisers acted as heads for the programs in social science and the use of English. There was a widespread conviction that as long as the U.S. government was paying the salaries of the staff for general studies, there was no assurance that the program had been accepted by the Nigerians.

By the time the 1966-67 University of Nigeria budget was formulated, it included positions for one senior lecturer, four lecturers, six assistant lecturers, and four teaching assistants. This seemed to demonstrate that the Nigerian community would accept general studies. In addition to teaching, this staff developed syllabi for each of the four courses—syllabi using Nigerian and African materials and concerned with Nigerian problems.

The problem of establishing a division of general studies at the University of Nigeria was solved by people who were willing to accept the normative dimension of reality as being equally important as the non-normative. They were concerned from the first with the goods of a broad-based education for all students. As such an education did not yet exist in Nigeria, it had to be created. Therefore, the project demanded creativity. Its founders were individual men, who, like Cap Edmonds, rebelled against the existing situation and worked for the realizations of goals they had set for themselves and the students. The goals were compromises between what was valued and what was possible. The program's founders were able to create in reality the program they had conceived to be right and were able to institutionalize this reality within the pattern of the University of Nigeria. The community came to accept general studies as part of the solution of its problem; therefore, the work turned out to be creative in the sense that the word is used in this book. Out of a number of groups holding different opinions, a clarification of positions resulted in realistic discussion of normative and non-normative possibilities.

It would be pleasant to be able to end this chapter with this success motif, but this is not in fact possible. In its conception, the University of Nigeria was looked upon as a truly national university. The student body represented all regions of the nation, and the faculty represented numerous Nigerian tribes. But between 1960 and 1966 the country outside the university became less and less unified. Crisis followed crisis in ever more rapid succession until January 1966 a group of young army officers staged a coup d'état in which the prime minster, the premiers of the north and west, the minister of finance, and numerous army officers lost their lives. Out of the coup came a military government, the head of which was an Ibo named Ironsi.

After the coup, each of the regions was administered by a military governor, and from January 1966 until July 1966, people in eastern Nigeria felt satisfied that the country was making giant strides forward in economic development and in the elimination of tribalism, corruption, nepotism, and government inefficiency. However, such a feeling was not nationwide. Dissatisfaction with the new government was felt particularly in the north, and in July 1966 Ironsi and the military governor of the west were both killed in a second coup d'état.

The new government set Colonel Gowen at its head. Many felt that Gowen represented an ideal choice since he was nominally a northerner but was actually from the middle belt and was a Christian rather than a Moslem. However, pent-up tribal animosities flared up against the easterners, who suffered large-scale attacks which the federal government was unable to prevent or control. At the end of months of futile negotiations, the eastern region declared itself the Independent Republic of Biafra and declared a secession from Nigeria. The declaration started a civil war. The University of Nigeria, located as it was in the area of most intense early fighting, could not open in the fall of 1967.

The intimate relationship between a university and the society within which it exists is brought forcefully to mind by the recent civil conflict in Nigeria. This conflict delineates the urgency for basing decision making upon realistic factors in both non-normative and normative dimensions and has made the goals for general studies for Africa seem more obvious today than they were in 1960.

Technical progress, medical facilities, economic development, and industrialization can be meaningless (if, indeed, they are possible) unless intellectual (including normative) development occurs at the same time. The British educators often acted as conditional normativists and positivists in their colonies. They assumed without question that the English values were the correct values for their colonies and that the way to achieve goals was the way in which they had been achieved in England. This resulted in neglect of the development of normative knowledge by Nigerians.

The Nigerians trained in England came home more British than the British. They wanted to teach in the technically backward context of Nigeria the same courses which they had been taught in England. In the typical British university college, the Nigerian student learned far more about law, geography, theology, economics, and political science as they apply in England than he learned about his own culture. Early rulers minimized the two resultant, polarized groups with different normative concepts as a factor in decision making, and no effort was made to find a common basis for discussion. Furthermore, inadequate attention was paid to the future careers of the students. Men who were to become prime ministers, premiers, legislators, and permanent secretaries were educated in such narrow specialties as chemistry, medicine, theology, and mathematics. By contrast, the general studies program looked upon every student as a potential leader and attempted to give him the sort of understanding of man and the world which would equip him to be a good prime minister or local leader as well as one who could be identified with a large community of interests.

Thus, as opposed to the conditional normativists, the advocates of general studies took values very seriously, and the values they took seriously were based on the logical analysis of normative experiences of Nigerians as well as the values of twentieth-century man. As pragmatists, they took seriously the criterion of workability. General studies programs were continuously evaluated in terms of their ability to solve the problems and achieve the ideals of the Nigerian community.

One of Nigeria's basic problems was to create a society which could define itself as a single nation. It is ironic, then, that some of the same men who were early nationalists and who founded the University of Nigeria to assist in promoting nationalism should, in 1967, find themselves the leaders of a self-declared rebel government trying to carve a second nation out of Nigeria.

While the institutionalization of general studies within the university had truly begun, the role of the total university within the body-politic of Nigeria had not had time to develop. The failures suffered by Nigeria in this connection can be instructive for all nations struggling toward national strength and economic development and for advisers to such nations.

The first lesson of this failure is that governments and educational systems cannot be transposed from one culture to another in the way physical objects can be transposed. The naive faith which the earlier nationalists had in the Westminster model of democracy and the London University model of education has proved to be without foundation. Whatever government and education will ultimately be successful in Nigeria will be the result of creative producers of new programs geared to an understanding of the past and to the changing ideals, needs, goals, aspirations, and worldviews of Nigerians.

The second lesson is that it is not possible to unify cultures as heterogenous as those in the geographical area called Nigeria simply by declaring them to be one nation. Both normative and non-normative factors work against such unity unless there is a generally recognized goal in such unity. In 1964 Dr. Nnamdi Azikiwe, who was then president of Nigeria, gave a talk at the University of Nigeria in which he spoke of tribalism as a pragmatic instrument for national unity. The gist of his lecture was that unless the federal government was able to demonstrate by specific, concrete services to the hetrogeneous sections of Nigeria its capacity to help them achieve their own diverse goals, tribalism would destroy Nigeria. Never has a perceptive prophet been more without honor in his own country. Tragically enough, Azikiwe was more honored among the leaders of other tribes than he was among his fellow Ibos. His insight that a government must *work* in order to be stable was and is one that grew out of his solid grounding in pragmatism.

The third lesson is that an educational infrastructure is a sine qua non for stable economic development, even as a stable economic development is a sine qua non for an educational infrastructure and that uneven educational levels of achievement and uneven economic development can be disruptive in any nation's quest for a meaningful nationalism. The myopic ideal of achieving economic development by importing or training a small coterie of experts who can then transform a traditional society into a modern society must be replaced by a more realistic ideal of changing the intellectual (including normative) quality of a high proportion of the population. Without such change, traditional society will remain traditional regardless of the advice and expertise of specialists.

The fourth lesson is that far more respect must be paid to the factor of tribalism or regionalism in some of the emergent nations than has been paid in the past. A group's loyalties represent a basic element in the psychology of each individual in the group and, unless this is understood, the development of new patterns in politics, economics, or education is made difficult if not impossible. Individual and group loyalties are not easily or quickly changed, and this is a fact which leaders among advisers to new nations need to recognize. Such loyalties change with the individual's acceptance of data on extensive normative and non-normative experiences as relevant to his own and his group's well-being.

In instituting a program of general studies, a serious attempt was made to keep each of these lessons in mind. For example, a primary purpose of the humanities course was to give the student an opportunity to understand his own past experiences and those of others and to participate in further significant experiences with both the normative and non-normative dimensions. The concretion of experience was part of that intent. The experience of art was made possible by the presentation of paintings, musical recordings, and literature which were discussed by artists, musicians, and writers. During two lectures a week, it was possible for the student to enter empathically into great periods of history, both African and non-African, as they are reflected in cultural expressions.

African students are sometimes inclined to overemphasize the uniqueness of their world (their moral community) and to fail to recognize its similarities to the Asian and European worlds. In religion and philosophy, for example, there has been a tendency to make a bifurcation between Africa and the rest of the world. (This overemphasis is repeated, it should be noted, in the Black Nationalist and Black Power movements in the United States.) Part of the bifurcation is the result of the fact that people outside of Africa fail to understand the actual native African philosophy and religion, while part of it is also the result of Africans' failure to understand other cultural patterns. By contrast, intimate relationships were found to exist between the African world and the worlds of Asia and Europe in the general studies course in humanities.

Education must attempt to overcome the regretable chasm brought about by the circumstances of Africa's history. Colonialism, slavery, and racial bigotry made impossible normal cultural movements and crossfertilizations. While the early invaders of Africa had a quick and keen awareness of the material wealth of the continent and were eager to exploit it, they ignored or failed to appreciate its human and aesthetic wealth. But, in the twentieth century, independence has been accompanied by the demand for cultural recognition. Education, to be effective and appropriate, must promulgate such recognition.

In instituting the general studies program, it was recognized that a university student must understand the complex social world of which he is a part, and this understanding must be based on past and future projections as well as on the present. No man can separate himself from this social world. He cannot exist without his fellow men because his very nature and character are formed by the social groups to which he does or does not belong. To recognize this fact and to choose, on the basis of knowledge rather than chance, the group to which he belongs is a distinguishing feature of an educated man.

The social science course studied the social life of man and attempted to relate the student articulately and explicitly to the many groups which exist today. It was concerned not only with how man in fact lives in society (a question involving only non-normative knowledge) but also with how he ought to live (which also involves normative knowledge). Because of this concern, both normative and non-normative material was included from ethics, psychology, sociology, economics, and political science as well as the more purely non-normative information from the physical and biological disciplines. In each of these disciplines, an effort was made to help the student see how the fundamental principles of social science apply to some of the basic problems which confronted him as a citizen of a new nation with an old culture, a nation that is in a hurry to change itself from a traditional society into one which can properly be called a society of economic and social maturity. On each question, traditional subject matter was chosen that would have particular relation to the students. In presenting the topic of what psychology is and what psychologists do, the psychological problems of present-day Nigeria and Africa were emphasized: prejudice, tribalism, racism, motivation, frustration, and cultural schizophrenia.

In sociology, terms like *community, association, institution, culture, caste, class,* and *social role* were analyzed. Traditional society was contrasted with modern man's society. In economics, the basic normative and non-normative concepts and laws of the discipline were studied in topics associated with economic development in Nigeria. The principles of political science were illustrated by material on the political evolution of Nigeria from its traditional and colonial forms of government into an independent nation. There was also concern with giving a perspective of Nigeria's place in the world community of nations and her role as an actual or potential leader in various African international blocs.

In natural science, an attempt was made to overcome some of the ancient superstitions, provincialisms, and intolerances that plague African society. The dean of education, Babs Fafunwa, expressed the matter thus: "For African schools today, the major problem is the race between the magician and the teacher as to who gets the child first." Teachers in natural science were primarily concerned with showing the role played by hypotheses, explanation, imagination, and theory construction in science. Students who otherwise would not have had an opportunity to get an understanding of laboratory work were put into laboratories to participate in the sort of activity that makes up the modern world of science. Einstein once said, "If you want to find out anything from theoretical physicists about the methods they use, I advise you to stick closely to the principle: Don't listen to their words, fix attention on their deeds." The teachers in natural science tried to go one better than this and to make their students actually *do* some scientific *deeds*.

The philosophic glossary in chapter 1 defines instrumental value as "the meaning of a concept of goodness or badness insofar as it is derived from more basic values." In this respect the general studies course in the use of English had instrumental value. For most Nigerian students the English language is a second or even third language, and mastering it is a means to achieving the kind of understanding acquired in social science, physical science, and humanities. Written and spoken English was practiced extensively to facilitate comprehension and communication.

Summary

In this chapter, the practical problem of establishing a general studies program at the University of Nigeria has been discussed. We have seen the importance of creativity in solving this problem. We have also discussed how the program achieved institutionalization within the university community and some of the problems associated with establishing the university itself.

Throughout the discussion, we have stressed the importance of taking normative reality seriously and avoiding the restrictions of positivism and the necessity for a realistic sort of pragmatism and for creating a moral community of men sharing a common conviction. In spite of the disruption the recent civil war has caused at the University of Nigeria, we are persuaded that there has been some success in implanting the idea of general studies in the minds of a number of leaders in African education, and it is encouraging to note that as efforts are made by the Nigerian leaders to reestablish the University of Nigeria general studies is a recognized part of the curriculum.

IX | Research on Nigerian Rural Development

Each of the chapters contained in this book is a historical case study. The previous chapters have all dealt with attempts of agricultural economists and others to deal with important practical problems. In a number of instances, these investigators have encountered theoretical problems involving the attainment of: (1) interpersonally valid welfare measurements; (2) a common denominator in terms of which multitudinous goods and bads could be measured as a basis for maximizing the difference between goodness and badness attainable from alternative proposed solutions to the problem; (3) the second-order conditions mathematically required for the existence of a maximum difference between goodness and badness; and (4) an appropriate basis for choice in selecting that alternative course of action which would best solve the problem they face.

The case considered in this chapter—that of doing practical research on rural development problems in Nigeria—involves these four theoretical problems so often and so clearly that the investigators were forced to try to find a way of handling them almost as a prerequisite for tackling the practical problems under investigation. Thus, this chapter indicates very clearly the nature of certain theoretical problems that must be solved as prerequisites for attacking practical problems.

History of Rural Development Research in Nigeria
Supported by the U.S. Agency for International Development

This section will deal briefly with the experience of one of the authors at the Economic Development Institute (EDI) of the University of Nigeria. It will then consider the creation and operation of the Consortium for the Study of Nigerian Rural Development (CSNRD). The importance of the four theoretical problems mentioned in the introduction will become apparent in the final portion of this section.

The Economic Development Institute

Dr. Glenn Johnson began work in Nigeria in the fall of 1962 and served for 19 months as Director of the Economic Development Institute of the University of Nigeria.[1] During his tenure in this position, he developed a keen interest in Nigeria and gained considerable knowledge of the structure of the Nigerian economy. He accepted the position as director of the Economic Development Institute with the general understanding that he would probably maintain a long-term association with the country.

The Consortium for the Study of Nigerian Rural Development

As a result of his work, Dr. Johnson was later asked to head a Consortium for the Study of Nigerian Rural Development. "Snerd," as the Consortium was popularly known, was either owned or controlled by Colorado State University, which had contracted with the Agency for International Development (AID) to assist the agricultural research, extension, and public service activities of the Eastern Nigerian Ministry of Agriculture; Kansas State University, which had contracted with AID to assist the faculty of agriculture at Ahmadu Bello University in northern Nigeria; Michigan State University, which had contracted with AID to assist the entire University of Nigeria in eastern Nigeria, including its agricultural faculty; the University of Wisconsin, which had contracted with AID to assist the Agricultural Faculty of the University of Ife in western Nigeria; the Research Triangle Institute of North Carolina, which had contracted with AID

---

1 The EDI was supported financially by the University of Nigeria, USAID, and the Ford Foundation with the University of Nigeria and Michigan State University jointly responsible for staffing.

to assist the Nigerian Federal Office of Statistics conduct a Rural Economic Survey; and the United States Departments of Agriculture and Interior, which had Participating Agency Service Agreements (PASAs) to assist various Nigerian agencies with agricultural development projects ranging from range management and plant building to supervised agricultural credit.

Michigan State University was the prime contractor for the consortium and, as such, accounted for the money and made subcontracts and agreements with the university members of the consortium (including itself) to support CSNRD research programs. CSNRD had responsibilities to AID under contract AID/afr. 264 to "render technical advice and assistance to AID for the purpose of providing an intensive examination and evaluation of the agricultural development program" of Nigeria and "of the USAID program of technical agricultural development" in Nigeria "in order to provide a sound basis for planning such programs for the future."

Some persons thought of CSNRD as an organization comprising four universities, one research institute, and two government agencies involved in evaluating their own contracts or Participating Agency Service Agreements which they were operating in Nigeria. Some people thought that it would have been better if these contracts and Participating Agency Service Agreements were studied by an agency not involved in Nigeria.

There were, however, advantages in having the agencies which were working in Nigeria involved in the evaluation of USAID projects in that country, for it was precisely these agencies that knew the most about Nigeria and about the problems of the country. In one sense, the choice appears to have been one between uninformed objectivity on one hand and informed bias on the other hand. These are not the two alternatives, however. Instead, it appears that by involving government and universities, and Nigerian and U.S. personnel, and by calling freely on others, one can get *informed objectivity*. (See chapters 1 and 11 for the definition of objectivity as used here.)

An advance planning team went to Nigeria to work with Nigerian and U.S. agencies and people to plan the main research program of CSNRD. The work of the advance planning team was referred to as Phase I work. The research plan which the Phase I team devised was referred to as Phase II work. The advance planning team consisted of Dr. Raymond Christensen from the USDA, Dr. Lynn Hodgdon from Colorado State University, Dr. John Nordin from Kansas State University, and the director, Dr. Johnson. In addition, it had the benefit of assistance, consultation, and advice from Mr. Francis Jones of the USAID/Lagos, Dr. Vernon Johnson from AID/Washington, and Dr. Gerald Tichenor of the USDA.

The director went to Nigeria ahead of the advance planning team to talk with personnel in Nigerian and other agencies concerning the activities of the team. His purpose was to get Nigerian, contractor, and USAID assistance in deciding whether or not CSNRD should go ahead and, if so, how it should go about doing what. A great deal of valuable, much appreciated help was obtained.

Along with this help, he encountered the strong opinions of the directors of the Nigerian Institute of Social and Economic Research and of the Economic Development Institute at the University of Nigeria. Similar opinions were expressed by Mr. A. A. Ayida, permanent secretary of the Federal Ministry of Economic Development; John Sjo of the Rural Economic Research Unit at Ahmadu Bello University; Francis Jones and others. Their strong opinions and resultant discussions with them greatly influenced planning for Phase II of CSNRD activities. Drs. H. M. A. Onitiri and Carl Eicher felt very strongly that Nigerians and Nigerian institutions should have a great deal to do with developing and executing the long-run research of CSNRD. On the other hand, USAID personnel, both in Lagos and in the regions, felt a strong need for rather immediate evaluations and recommendations concerning the USAID agricultural programs in Nigeria.

Thus, Phase II was divided rather naturally into parts *a* and *b*. Part *a* was to deal with research on problems encountered by the U.S. government in the administration and conduct of existing programs to aid the Nigerian agricultural economy. Part *b* was to deal with longer-term research. In connection with part *a*, it was recognized that the U.S. government had an immediate practical interest in these programs, and that CSNRD should proceed with its research work on these problems quite independently of Nigerian institutions, if necessary.

Part *b*, however, was recognized to be, in substantial part, the business of Nigerian governmental and academic institutions. After this became clear, a meeting was held that included Mr. William Lawless, USAID minister-director for Nigeria, and Mr. Ayida, permanent secretary of the Federal Ministry of Economic Development and the director of CSNRD. At that meeting, the division between part *a* and *b* was agreed upon. The Phase I advance planning team then concentrated on developing a set of projects and administrative studies dealing with the problems of USAID agricultural development in Nigeria plus one additional project.

The USAID program of assistance to Nigerian agriculture which was to be evaluated by CSNRD concentrated first on long-term assistance in education and extension and second on a shorter-term program dealing mainly with the nonexport sector and concentrating on both replacing imports and improving nutrition. At the university level, AID support was being given to the agricultural faculties at the Universities of Nigeria and Ife and at Ahmadu Bello University. In addition, a participant training program was being phased out at the bachelor-of-science level as the indigenous universities acquired capacity to conduct domestic training. Support was also being given to nondegree programs and to various agricultural schools for the training of personnel to work in agricultural ministries, at farm training centers, at farmer institutes, and in the veterinary training centers. Research assistance had been given for cocoa and rubber and for the nonexport crops.

The Nigerian USAID agricultural program was one of the largest in the world and the total USAID program for Nigeria was the world's second largest. For instance, the Northern Nigeria/USAID program alone was larger than the USAID program in any African state other than Nigeria. In the north and west, extension assistance was largely by direct-hire USAID personnel. In eastern Nigeria, extension assistance was rendered largely through the University of Colorado contract to support the Eastern Ministry of Agriculture. Attention was being given to land and water resource development through PASAs with the U.S. Departments of Agriculture and Interior. Substantial assistance was also being given to the development of livestock and poultry, and good work in the area of rinderpest eradication had been accomplished.

In the field of credit, consultant surveys had been conducted and direct aid had been rendered in the eastern and western regions largely along FHA lines. In the west, considerable assistance had been given to credit cooperatives. In the field of economics some aid had been rendered in the areas of farm planning and marketing and in the drying and storage of grain. A major contract with the Research Triangle Institute of North Carolina provided support in conducting a rural economic sample survey which produced basic, primary data on yields and production. It involved approximately 175 men and accounted for a high percentage of USAID assistance to Nigeria, which was scheduled to run at $225 million for the six-year period, 1962-68.

Both the United States and Nigeria felt the need for this large USAID program. The public decision makers in both governments were concerned that USAID assistance to universities and research agencies would create an unfrastructure which the productivity of the Nigerian economy would not be able to support. In addition to this and other questions about the distribution of USAID assistance, questions arose concerning the possible duplication of or conflict between projects. Further, both countries were gravely concerned about the rate of growth of the Nigerian agricultural economy relative to its needs for foreign exchange and for better foods to improve the nutritional standards of the populace.

Originally, there were nine CSNRD Phase IIa projects and three administrative studies. A tenth project provided financing for seminars to develop Phase IIb projects. The accompanying table provides the titles of the original nine projects and three administrative studies and indicates the sponsoring U.S. university or institution and the Nigerian institutional home for each project.

Projects 1, 2, and 6 (those dealing with agricultural education, training, and research) were all conducted in more or less parallel fashion under the direction of three capable administrators from the contracting universities. In addition to providing a "rolling appraisal"—that is, one adjustable to the changes in the country's institutional structure—with respect to these three kinds of assistance, these three projects gave a number of persons one- to two-year assignments in Nigeria. Dean Glen Pound from the University of Wisconsin gave James Long such an assignment. Director Lowell Watts from Colorado State University placed Dr. James Kincaid, R.

CSNRD Projects

Item	Sponsoring U.S. Institution	Sponsoring Nigerian Institution
Project number and title		
1. University Level Agricultural Education	University of Wisconsin	National University Commission
2. Sub-University Level Agricultural Education	Colorado State University	Federal Ministry of Agriculture and Research
3. Direct Public Investment	Michigan State University	NISER and Federal Ministry of Economic Development
4. Direct Private Investment	Michigan State University	EDI and Federal Ministry of Economic Development
5. Modernizing Northern Beef	Kansas State University	Ahmadu Bello and Northern Ministry of Agriculture and Forest Research
6. Agricultural Research	Kansas State University	Federal Ministry of Agriculture and Research
7. Agricultural Credit	Ohio State University	Federal Ministry of Agriculture and Research
8. Traditional Restrictions on Rural Development	Colorado State University	Undecided
9. Agricultural Marketing	Michigan State University	NISER
Administrative study number and title		
1. Development Theories	CSNRD	None required
2. Impact of AID Contracts on U.S. Universities	CSNRD	None required
3. Forms of USAID Assistance	CSNRD	None required

D. Butler, and David Kidd in Nigeria, and Vice President Glenn Beck from Kansas State University placed Drs. Wilfred Pine, Everett Peterson, and Omer Herrmann there. These men carried out detailed investigations of projects and of Nigerian needs.

The two educational projects were cooperative with EWA (Education and World Affairs) and with the CIC (the Committee on Institutional Cooperation, which includes the Universities of Indiana, Ohio, and Wisconsin and Michigan State University) project on agricultural education. The two direct investment (public and private) projects were under the coordinated direction of Mr. Ayida, Permanent Secretary, Federal Ministry of Economic Development. Professor T. W. Schultz and Dr. Forest Hill served as consultants. Mr. Herbert Kriesel and Drs. Kenneth Laurent, Malcolm Purvis, Gerald Saylor, and Dupe Olatunbosun were assigned to these projects.

Researchers used in the field of agricultural credit included a representative of the International Bank for Reconstruction and Development (IBRD), the United States Federal Reserve Banks, the Farmers Home Administration, and the Farm Credit Administration, all working under Dr. Mervin Smith and Ted Jones from Ohio State University's agricultural economics department.

The administrative studies were under the direction of CSNRD administrators. The subject matter of these studies was of general interest to administrators and academic economists working on developmental research in connection with a program such as USAID's.

As will be pointed out later, CSNRD investigated the use of simulation models under administrative study No. 1. Activities under administrative study No. 3 were merged with projects 3 and 4 where forms of USAID assistance turned out to be a determinant of success for investment projects.

The complications encountered by the Consortium arose mainly in the nature of Nigeria's institutional structure, in the nature of U.S. institutions operating in Nigeria, in English-American relationships, in the prejudices common to both U.S. and Nigerian civil servants, in the prejudices common to both U.S. and Nigerian academicians, in the operation of American foundations and other donors, in AID's problems with the U.S. Congress, and in the military coups which were themselves an outgrowth of the complications among Nigerian institutions. The overriding complication of Nigerian institutions has been regionalism which is closely based on tribal, political, and religious ties.

Under the precoup Nigerian constitution, agriculture was the province of the regional governments. There was a Federal Office of Research which dealt with agricultural research, but there was no federal extension program and no ministry of agriculture. As a result of an FAO report, a Ministry of Natural Resources and Research was formed in late 1965. Because "mines and power" were lodged in another ministry, the Ministry of Natural Resources and Research was largely an agricultural ministry, although not so named for constitutional reasons. Since the coups, the Ministry of Natural Resources has been renamed the Ministry of Agriculture and Natural Resources.

Prior to the civil war, Nigeria was characterized by rather complex relationships among heads of universities and among faculties of agriculture in four universities. Similarly, competition existed among the university faculties of agriculture and the ministries of agriculture of the respective precoup regional governments. This competition occurred with respect to research, subuniversity education, and extension work proper. There was also competition between the Ministries of Economic Development and of Economic Planning on the one hand, and the Ministries of Education and of Agriculture on the other. In one of the regions, there were both Ministries of Agriculture and of Animal and Forest Resources.

The U.S. situation was also multidimensional. AID/Washington had several divisions: technical cooperation and research, the African bureau, and program coordination. In USAID/Lagos, there were divisions of program, agriculture, and education. The numerous American universities and agencies operating in Nigeria also created complications. In addition, the U.S. Departments of Agriculture and Interior had to be reckoned with, which is not to mention the relationships among direct-hire USAID, PASA, and contract personnel.

Although there is good overall cooperation between English and American agencies and the topnotch workers from both countries respect and complement each other, there were complicating, undesirable kinds of relationships among less competent personnel from both countries. The dedicated workers from both countries have basic philosophical differences about which there is legitimate disagreement and which are a prime concern of this book; for instance, American educators and researchers tend to be more pragmatic than their Nigerian and British counterparts who are more positivistic.

The work of the Consortium was further complicated by reciprocal kinds of prejudices held by governmental and academic workers. On both the Nigerian and U.S. side, academicians sometimes displayed damaging, disruptive, antigovernmental biases. Similarly, there sometimes were misunderstandings on both sides, and governmental workers often had antiacademic prejudices.

The situation was not simplified by the operations of American foundations and of donors from other countries. Here too, competition and lack of coordination created problems in the total rural development program for Nigeria. American foundations seemed to be highly selective about the kinds of projects they would support. Generally, they tended to avoid high-risk, controversial projects. This selectivity sometimes resulted in uneven, and, in some instances, uncoordinated support of Nigerian rural development projects and institutions.

The whole situation was made even more difficult by the first coup (January 15, 1966) which grew out of the regionalism mentioned earlier. Between the first and the second coups, the country was operated under a military government. There were major national committees and commissions on the new constitution, agriculture, education, and judiciary system. The tendency was toward a more unitary, as contrasted to a federal, government.

Because of a lack of consensus among the population and the dominant leaders, the situation which grew out of the first coup was basically unstable. A second coup destroyed the unitary government established under the first, and the country moved to a loosely held military federation from which the former eastern region attempted to secede. During the resultant civil war, the military government of Nigeria was again substantially centralized and strengthened.

Obviously, CSNRD research in support of USAID technical assistance and development had to be conditioned by the kind of government and the constitutional relationships which might exist in the future among the government, universities, and research agencies. This complication of rapidly changing, fundamental institutional arrangements meant that much of CSNRD evaluative and developmental research had to be in the nature of a "rolling appraisal." As such, it had to be readily adjustable to the rapidly changing institutional structure of the country, because several of the Phase IIa CSNRD projects dealt with USAID projects to improve the institutional structure of the country.

At about this time in the history of CSNRD, AID appropriations encountered serious difficulties in the U.S. Congress. The appropriation cuts, as well as the image of Nigerian political instability, resulted in the imposition of severe budget restraints on CSNRD. As a result, CSNRD, USAID/Lagos administrators, and Nigerian officials were forced to assign priorities to CSNRD activities. Phase IIb projects were consolidated, speeded up, or eliminated. More specifically, projects 3 and 4 were consolidated while project 9 was reduced in scope and then consolidated with projects 3 and 4. Initiation of project 5, on beef, was postponed indefinitely, and project 8 was eliminated entirely.

Projects 1, 2, 3, 4, and 6 were speeded up, and CSNRD assumed responsibility for putting together the research results produced under the separate projects and other generally available information on Nigeria in an overall report on Nigerian rural development for the guidance of USAID. Under the terms of the contract, as previously indicated, this guidance was to include the rendering of "technical advice and assistance to AID for the purpose of providing an intensive examination and evaluation of the agricultural development program" of Nigeria "and of the USAID program of technical agricultural development" in Nigeria "in order to provide a sound basis for planning such programs for the future."

In providing such an intensive evaluation of the Nigerian agricultural development program and of USAID's agricultural development program in Nigeria, four specific empirical difficulties arose repeatedly for CSNRD. One of these was the problem of evaluating programs that damage some persons in order to confer benefits on others. Most of the rural development projects operated by the Nigerian government and supported by USAID fell in this category. For instance, much of the Nigerian financial support for rural development projects came from marketing board revenues (taxes) imposed on Nigerian cocoa, palm produce, and groundnut producers. Even USAID support for one project often came at the expense of alternative Nigerian projects, thereby hurting the alternative potential beneficiaries in order to confer benefits on the beneficiaries of the project which USAID supported. In the jargon of economists, such problems have only non-Pareto-better in contrast to Pareto-better solutions, i.e., they have no solutions that make one or more persons better off without making someone worse off.

The second difficulty involved inability to isolate any one thing, such as gross national product or utility, which could be used as an index to determine whether a given program or program proposal was right or wrong. This problem was apparent from the multiplicity of goods sought and bads to be avoided in connection with any problem involving, say, Nigeria's university-level agricultural education program. The number and variety of goods and bads often prevented their immediate reduction to a common unit of measurement which would permit an analyst to subtract the bads from the goods as a basis for maximizing the difference to determine a right program.[2]

The third difficulty involved the basis for choice. It was difficult, for example, to determine if programs should be judged on the basis of the maximum of some measure of the average excess of goodness over badness, or on the basis of some satisficing criteria, or on the basis of whether the choice appears to involve that course of action for which the worst that can happen is best. Because of the difficulties of evaluating programs and isolating an index for rightness or wrongness, and in the absence of an agreed on basis for choice, it was most difficult for practical researchers to ask the crucial question or state a research problem so that there would be a determinable right solution. It was also difficult for the public decision makers who were served by researchers to ask the correct question.

---

2 The terminology used here is in strict accord with the definitions presented in chapter 1.

The fourth difficulty involved the mathematically necessary, second-order conditions for the existence of a maximum difference between the goods being maximized and the bads being minimized. In static production and consumption, these conditions are ensured by the presence of fixed resources and real income constraints of firms and households, respectively. Hence, as firms expand their use of variable inputs and households expand their use of variable products, the laws of diminishing productivity and utility ensure the existence of the second-order conditions which, in turn, establish the existence of a maximum profit or a maximum of utility over disutility. However, the Consortium dealt with the creation of technology (project 6), of institutional change, and with education. Neither the law of diminishing productivity nor the law of diminishing utility could be invoked to guarantee the existence of optima with respect to casual orderings of such activities.

Ways of circumventing the four difficulties just discussed had to be found in order to fulfill CSNRD's contractual obligation "to evaluate as a basis for improving the agricultural development programs of both USAID and the Nigerian government." CSNRD administrators took two actions: first, they set up a makeshift method of simulating the operation of the Nigerian agricultural economy within CSNRD and, second, they took steps to establish a long-term, special research project outside of CSNRD to conduct computer simulation of the Nigerian economy as a means of tackling the four theoretical problems.

The short-term simulation within CSNRD was fundamentally nothing more or less than a common-sense, paper-and-pencil simulation (construction of projections) of the operation of the Nigerian agricultural economy under alternative policies and programs at three points in the future—1970, 1975, and 1980. The following is the memorandum setting up these projections:

It was agreed that projections should be developed for the following dates:

1. January 1, 1970
2. January 1, 1975
3. January 1, 1985

With respect to 1970, it was agreed that projections would be developed showing likely developments under three alternative sets of assumptions:

1. Continuation of present policies and programs as they affect agriculture.
2. A shift as of January 1, 1968 of present policies and programs to what CSNRD would recommend.
3. A shift to a more adverse set of policies and programs.

The 1970 projections were "intended to cover a two-year reconstruction planning period" . . . under consideration by GON.

With respect to 1975 it was agreed that projections would be developed showing likely developments under three sets of alternative assumptions:

1. Continuation of present policies and programs as they affect agriculture.
2. A shift of present policies and programs to what CSNRD would recommend.

The shift is assumed to take place as of two different dates:

a. January 1, 1968
b. January 1, 1970

In neither case will expanded financial support of infrastructure for agriculture start until 1970.

3. A shift to a more adverse set of policies and programs:

a. With expanded infrastructure programs to support agriculture starting in 1970.
b. Without expanded infrastructure programs to support agriculture.

With respect to 1985, the main interest was in seeing the consequences of introducing population control. CSNRD recommendations on policy and infrastructures were assumed to be attained under two cases:

1. Without population control
2. With population control

The above provides for twelve different sets of projections. It was agreed that the nonfarm economy would be taken as given initially. If the construction of projections revealed that this procedure would be unfeasible, it was to be changed. In this connection, nonfarm employment, capital, and output were taken as given at levels to be set in consultation with Anson Chong, Dr. Onitiri (of NISER), and personnel in the Ministry of Economic Development. Dr. O. J. Scoville accepted responsibility for doing this in close cooperation with Dr. Gerald Saylor. The first set of assumptions were to be available by November 15.

The formuation of alternative policy and program assumptions was the responsibility of Mr. Herbert Kriesel. A first statement of those assumptions was to be available November 15. The first set of projections was to be available for use in CSNRD/Nigeria and for mailing to East Lansing by December 1, 1967.

Responsibility for constructing and updating the estimates to reflect the results of new information from ongoing CSNRD research and other sources fell primarily on Dr. Scoville, Mr. Kriesel, and Dr. Kenneth Laurent, as Dr. Saylor was to leave Nigeria shortly. Mr. John Whitney had heavy assignments in connection with Dr. Mervin Smith's work, and Dr. Malcolm Purvis was badly needed to carry out investigations for the investment projections. More specific assignments were to be made by Dr. Scoville.

Each of the 12 sets of projections was to include:

1. Population projections—farm, nonfarm, sex and age distributions, and the farm labor force with adjustments for war and the smallpox/measles vaccination campaign.
2. GDP or GNP projections (totals)
   a. Nonfarm
      1.) Government
      2.) Private
   b. Farm
      1.) Government versus private
      2.) Export
         a.) Eventually, the total was to be checked with realistic estimates for cocoa, oil palm produce, rubber, cotton, groundnuts.
      3.) Domestic food
         a.) Eventually, the total was to be checked with realistic estimates for maize, yams, rice, poultry, beef, guinea corn and millet, and sugar.
      4.) Industrial raw materials
         a.) Eventually, the total was to be checked with realistic estimates for tobacco, kenaf palm kernels.
3. "2" was to be expressed on a per capita basis.
4. Price data in constant and current monetary units
   a. Farm, nonfarm
   b. By major farm commodities and farm inputs

    5. Foreign trade data
       a. Export table by major commodities
         1.) Cocoa, rubber, oil palm produce, groundnuts, cotton
       b. Import table, food, nonfood, with emphasis on agricultural inputs
         1.) Food, fertilizers, pesticides, herbicides, agricultural drugs, machinery, and equipment
       c. Exchange reserves
       d. Trading balance
       e. Terms of trade index—total and agricultural
    6. Nutrition levels (per capita)
       a. Caloric intake
       b. Protein intake
         1.) Plant origin
         2.) Animal origin
       c. Fat intake
       d. Vitamin A intake
    7. Investment
       a. Agricultural, total
         1.) Foreign
         2.) Domestic
           a.) Government
           b.) Nonfarm
           c.) Farm-saving and farmer-created agricultural improvements
       b. Nonfarm

From the standpoint of the philosophy of science, it is interesting to note the use of the consistency criterion in making the projections outlined in the above quotation. Sections 1, and 2 *a, b,* and *c* all require that totals check with realistic estimates for components. In addition, three separate complementary subprojects were established, partly with CSNRD's funds and partly with others', to ensure consistency between (1) projected manpower requirements and the output of educational and training institutes; (2) the projected production of export and domestic food crops on one hand, and the projected demands of the country for foreign food crops on the other; and (3) the projected production of various export crops and effective international demands for those crops.

Even rough, makeshift simulations, such as those outlined above, contain some means for circumventing the four theoretical problems which CSNRD researchers encountered in doing their practical research on the development of Nigerian agricultural economy. When a simulation (set of projections) predicts the consequences of following alternative policies and programs at different points in time, it is possible to display to the real decision makers (1) evidence as to who would be damaged and who would be benefited by non-Pareto better solutions which impose damages on some persons in order to confer benefits on others, and (2) the extent to which certain goods are attained and certain bads are incurred as a result of following the alternative policies and programs under investigation. When such evidence is displayed to the relevant public decision makers, they can, in turn, help select or develop a basis for choice to be used jointly by the researchers and themselves in developing evaluations and recommendations to solve the problems they face. In addition, such simulations or projections permit them to circumvent the problem created by the possible absence of the second-order conditions for maximization by restraining them from attempts to maximize with respect to processes for which mathematically necessary, second-order conditions for maximization are not likely to hold.

Makeshift pen-and-pencil projections of the type used by CSNRD have proven effective in the work of the Council of Economic Advisers to the President of the United States and for the former Bureau of Agricultural Economics in its work with agricultural leaders of the U.S. Congress and the administrators of the Department of Agriculture. The effectiveness and extent of such projections, however, have been limited by the amounts of time required to work them out with paper, pencil, and desk calculators. CSNRD projections were similarly limited. However, as demonstrated by Secretary Robert McNamara and by a number of agricultural economic researchers, it is possible to formalize the process of making such projections into simulation procedures which can be put on large-scale, electronic computers.

Once techniques are developed for placing such formal simulations on large-scale computers, much larger, more effective, and more detailed sets of projections should become possible and feasible. While there was not time for CSNRD to gear up for such computations, CSNRD administrators took the lead in establishing a long-term AID project to develop and employ such techniques. The development of that project and its operation are the subjects of the third and last section of this chapter.

A Project for Computer Simulation of the Nigerian Agricultural Economy

As indicated above, the idea of simulating the Nigerian agricultural economy grew out of the needs of CSNRD in its work on practical problems of Nigeria. It did not arise from a burning desire to develop a new methodology, nor did it develop from a desire to illustrate the application of simulation techniques. Instead, the need for solving theoretical problems grew out of the very practical kind of investigation being carried out in Nigeria by CSNRD.

Simulation, whether makeshift or formal, is a means of computing through time the consequences of what are known and contemplated as possible courses of action. It is not primarily a means of producing adequate data. Instead, it is a way of extracting meaning from available data and of testing the sensitivity of the results to possible errors in existing data. Simulation is also a likely means of increasing the efficiency of efforts to accumulate data, because it concentrates one's efforts on relevant data.

Simulation, in addition to providing assistance in getting along without data (*Planning Without Facts*, to use Wolfgang Stolper's title) and in obtaining data, does not necessarily require the maximization of the difference between costs (badness) and returns (goodness) as a basis for defining a right action. As such, it circumvents some of the basic theoretical issues by not requiring (1) that the goods sought and bads avoided be reduced to some least common denominator, or (2) that some basis for choice, such as maximization of averages, minimaxing, satisficing, etc., be used in choosing a right program, or (3) that the mathematically necessary, second-order conditions required for the existence of an optimum be present.

Although, as a consequence, simulation does not answer direct questions about which programs are right or wrong, it does display the likely consequences through time of following alternative programs and policies. When these consequences of alternatives are expressed in terms of a multiplicity of attainable goods and avoidable bads and in terms of who is benefited and who is damaged, they can be shown to program designers and policy formulators. Such displays tend to stimulate the interaction of researchers and policy makers in making choices (1) without least common denominators, if need be, and (2) on the basis of any of a wide variety of decision rules (bases for choice) that might seem appropriate for each problem. These attributes of simulation prompted CSNRD and Michigan State University administrators to convene a seminar on the possible use of formal simulation in studying Nigerian rural development.[3] What follows is a paraphrase of the report of that workshop.

While much information was exchanged concerning the nature of simulation models, characteristics of the Nigerian economy, and results of past applications of simulation models in economic development, the main conclusions reached were:

1. That (formal) simulation models were of questionable operational value for economic development research at that point in time
2. That computer languages (soft ware) needed substantial development and that efforts were needed to adopt and

---

[3] Participants included: Dr. Irma Adelman, Department of Economics, Johns Hopkins University; Mr. John Bishop, Department of Economics, University of Michigan; Dr. James O. Bray, Stanford Research Institute; Dr. Douglas Caton, Agency for International Development; Dr. Richard H. Day, Department of Economics, University of Wisconsin; Dr. A. Halter, Department of Agricultural Economics, Oregon State University; Dr. Ronald (Wade) Jones, Department of Agricultural Economics, University of Wisconsin; Mr. Frank Lehan, President, Space-General Corporation; Dr. Wolfgang Stolper, Department of Economics, University of Michigan; and Dr. Sylvester Ugoh, Deputy Director, EDI, University of Nigeria. The participants from Michigan State University were: Dr. Robert Gustafson, Department of Agricultural Economics; Dr. Jerome Herniter, Department of Markets and Transportation Administration; Dr. Eugene Jacobson, Assistant Dean, International Programs; Dr. Glenn L. Johnson, Director, CSNRD; Dr. Jan Kmenta, Department of Economics; Dr. Herman Koenig. College of Engineering; Dr. Mordechai Kreinin, Department of Economics; Dr. Lester Manderscheid, Department of Agricultural Economics; Dr. David Milstein, Department of Resource Development; Mr. William Ruble, Computer Center; and Dr. Robert Stevens, Acting Director, EADI.

extend existing simulation models for use in economic development

3. That simulation research should not interfere with more conventional problem-solving, feasibility, and descriptive research on developing economies such as that being done by CSNRD in Nigeria

4. A project was prepared for submission to AID/Washington with these objectives:

  a. To assess existing computer models for use in doing research on interrelationships between substantial numbers of separate problems involving technical assistance for rural development

  b. To evaluate the models considered in relation to total development models, involving components for such things as population growth, foreign trade, and fiscal operations

  c. To produce plans, if judged feasible, for the development of operational research models to assist policy and decision makers handling specific problems involving agricultural research, agricultural education, investments in crop and livestock production, and investments in other agricultural infrastructures

The project statement indicated that an attempt would be made to develop broad *but simple* models to use in determining the overall effects and interrelationships of results such as those obtained by CSNRD's feasibility and more conventional studies. Although such results would be useful to the USAID/Lagos Mission and to Nigerian agencies, the main design strategy was to be theoretical; that is, its object would be to develop an aggregate model capable of being partitioned and extended to include more detailed submodel components which would handle, on a more formally interrelated basis, a number of decision-making and policy problems of the kind now assigned to CSNRD. An attempt was to be made to maintain linkage between the aggregate model and the related submodels so that reaggregation would be possible.

After this was completed, the feasibility of using simulation models to answer specific questions about developmental problems was to be determined. This consideration was to include an evaluation of the effect of key relationships on rates and levels of rural development for the specific components or rural sectors. The purpose of this assessment was to conclude whether a justification existed for continuing the investigation of simulation models for this purpose.

Practical versus theoretical issues and simulation

In the negotiations with AID for contractual support of simulation research, AID officials quickly recognized a difference between CSNRD's research and the new proposal. Officials responsible for AID's operational programs in Nigeria and Africa sensed, at once, that the simulation proposal did not deal directly with the task of deciding on the right policies and programs of USAID and the Nigerian governments to develop Nigerian agriculture. As the practical interests of their operational agencies were not being served directly, AID officials correctly raised grave questions about whether such research could be supported by the "Nigerian Desk" of AID with its direct operational responsibilities.

On the other hand, the Technical Cooperation and Assistance Office (TCA) of AID had responsibility for supporting more disciplinary kinds of research. For TCA, the question was not one of whether or not the research involved practical or disciplinary (theoretical) problems but, instead, one of whether or not the proposed research was relevant. Because CSNRD research and the Lagos/USAID mission experience and Nigerian Desk operations had established the relevance of the proposed disciplinary research, the question of whether or not such work should be supported was easily answered. However, the question was raised about whether or not a second contract should be placed under the control of the director of CSNRD who, incidentally, devoted 40 percent of his time to the Consortium. Some officials argued that the director's time and interests would be diverted from his responsibilities for practical research by a simulation contract, while others, without saying so, seemed to feel that the director's involvement in CSNRD's practical research on AID's problems had more or less disqualified him for more academic, disciplinary work.

The arguments involved in settling this latter question are of substantial interest to students of the philosophy of science, because they support the contention that disciplinary and practical work are interdependent although formally differentiable. In the end, the idea prevailed that the Nigerian experience of CSNRD and its director would improve the quality and relevance of the disciplinary results which would be obtained. Another argument of less serious philosophic meaning was that work on practical problems should not be penalized by the refusal of financial support for more fundamental disciplinary work, especially when the practical work had revealed the need for the disciplinary work. Perhaps the most telling argument was that an awareness of problems is necessary in order to handle disciplinary questions involving (1) interpersonal validity of welfare measures, (2) the lack of a common denominator among competing goods and bads, and (3) the lack of agreement on which basis for choice to use.

Summary and Conclusions

In this chapter, we have seen how a problem-oriented, practical research effort encountered four disciplinary, theoretical problems that had to be handled before solutions to the practical problems which were under consideration could be reached.

Of the four disciplinary problems, two were normative and two were both normative and non-normative. The two normative problems involved (1) the apparent absence of interpersonally valid welfare measures and (2) the difficulty of finding a common denominator for the various goods being sought and bads being avoided in connection with Nigerian rural development. The mixed problems involved the selection of appropriate bases for choice and the problem of second-order conditions.

As a practical matter, given CSNRD's limited budgets of time and money, these four problems were circumvented by a more or less makeshift resort to paper-and-pencil, desk-calculator type of simulation to produce projections for a number of important variables under alternative possible policies and programs for 1970, 1975, and 1985. At the same time, it was recognized that the disciplinary and theoretical problems were general in nature and encountered in many different countries and contexts. Consequently, steps were taken to establish an AID-supported project devoted primarily to disciplinary problems rather than to the practical problems considered by CSNRD. While establishing this project, CSNRD, Michigan State University, and AID administrators readily differentiated between the two types of problems, but eventually they recognized a degree of interdependence between the two kinds of efforts required by lodging the contract for the more theoretical kinds of work with MSU and the director of CSNRD.

X | Selecting a Survey Sample Size

The "scientific" agriculturalist is not likely to recognize the essential normative aspects of decisions involving sample sizes. Fundamentally, the practical problem of deciding how large a sample should be is like any other problem involving multidisciplinary information, both normative and non-normative. And, like any other practical problem, the solution to the problem of sample size can be complicated by competing values and by conflicts among various numbers of people interested in the sampling results. Moreover, this problem, like any other practical problem, requires that the normative and non-normative information be processed through some decision-making mechanism.

Rudner[1] has pointed out that scientists *as scientists* cannot avoid making value judgments in connection with such decisions. Generally speaking, the probability of making an empirical error of a given size decreases at a decreasing rate as sample size increases. How large the sample should be depends, obviously, on both how the value of reducing the size of error and the probability of making it increases and on how costs (badness) increase with sample size.

Rudner points out that specification by an "unscientific outsider," such as a researcher's employer, of both the size and probability of error which are acceptable does not make it possible for the researcher to avoid the normative. Such specification leaves the researcher with the problem of deciding on a sample size suitable enough *for him* to maintain acceptable—to him, the researcher—probabilities of coming

1 Richard Rudner, "The Scientist *qua* Scientist Makes Value Judgments," *Philosophy of Science*, XX (Jan. 1953), 1-6.

within the acceptable range specified by his employer. The acceptable range depends upon the badness and goodness of meeting or not meeting the employer's specifications—badnesses involving possible loss of professional reputation, of employment, or of pride of workmanship, to mention only a few, and goodnesses involving such things as pride of workmanship, possible salary increases, or renewed research contracts accompanying accurate estimates.

Sample Size for the Interstate Managerial Survey

The particular case to be examined here involves the determination of sample size for an actual empirical study of managerial processes employed by midwestern farmers.[2] The sample size varied from subpart to subpart of the study and was determined by a committee of agricultural economists working in consultation with statisticians and sociologists. Study of the actual processes employed and decisions made reveals how a group of economic researchers (some of whom deny the possibility of objective normative knowledge) did, in fact, use normative knowledge to solve the practical problem of deciding how large a sample would be employed.

The practical problem involved selecting the best combination and amounts of various kinds of empirical information and the best levels of expenditures to obtain those different kinds of information. Ten broad kinds of information were judged to have value. These included:

1. Data for testing hypotheses about the interrelationships between the characteristics of the managers and performance of the managerial process. Included under this heading is information on tenure status, size of farm, type of farm, contacts with the extension service, contacts with farm organizations, background, education, vocational training, farming experience, nonfarm employment, family responsibilities, employer status, income, assets, liabilities, and net worth.

2. Data on types of information used by farmers in managing farms.

---

[2] Glenn L. Johnson, et al., eds., A Study of Managerial Processes of Midwestern Farmers (Ames, Iowa: Iowa State University Press, 1961), pp. 16f.

3. Information on the analytical processes performed by farm managers.

4. Data on the sources of information used by farmers in assembling information to solve their problems.

5. Information on expectation models employed by farmers in forming predictions of prices received, prices paid, human behavior, institutional changes, and technological advance.

6. Information on insurance strategies used by farm managers.

7. Information on the degrees of knowledge possessed by farmers at various stages in the decision-making process.

8. Information on personal strategies employed by farmers.

9. Information on the propensities of farmers to insure and the disutility which they attach to losses in income and in assets.

10. Information on the propensities of farmers to take chances and the utility they attach to gains in incomes and assets. . . .

The ten types of information acquired in the Interstate Managerial Survey can be grouped into six major areas, each of which is related to an important phase of the managerial process.

1. Types and sources of information used by farmers.

2. Analytical processes employed by farmers.

3. Knowledge situations.

4. Expectation models.

5. Strategies employed by farmers.

6. Insurance, chance taking, the utility of gains and the disutility of losses.[3]

Additional information about each of these different phases of the managerial process was regarded as valuable. These values, however, were far from uniform. Knowledge then existing about the different phases was very unevenly developed. In some instances, clear-cut hypotheses were awaiting testing. In other instances, insights were sought about poorly understood aspects of the process. Several questions on the survey presupposed that ex ante empirical classifications would be established on the basis of the data secured.

In a real sense, discovering the value of different kinds of information was an objective of the sampling procedure. Thus, a priori determination of the value of additional

---

3 *Ibid.*

amounts of the different kinds of information was difficult. Obviously, the value of establishing the empirical relevance or irrelevance of an abstract classification or category depended on which other abstract categories were revealed to be empirically significant and to have value.

The value of information useful in establishing a new concept depended on the consistency of the information with the new concept, with old and accepted concepts, and with new concepts of decision-making structures that would grow out of the empirical work. This was clearly true of concepts and information concerning degrees of knowledge possessed by managers at different points in the decision-making process. Thus, there was considerable evidence that non-normative and normative concepts were interrelated and that pragmatism was a relevant philosophic approach.

On the other hand, some concepts and hypotheses were well enough established and their value in managerial theory so well understood that descriptive non-normative work independent of the normative analyses based on the survey was impossible.

Economists and philosophic value theorists commonly encounter difficulty in making interpersonally valid measurements of goodness and badness. This difficulty was acute in establishing the Interstate Managerial Survey (IMS) sample size. Representatives of seven different midwestern states were involved, each valuing differently information about various aspects of the managerial process. Although these differences created problems, they were less pronounced than they would have been had the cooperating personnel not been a voluntary group having similar interests and experience in studying the managerial process.

In the processes of developing the survey schedule, designing the survey, and deciding on sample size, the degree of consensus on the values of different kinds of information widened among cooperators. In a far from orderly manner, cooperators discussed the value which they had found (experienced) to be associated with different kinds of information, especially different kinds of information in relation to each other. Duplicated information was eliminated in some instances.[4] Some persons argued that behavioral data, but not

---

[4] Note the omission of question numbers from the master questionnaire in *ibid.*, pp. 186-204.

attitudinal data, were of value in predicting managerial behavior. This inconsistency was eventually worked out in a set of conclusions about the value of the two kinds of data.[5]

Time and time again, the question of the usefulness of the information in solving problems was raised in determining the relative values of different kinds of information. The widening of consensus, which grew out of these discussions, reduced but did not eliminate the need for interpersonally valid appraisals of goodness and badness. In some instances, differences in value attached to the same kind of information by different representatives were disregarded by the representatives in order to reach a decision on the practical question of sample size.

Some Positivistic Questions

Just as various questions about the goodness and badness of different kinds of information were present, so important non-normative questions were present. A statistician will use certain non-normative concepts when computing the sample size required to ensure that an error of a given size will not be expected to occur more than a given proportion of times a given estimate or choice is made. These concepts pertain to the nature of the probability distribution involved and the magnitude of its major parameters in the universe to be sampled.

Answers to such non-normative questions were not always available for the kinds of information sought in the IMS sample survey. Thus, even had IMS researchers been able to tell a statistician what size of sampling error and probability of error would be acceptable, the statisticians would not have been able to compute the optimum sample size, even for one type of information, without first carrying out some empirical and conceptual investigation of certain questions about the probability distributions involved.

The similarity of questions about the normative and non-normative did not end at this point. Just as questions about interpersonally valid, normative concepts arose, so questions arose about the interpersonal validity of non-normative con-

---

5 *Ibid.*, p. 181, item 25A, 1-5.

cepts. These questions seemed to originate in the doubt which exists about the correspondence between any abstract mental concept of reality and reality itself, the latter being viewed only conceptually.

If such doubts are recognized, each person's concepts of reality become questionable, and the problem of interpersonal validity which arises must be settled by (1) the appeals to consistency among both related existing concepts and new concepts continually being created out of experiences, (2) attempts to clarify the meaning of concepts and communicate them to other people, some of whom hold conflicting concepts, and (3) demonstration of the workability or non-workability of certain concepts in the solution of problems.

Discussions of such problems indicated that introspection, empathy, and pretesting were important in obtaining the consensus required to overcome questions about the interpersonal validity of factual concepts. Discussion often revealed logical inconsistencies among concepts. Introspection and empathy with respect to one's own managerial activities often tended to confirm the correctness of both another's and one's own assertions about the empirical adequacy of both normative and non-normative concepts. Pretesting furnished experience to establish the relevance or nonrelevance of certain concepts. In fact, certain concepts embodied in certain questions did not survive the pretesting that established their irrelevance.

Basis for Choice

When only one kind of information is sought, the basis for choice in deciding on a sample size is often that sample size which will ensure that the expected proportion of errors of more than a given acceptable size will tend to approach a given acceptable proportion as the number of times the sample is drawn increases toward infinity. In determining IMS sample size, several kinds of information having values that are different and, perhaps, not comparable were sought by a number of different people attaching different values to the different kinds of information. Thus, the situation was much more complex than the simple problems often considered by statisticians, in which only one kind of information is sought. Even so, no statistical formulas were available to the IMS research group or others for computing an optimum sample size for even a single kind of information which would take into account the values of one or more people planning to use the information.

In the case of the IMS sample size, additional complications grew out of the costs of giving up attainment of one kind of information having one kind of value in order to obtain different kinds of information having other values and out of the value of obtaining one kind of information advantageously produced in conjunction with a second type having a different value not comparable with the first.

In general, three approaches were followed in these difficult cases: (1) consensus about an acceptable sample size was sought through logical discussion, experience, exposition, and application of the test of workability; (2) arbitrary choices were made almost at random in those instances where it could be agreed that reaching a decision was more important than the disadvantages of not agreeing upon a choice; (3) compromises were tried until a proposed action (size of sample for a particular purpose) was regarded as barely acceptable to everyone even though, perhaps, no one regarded it as the best sample size for his particular purposes; and (4) in the case of one question, one state used a different sampling rate than used in the other states.[6]

Eventually, 66 questions, some involving complex sets of subquestions, were formulated to obtain the various kinds of data described earlier. As a result of normative and non-normative investigations of various types (logical and experimental), several of these questions were modified and a sample size determined for each.

Resultant Decisions about Sample Size

In all, six different sample sizes were selected as right or acceptable. In total, 1,075 farms were surveyed. Some of the 66 questions were addressed to:

1. All 1,075 farmers

---

6 "(Iowa interviewers will substitute 'for profit' in place of 'to get the most out of life.')" *Ibid.*, p. 188.

2. An estimated 537 or 538 farmers

3. An estimated 895 farmers

4. An estimated 358 farmers

5. An estimated 179 farmers

6. No farmers

Still further, the concepts of the seven representatives from the seven states varied widely with respect to sampling variances and the importance of geographic differences for studying managerial processes. As a result, some state representatives elected to sample small, rather homogenous areas quite intensively, while others sampled large, obviously heterogenous areas quite extensively. In one sampling area, 8 percent of the eligible farmers were included, while in another, only .6 percent of the eligible farmers were included.

Philosophic Conclusions

This brief recapitulation of the procedure whereby the Interstate Managerial Survey Committee decided upon survey sample sizes indicates some interesting aspects of the roles played by the five philosophic positions given special consideration in this book. The committee included mainly persons inclined to be conditional normativists. Nonetheless, committee members also practiced positivism (both ordinary and logical), outright normativism, and pragmatism on various occasions. The committee definitely had to reach conclusions about what should be done in order to get into the field with a survey schedule to gather the data required in its reserach. The question about what should be done involved problems encountered by the committee in actually doing its research.

Non-normative questions were asked about variances in the population and how these variances would influence sample sizes. Such questions also involved the use of statistical theory and could definitely be described as logically positivistic (non-normativistic). While positivistic procedures were followed in answering such questions, the entire approach of the committee cannot be regarded as positivistic because definite attention was given to questions of value. For instance, as the committee began to consider questions about the desired reliability of the estimates which it planned to produce, questions arose repeatedly about the goodness and badness of different kinds of information. Some of these questions of goodness and badness appeared answerable directly and independently of answers to non-normative questions, while others appeared to be means to still more ultimate ends.

When questions arose about the instrumental goodnesses of certain kinds of information as means to more ultimate ends, the philosophy of the pragmatist was often employed to answer them. For instance, descriptive investigation of the decision processes of managers indicated that farmers followed procedures not previously conceptualized. Such discoveries established the instrumental goodness of certain kinds of information not previously regarded as having value in attaining the more ultimate good of understanding the decision-making processes of farmers.

In other instances, the committee attacked questions of goodness and badness without encountering problems of interdependence between answers to non-normative and normative questions. In a number of closely related instances, answers were sought to questions about what ought to be done with respect to sample size. The solutions to some such questions appeared to turn simultaneously on answers to both normative and non-normative questions.

This simultaneous dependence on normative and non-normative information did not establish a general interdependence between answers to normative and non-normative questions. Instead, this dependence indicated that answers to practical problems about what ought to be done depend on both non-normative and normative considerations. Thus, it would be hard to argue on the basis of the IMS experience that a pragmatic philosophy was universally required in seeking answers to questions about what size sample should be employed.

Conditional normativism was often employed. Unlike positivism, it had the advantage of taking values into account to define as well as help answer practical questions, yet it could be as effective as positivism in dealing with non-normative questions. In contrast to pragmatism, conditional normativism was simple and workable, despite the emphasis of pragmatism on workability. By definition, conditionally normative procedures, of course, do not produce answers to normative questions, i.e., of goodness and badness per se.

IMS committeemen found it difficult to determine a basis for choice in deciding what ought to be done; hence, they used various bases. Reaching consensus about the external and internal consistency, clarity, and workability of both normative and non-normative concepts made it much easier to agree on a basis of choice. In several instances, agreement in these three areas made it unnecessary to assign weights to the opinions of committee members. In other instances, opinions were weighted by the professional, personal, and other kinds of authority possessed by the committee members holding the opinions. In still other cases, opinions of different people were given equal weights.

In several cases, the cost of not reaching a decision exceeded the costs of any likely erroneous decision, and essentially random choices were reached by quite arbitrary methods. Although it was never recognized, the need to assign weights to the opinion of different committee members existed when objective concepts could not be reached, i.e., when consensus did not arise from the attainment of consistent, communicatable, workable concepts.

XI | Summary and Philosophical Generalizations

One may well ask at this point whether any patterns emerge from the cases we have been examining. The answer is yes, and the patterns discovered are obviously complex. But there is little virtue in a simplicity that distorts reality. One of the arguments of the previous chapters has been that attempts to make decisions are unsatisfactory when based on schemes that are oversimplified in the sense that they omit the complex and difficult dimension of normative investigation.

In this chapter we shall first evaluate the five philosophic positions outlined in chapter 1 as relevant to the work of agricultural economists.[1] This will lead to a discussion of the roles of projections and simulations in problem-solving activities of agricultural economists. We shall then stress the difference between theoretical and practical beliefs. This will be followed by summary discussions of objectivity, creativity, and the role of community in obtaining acceptable solutions to practical problems.

An Evaluation of the Five Philosophic Positions Described in Chapter 1

Chapter 1 distinguished four approaches of agricultural economists to obtaining knowledge for use in solving problems: positivism, outright normativism, conditional norma-

---

[1] This chapter should not be read without reference to the glossary in chapter 1 and without reading at least one or two of the case study chapters.

tivism, and pragmatism. A fifth philosophy, existentialism, which is less concerned with attainment of knowledge than the other four, was also considered. Our investigations indicate that each of these philosophies appears to make an important contribution to the solution of problems, yet there is danger that each may become unduly restrictive.

In the introduction to this book, we saw that the positivist limits knowledge in such a way as to exclude investigation of normative questions. The case studies in this book clearly show the foolishness of such a restriction. Positivism is acceptable as an approach, then, insofar as it is not negative; but when it becomes restrictive it loses its usefulness and "blocks the road to inquiry," to use Charles Sanders Peirce's felicitous phrase, into normative questions.

On the other hand, outright normativism makes a contribution to decision making by calling attention to the importance of analyzing and understanding the place of values in decision making. However, when the normativist attempts to answer questions about right and wrong actions independently of non-normative information, his work also becomes restricted and unrealistic. (See the glossary in chapter 1 for the distinction between right and wrong on one hand and good and bad on the other.) For example, despite the goodness of higher incomes, a realistic agricultural economist cannot recommend that it would be right to increase Nigerian average per capita incomes $280 in one year while disregarding non-normative information concerning the impossibility of making such an increase.

Conditional normativism recognizes the inadequacy of positivism by clearly recognizing that values must be taken into account. Our disagreement, however, is with the way in which conditional normativism accounts for values. To treat values merely as data assembled by the investigator is a kind of defeatism in social inquiry. As we have attempted to show in our preceding analysis, values can be examined and subjected to the same criteria for objectivity as non-normative information. Failure to do this is to leave some of the most important problems of social science unattended. One important contribution of the conditional normativist's position is that it provides convincing evidence for the incompleteness of the positivistic point of view.

The fourth philosophical position to be judged is pragmatism. The pragmatist has been more willing than the positivist to attempt the sort of dialectic of purposes which ethics amounts to. This sort of ethics is in the mainstream of American philosophy and is to be found in such writings as George Santayana's *Life of Reason*, R. B. Perry's *General Theory of Value*, and M. R. Cohen's *Reason and Nature*.

In ethics, John Dewey holds that one cannot distinguish between ends and means. This is, at best, misleading. While it is true that the same action may be a means in one situation and an end in another, this does not mean that one cannot distinguish objectively between the two. One might argue analogously that there is really no distinction between premises and conclusions because the same proposition may be a premise in one argument and a conclusion in another argument. Although this is true, it is nevertheless the case that premises and conclusions are different, and different in objective ways.

There is, however, a basic inconsistency in Dewey's thoughts on this topic, for often he writes as if the good were the satisfaction of social interest. This notion of goodness that is experimentally determined as the intelligent satisfaction of human needs and desires is never, to our knowledge, a mere means-end in Dewey's philosophy. Thus, the utilitarian conception of goodness is incompatible with his means-end continuum.[2] As we have seen, however, normative and non-normative issues are often closely involved with each other, and the pragmatist's emphasis on workability as a criterion for truth and objectivity has been a significant philosophical contribution.

The last philosophic position considered was existentialism. The emphasis in existentialism is on the existence and identity of individuals—on human beings rather than on the essences, normative or non-normative, of conditions, situations, and things, including men as things. Hence, existentialism, unlike the other four philosophic positions, is not primarily concerned with the nature of abstract, descriptive, and/or prescriptive beliefs. Our case studies indicate that

---

2 Glenn L. Johnson and Lewis K. Zerby, "Values in the Solutions of Credit Problems," *Capital and Credit Needs in a Changing Agriculture*, ed. by E. L. Baum, *et al.* (Ames, Iowa: Iowa State University Press, 1961), p. 277.

attention must be given to the problems of individuals. This was learned a long time ago in agricultural extension work. It was also learned in establishing the general studies program at the University of Nigeria and still again by the authorities and legislators concerned with establishing the Sleeping Bear National Recreation area. It is likely that it will have to be learned time and time again in such future work as the elimination of rural poverty, the conservation and improvement of the quality of the environment, a more appropriate combination of public and private control over production, and agricultural investment and output.

However, even when the agricultural economist uses all of the philosophic approaches to knowledge mentioned above and does not limit himself to a single approach, he still faces difficulties. Many economic problems are solved by the functioning of the market, but some are not. In the introduction to this book we noted four fundamental difficulties in defining right actions, none of which are present for an economist who defines a right action as one which maximizes profits. The question we must ask and answer is: How does an economic researcher conduct research on problems involving—

1. concepts of goodness and badness not reducible to a common denominator in such a way as to permit maximization of the difference,
2. absence of the second-order condition mathematically necessary for the existence of a maximum difference between the goodness and badness, and
3. lack of agreement on the appropriate decision-making rules to follow in choosing a right action under risk and uncertainty?

Computer Simulations and Systems Analysis

While examining the research of the problem-solving agricultural economists, we noted repeatedly that they and others tackled problems—provided that they were not blindly committed to maximization or to some restrictive philosophic approach—by trying to envision (often jointly with the relevant decision makers) the consequences through time of following various alternative programs and policies. These consequences were often expressed quantitatively, as projections, in terms of attainment or avoidance of conditions, situations, and things that were valued either positively (goods) or negatively (bads). Later we were struck by the common-sense similarity between the old technique of making pen-and-paper projections and the modern techniques of mathematical simulation and systems analysis.

Allen Newell and Herbert Simon define simulation as "a method for analyzing the behavior of a system by computing its time path for given initial conditions, and given parameter values."[3] With respect to system analysis, Anatol Rapoport writes, "General systems theory is best described not as a theory in the sense that this word is used in science, but, rather, as a program or direction in the contemporary philosophy of science. . . . all the variants have a common aim: the integration of diverse content areas by means of a unified methodology of conceptualization or of research."[4]

Mathematical simulation and systems analysis offer a multidisciplinary approach for interrelating the different aspects of complex problems to see the consequences through time of alternative policies and programs (as reflected in different initial conditions and parameters). The promise of these methods captures the imaginations of researchers who have studied the muddling of agricultural economists in one problem after another—at the University of Kentucky, in the TVA, in Michigan, in Thailand, and in Africa.

When we look back at the contribution that researchers have made with their projections, we see that the following are the essential strengths of the process:

1. Projections are objective estimations of the consequences through time of alternative possible actions in terms of attaining several different relevant goods and incurring several different relevant bads.

2. Such researchers show willingness to work objectively (as defined later in this chapter) with the normative as well as the non-normative.

3. Such researchers also show a willingness to estimate the

---

[3] Allen Newell and Herbert Simon, "Simulation," *International Encyclopedia of the Social Sciences*, XIV, 262.

[4] Anatol Rapoport, "Systems Analysis: General Systems Theory," *International Encyclopedia of the Social Sciences*, XV, 452.

future consequences of actions without being constrained by the economists "trained in" disciplinary propensity to maximize. At the same time, these researchers do not necessarily avoid maximization.

4. The process involves team work among interdisciplinary researchers, administrators, and legislators which, in effect, makes the decision makers a part of an objective investigation in such a way as to stimulate originality and creativity.

Below are the advantages that we see for formal mathematical simulation and systems analysis as opposed to seat-of-the-pants, common-sense projections of the type used in most of the case histories examined herein.

1. The computer is vastly superior to paper, pencil, desk calculators, and clerks. Instead of dealing with a few alternative policies for two or three periods of time, as was done by the Nigerian Consortium, the computer can deal with dozens. Furthermore, it can calculate results for, say, every tenth of a year as far into the future as one dares to let it run instead of for 1970, 1975, and 1985 as was done by the Nigerian Consortium pen-and-paper projectionists.

2. In mathematical simulation work for the Nigerian beef industry, the requirement that team members contribute specific kinds of information to a specific system proved to be good discipline for both empirical work and conceptual efforts. It also speeded up the rate at which team members obtained an organized systematic concept of how the Nigerian beef economy (system) works, and it promoted multidisciplinary cooperation.

3. There are really no fewer data requirements for pen-and-paper, common-sense projections than there are for mathematical simulations of the same degree of complexity. Requirements also seem to be about the same for theory, original ideas, and creative activities, or for any given amount of work. However, because simulation can range from small amounts of work—such as that done by CSNRD researchers in projecting the consequences of three policies at three points in time—to work on huge systems, requirements for data theory and

new creative ideas can become staggering and impossible to fill. We conclude that data requirements are more a function of the size of the job undertaken than of whether or not computers are used.

4. Requirements for mathematical and computer skills are much higher for mathematical programming.

5. Pen-and-pencil projections, mathematical simulation, and/or systems analysis should not be viewed as single, specialized techniques; they are better viewed as approaches that can encompass any combination of quantitative techniques and disciplinary skills needed to attack a given problem. Thus, these approaches are processes for using techniques rather than techniques themselves. One can be enthusiastic about projections, simulations, and systems analysis without running the danger of becoming technical (as contrasted to problem-oriented), a danger against which we have repeatedly warned in the past.[5]

6. When mathematical simulation is employed, researchers, decision makers, administrators, and lawmakers seem to have no insurmountable problems in working together as a team. As far as multidisciplinary cooperation among physical scientists, social scientists, and humanists is concerned, the projection, simulation, and systems analysis approach seems almost ideal both in theory and in practice.

7. We conclude that, in the very near future, computer simulation and systems analysis will be superior operational ways of making projections to deal with the very sensitive issues which arise when we tackle those extremely important practical problems that cannot be left to the operation of a free-market mechanism whether these are problems of the U.S. agricultural economy, of agricultural development abroad, or of disadvantaged persons in urban areas.

---

[5] Glenn L. Johnson, "Stress on Production Economics," *Australian Journal of Agricultural Economics*, VII (June 1963).

Practical versus Theoretical and Disciplinary Beliefs

In terms defined in our glossary, practical beliefs or practical pieces of knowledge are both descriptive and prescriptive. They are concerned with the rightness and wrongness of possible actions as solutions of specific practical problems. Such beliefs or pieces of knowledge are functions of, or depend on, nonprescriptive beliefs about the nature of normative and non-normative reality. Descriptive beliefs about the nature of normative or non-normative reality, as contrasted to beliefs about the rightness or wrongness of possible actions as solutions of problems, are termed nonprescriptive and are not of practical value until they are structured with prescriptive theoretical knowledge to yield descriptive prescriptive knowledge.

Along with this distinction between the prescriptive and nonprescriptive is a corresponding distinction between practical and disciplinary problems. If a problem is practical, decision is unavoidable. A person must act or fail to act, and if he acts, he must act in one manner or another. The pickle packers (chapter 6), the members of MSU's agricultural economics department (chapter 7), and the state department consultants in Thailand (chapter 2), were all confronted with practical problems, as was Cap Edmonds in western Kentucky (chapter 3).

Disciplinary problems, on the other hand, are problems of belief about whether alternative normative and non-normative concepts describe or might describe reality. Disciplinary decisions can be made now or postponed indefinitely. Whether or not limestone would lower the acidity of western Kentucky soils was a different problem from that of acting in one way or another with respect to salvaging available supplies. The disciplinary problems connected with using migrant labor to produce pickles could be discussed and argued about whether or not a practical problem existed in the realm of pickle picking.

However, we must stress that nonprescriptive beliefs are required in making sound practical judgments. The history of practical agricultural research is a record, by and large, of the successful application of theoretical and disciplinary beliefs (normative and non-normative) in the solving of practical problems.

Objectivity and Creativity

Thus far, we have distinguished between practical and theoretical or disciplinary problems and have shown the necessity of answering theoretical questions, both non-normative and normative, as prerequisites for solving practical problems. We have further recognized the usefulness of projection, simulation, and systems analysis in solving problems not solved by the functioning of the market. However, problem solving cannot be discussed adequately unless we recognize that the application of knowledge in solving problems is a creative enterprise requiring objectivity. It becomes necessary, then, to discuss some of the social and psychological factors that impede creativity and objectivity and some that implement them.

Among the factors that impede creativity we should perhaps list four:

1. Emotional disorders[6]

2. Lack of knowledge

3. Improperly structured knowledge

4. Repressive social forms

Each of these factors prevents one from achieving the sort of objectivity and creativity that is necessary for solving problems effectively. But objectivity is a word with many meanings, and it is important to clarify its use in the present book before discussing how to attain it.

Objectivity

The term *objectivity* is used to describe both the attitude of an investigator and the kind of knowledge which results from objective investigation. An investigation is called *objective* when the investigator refrains from identifying himself and his prestige with some particular concept so that, in the

---

6 Since the present book is not a treatise on psychology, we shall not consider at greater length the problem of emotional disorders. The problems of this book are problems of relatively undisturbed men, and emotional disorders were not encountered.

absence of pride or humiliation which comes from being identified with a concept, he will be willing to subject any relevant concept to various tests of objectivity. Thus, the objective investigator must detach himself from his conceptual work enough to submit it to impartial testing and must be willing to reject and revise a concept that is not objective in terms of tests for the objectivity of concepts to be presented below. We noted, in passing, that emotionally disturbed persons are often incapable of achieving such impartiality since they persist in injecting themselves into their work.[7]

The term *objectivity* is also used to modify concepts or knowledge. Some investigators hold that a concept or bit of knowledge is objective when it corresponds to reality. At first blush, this seems to be an acceptable and even common-sense meaning of objectivity. According to this view, the objectivity of a concept is readily testable. All one has to do is to compare the concept with reality to see whether or not it is, in fact, an accurate representation of reality. Some forthright people refer to this as the snapshot test. Somewhat deeper philosophic reflection on this point, however, will indicate that the only thing we have with which to compare a concept based on experience is another concept based on more experience. Thus, the comparison of one concept with another concept describing another experience never really gets beyond concepts, and thus a meaningful direct check can never be made on the correspondence between a concept and reality itself. The comparison of one concept of reality with another concept of it does not really give us a comparison between a snapshot and what a snapshot is of, but only a comparison of one snapshot with another. We are testing the consistency of concepts rather than a correspondence between a concept and a nonconceptual reality.

A similar criticism could be made of the proposition that a sentence is objective if it is true. Usually the notion of truth turns out to involve the same sort of unsatisfactory notion of the correspondence between snapshot and reality just discussed.

It seems to us that a satisfactory conception of objectivity would define as objective those concepts (bits of knowledge)

---

[7] See footnote 6.

that would pass tests based upon rules of evidence and valid means of justification. We assert and note that practicing agricultural economists establish that a concept is objective by showing that it—

1. is not inconsistent with other previously accepted concepts and with new concepts based on current experience,

2. has a clear and specifiable meaning, and

3. is useful in solving the problems with which one is confronted.

The *test of consistency* is both an internal and an external one. Internal consistency is a logical or analytical matter. The internal test required that a set of concepts must bear logical relationships to each other whether they pertain to the past, the present, the conditional future (if . . . , then . . .), or the unconditional future. There is also an external test for consistency. This is the test of experience. As such, it is synthetic (derived from experience) as well as analytic (deduced by logic from propositions). Experience provides a basis for forming new concepts. In order to apply the test of external consistency an existing concept is compared with concepts based upon new experience. While the new concept is synthetic, the process of comparison is likely to be analytic.

A new or independent experience (one which is outside a presently accepted body of knowledge) consists, essentially, of observations derived from either the operation of an on-going system such as a farm; the universe of planets circulating around the sun; the chemical, biological and physical activities going on in a cubic foot of soil; the operation of a biological organism; or the experience of family members with the "goodness" of life. Observations may also be generated by controlled experiments. In either case, observations or experience provide a basis for formulating new concepts which must be consistent with a given body of concepts if that given body of concepts is to pass the test of external consistency. Degrees of freedom in statistics can be regarded as "extra" observations whose consistency, or lack of consistency, with a fitted line of relationship are external to the line; we recognize the independence of these observations from the fitted line by referring to these extra observations as "degree of freedom."

The *test of clarity* is both simple and difficult. One knows when a concept passes the test of clarity and can be communicated between people. Ambiguity and vagueness block such communication. It is difficult, however, to indicate the exact nature of the test of clarity. A concept is clear if it can be understood and communicated from one person to another. If a concept is not understandable and cannot be communicated between people, it does not pass the test of clarity.

The *test of workability* is a pragmatic test. Concepts are used to solve both theoretical and practical problems. Concepts are often used to predict positively that a certain outcome will be forthcoming. If that outcome does not materialize, the concept used in predicting it has failed to pass the test of workability or usefulness. Similarly, if a normative concept of goodness is used in selecting a right goal, the goal must turn out to be as good as predicted when realized or the normative concept flunks the test of workability. Thus, the test of workability is pragmatic and rather closely related to the test of external consistency.

A moment's reflection will indicate that the meaning of objectivity just discussed is such that objectivity is not limited to the physical and to the biological sciences. It is as easy for concepts in the social sciences to be objective in the sense that they possess internal and external consistency, clarity and workability as it is for concepts in the physical and the biological sciences to be objective. In either case, failure to pass any of these tests calls for reformulation.

Similarly, it is also obvious that objectivity is not confined to "positive" non-normative, as contrasted to normative, concepts. Both "positive" and normative concepts may or may not pass the tests of internal and external consistency, clarity and workability. The test of external consistency with respect to a normative concept is more easily applied than is commonly supposed. For instance, we recall vividly having one of our colleagues come into my office after a period of illness with an unusually severe case of chicken pox. We had discussed the question of whether there were normative experiences which would permit a normative concept to be subjected to the test of external consistency. Our colleague's comment simply was "Egad, you're right. Chicken pox is bad!" He had experienced chicken pox and found the experience consistent with the generally held normative belief that chicken pox is bad.

Further reflection on the above meaning of objectivity will indicate that beliefs in "absolute" concepts, either positive or normative, are not objective. Willingness to accept or reject concepts on the basis of workability tests indicates that concepts are likely to work for some purposes but not for others. Thus, for purposes of sighting a rifle, I find the positive concept that light travels in a straight line to be adequate. Yet Einstein found it necessary to modify this positivistic concept for *his purposes*. The goodness of butterfat depends on whether one is dealing with certain heart diseases or not. Neither normative nor positivistic *absolutists*, then, can be classified as objective. One of the least objective arguments which can be advanced is that of the positivistic absolutist who argues that there cannot be an objective normativism, because there can be no absolute norms derived from observations of reality. One of the more objective arguments which can be advanced is that both normative and non-normative concepts are tentative and likely to flunk the tests of external consistency.[8]

When the economist makes projections and when simulators are asked about verification techniques for their work, it is significant that they, too, apply the tests listed above. Discussion of verifying a simulation involves its credibility or objectivity. Projections, simulations, and systems analyses deal with future or hypothetical consequences of following alternative policies, programs, and designs, some of which have never been used (such as, for instance, a new type of agricultural credit agency). Because of this characteristic of so many projections and simulations, direct experiential information is often not available for testing them. As a consequence, simulators and projectionists verify or establish the credibility of their estimates in several ways.

One way is to evaluate the data on which the estimates are based in terms of experimental data and recorded observations of operating systems. Another way is to investigate the logic relating such data to the estimates and to examine the consistency between the projections and other accepted concepts. Such logical investigations often draw heavily on the theories of disciplines such as economics, genetics, physics, chemistry, biology, botany, ecology, political science, and sociology. Simulators and projectionists who want their results to be used are also aware of two other ways in which their credibility is influenced: first, the nature of the projections and simulations must be clearly understandable to potential users or they will not be accepted; and, second, competent men experienced in the field being simulated must be convinced that the design, policy, or program being simulated will actually work more or less according to the model used. A moment's reflection on the part of the reader will reveal the similarity between the verification criteria and

---

[8] Glenn L. Johnson and Lewis K. Zerby, "Some Philosophic Thoughts about NCR-4's Work" (paper presented at the North Central Farm Management Committee's [NCR-4] meeting, Chicago, Ill., 1961).

criteria of objectivity presented earlier. We assert that this similarity is both philosophically interesting and significant.

Originality and creativity

In the philosopher's jargon, to define an abstract denotative word such as creativity or orginality is very difficult, as indeed it is difficult to define any abstract denotative word. When we try to define *freedom, equality, virtue,* or *justice,* we encounter a similar difficulty. It is easy in each case to define in a contextual manner the attributive word which is the correlate to the denotative word. Instead of defining *freedom* we may define a *free man* or *free government*; instead of *equality,* we find it easier to define *equal measures, considerations, rights, privileges,* or *punishments.*

If we approach the definition of *originality* in this manner, we can attempt to define the creative person. An original person is a person who first of all is willing to turn from an accepted behavior to a new mode of behavior. Although all rebels are original, not all rebels are creative. We believe, however, that all creative persons are original in the sense that they are willing to accept new modes of behavior. Thus, we have a start, but not an end to the process of definition. To be original requires a willingness not to conform, to rise above the routine or habitual.

Originality means the overcoming of inertia—an effort must be exerted to do something and to do that something differently. In this sense, original behavior may be opposed to both mechanical and repetitive behavior on one hand and plain inaction on the other. But originality may be destructive as well as constructive. Berserk gunmen are rebellious and, perhaps, original, yet most of us would hesitate to call them creative.

Creativity then is constructive originality. But when is originality constructive?

What original actions are judged to be creative depends, of course, upon the problems faced—and, hence, on both normative and non-normative knowledge. Knowledge is possessed by communities of men. Thus, we must add to our definition a reference to some community of men and the knowledge others possess and problems they face. Without such reference, we would be trying to define creativity in itself, and this is not possible. Taking these considerations into account, we may define a creative person as an original person who produces novel concepts taken to be important and of value by some community of men.

The above definition pays homage to the act of creation. An investigator is creative when he succeeds in conceiving of new ways of viewing physical reality, new designs for physical reality, new designs for social institutions, new understandings of goodness and badness, or new techniques and systems for deciding on right and wrong actions. His new conceptions are subject to the tests for objectivity described above. Anything that interferes with attempts to create and test such concepts interferes with the investigator's creativity and, hence, his ability to find new and superior solutions to both theoretical and practical problems.

Little attention is given here to emotional instability, the first of the four factors interfering with creativity that were listed at the beginning of this section, because, as pointed out, this book has dealt with case studies of the activities of relatively stable personalities.

The second and third factors interfering with creativity were lack of knowledge and improperly structured knowledge, which is to say the absence of knowledge which passes the tests of objectivity. This subject has been summarized rather fully in the subsection immediately preceding this subsection on creativity.

The fourth factor listed is repressive social forms. Our case studies have revealed two kinds of repressive social forms: (1) inappropriate conceptions of the nature of man and (2) inappropriate or inappropriately used philosophic approaches to the acquisition of knowledge.

Problems are not solved independently of human beings. It is always *men* who face the problems we are concerned with, and too often we become so preoccupied with the problems that we forget the men who solve and have them. A problem solver's conception of man is generally an important determinant of his conception of the problems faced by a particular man or group of men.

In the history of Western thought, two disparate conceptions of man are predominant. On the one hand is the concept of extreme individualism and on the other is that of organicism. The concept of extreme individualism views man as an isolated entity. From this viewpoint, which the subjectivity of existentialism illustrates, man has being and existence apart from the society in which he lives. Existentialism stresses the importance of the individual and of his freedom to establish his identity. According to these views, man is *in* society but not *of* society. Those individuals in Leelanau county who argued purely from the point of view of their own interest and refused to regard the welfare of their fellow men illustrate this point of view. But in most of the problems we have discussed we have seen individuals joining other individuals in a common effort. They have given up some individualism for the good of the community.

The second conception of man sees the individual as a mere cell in a social organism. Organicism of this sort is illustrated by either fascist or communist totalitarianism. Such a philosophy is as inappropriate as that of individualism for solving the problems of the agricultural economists.

The men who successfully solved some of the toughest problems discussed in the previous chapters thought of themselves as members of a moral community that was formed for the purpose of solving the problem. Thus, the members of the Interstate Managerial Study research team were selected because of basic common interests. (See chapter 10.) Some researchers from other regions were quite purposely left out of the project because they did not hold compatible beliefs. The members of the agricultural economics department at Michigan State University formed themselves into such a community in making their report. (See chapter 7.) Their differing beliefs were bracketed in order to write a report expressing a consensus. The U.S. technical assistance team in Thailand (chapter 2) joined with Thai officials because they held in common important values and were willing to disregard those less central beliefs which they did not hold in common.

These cases suggest, then, that neither the existentialist nor the organismic conception of man is very fruitful as a basis for the successful solution of practical problems. Thus, a third description of man is necessary. Such a description might make the distinctive aspect of a man his capacity to identify with other like-minded men to form moral communities. Particles cannot do this because they survive only as parts of a larger organism. According to this third concept of man, each man defines himself by identifying with a group of men with whom he shares basic beliefs. When a man is conceived of in this manner, he retains his individuality and yet is essentially a social being. If his sense of his own personal importance and uniqueness is too great, he loses his capacity to be a productive member of a moral community.

Thus, if the members of the Department of Agricultural Economics at Michigan State University, the Americans working in Thailand, the Agency for International Development advisers in Nigeria, the pickle producers, the residents of Leelanau county, and the farm advisers working to improve credit facilities had refused to identify with each other and to recognize the common values they stood for, none of the difficulties discussed in this book would have been overcome. Nor would they have been solved if the men facing them had lost their identities completely and become mere cells in a social organism. Each of the successful problem solvers of this book stood out as the leader of a group of like-minded men; yet he was also a member of the group which he led. He was successful and creative because he was a representative of a larger community in which he was only one of a number of members.

If we conceive of a man and evaluate his work in terms of the belief system that he represents, then the understanding of his belief system becomes an avenue for understanding the man. The burden of this book has been to show that the beliefs making up a belief system can be judged, and judged objectively, to be acceptable or unacceptable. This is true whether the beliefs concern the non-normative or the normative.

The nature of the community a man is a member of greatly affects the ease or difficulty with which objectivity is achieved. If a community is an open, free, and intellectually developed society, men are presented with a wide range of alternative beliefs from which to create their own belief systems, their own selves. In a closed society, on the other hand, the beliefs from which an individual may choose are limited by the nature of the society. In such a society the achievement of objectivity in the sense that we have described it is made difficult by the rulers of the social order. The moral community as a society in which men voluntarily participate is obviously impossible if men are compelled to adhere to beliefs dictated by other men, whether such beliefs are consistent and clear or inconsistent and unclear. Each man must choose his own values and beliefs and freely associate himself with others who have selected similar values and beliefs or there can be no *moral* community.

The difficulties faced by the individuals described in this book are, to a great extent, difficulties which could have been either avoided or lessened by a more adequate conception of self, society, and knowledge. Where solutions have been inadequate, we find that the inadequacy can be accounted for in terms of incompleteness of knowledge, an inadequate self-concept, and failure of imagination. Some incompleteness of knowledge springs from a simple lack of information, and this type is remedied in a relatively simple manner. However, another sort of incompleteness springs from a way of conceptualizing knowledge which makes unavailable to men some of the information they must have to solve their problems.

The possible restrictiveness of philosophic approaches to knowledge illustrated by the narrow positivism of men who refuse to allow serious, scientific study of normative questions is an example of such categorial incompleteness. One of the most basic concerns in this book has been to show the unsatisfactory character of such a philosophical position. While positivists have made basic clarifications in their analyses of non-normative knowledge gained from the empirical sciences and the formal knowledge exemplified by mathematics and logic, they have thrown roadblocks in the way of the advancement of what we have called normative knowledge.

The conditional normativists have likewise refused to take seriously the sort of intellectual enlargement that is possible in questions of value. They have recognized that man does not live by non-normative information alone but they have answered questions of value by arbitrary assumption immune from discussion and tests of objectivity and intractable to the creativity of man.

The close identification of conditional normativism with Pareto-better welfare economics also involves the restrictiveness of the individualistic concept of man discussed above. When the conditionally normative, Pareto-better, welfare economists refuse to evaluate alternative solutions that would leave at least one person worse off regardless of how many people are made infinitely better off, they are using an extreme, individualistic concept of man. Use of this concept does permit many problems to be solved, but not all kinds. Many solutions of important problems involving redistribution of rights and privileges (including, of course, such kinds of property as knowledge, technology, land, and wealth) are thus excluded from the conditionally normative, Pareto-better, welfare economists' investigations.

Pragmatism, too, is useful in solving many problems but restricts its users with its insistence on viewing both normative and non-normative concepts as well as means and ends concepts as necessarily interdependent. The restriction arises out of the imposition of this complex approach even on simpler investigations that could easily be handled with simpler approaches such as positivism or conditional normativism.

Creativity can also be restricted by the blind use of techniques, such as economists' maximization techniques that presume conditions which cannot be met in numerous instances without creative work.

Projections and simulations have been discussed earlier in this chapter with respect to their usefulness in problem-solving investigations and their criteria for objectivity. At this point, it is instructive to note the role which the simulation approach plays in freeing investigators from restraints on their creativity and, indeed, promoting creativity.

Unlike the Pareto-better welfare economist, the simulator or projectionist can estimate and help evaluate consequences of alternative policies which benefit some persons by damaging others. And, unlike the maximizer, the simulator or projectionist can estimate the consequences of different programs and policies in terms of several different conditions, situations, and things even though no common denominator is readily available in terms of which they can be evaluated. The generality of the approach also makes it unnecessary for the simulator or projectionist to be restricted by either the positivist's admonition to avoid the normative, or the normativist's possible admonition to avoid the positivistic. Similarly, he may or may not employ the techniques of the conditional normativist. He is also free to reap the advantages as well as to avoid the cumbersome disadvantages of pragmatism according to the nature of the problem under investigation.

Cap Edmonds (chapter 3) was not bothered by Pareto-better welfare economics in planning the future of the valley counties, nor were the agricultural economists who created the federal agricultural credit agencies of the United States (chapter 4). On the other hand, Pareto-better and positivistic doctrines were sometimes restrictive for the highly trained, well-educated agricultural economists planning the work of Michigan State University's Department of Agricultural Economics (chapter 7). Projections permitted CSNRD researchers (chapter 9) to avoid the restrictiveness of (1) Pareto-better welfare economics, with its stress on individualism, without embarrassing the equally restrictive extreme organization of totalitarian statism, right or left; and (2) maximization techniques of economists.

Simulation or projection can positively encourage creativity as well as permit investigations to avoid restrictions on creativity. As investigators and decision makers cooperate in estimating the consequences through time of using proposed designs, policies, and/or programs, their understanding deepens and new possibilities emerge. This deepened understanding is in both the normative and non-normative dimensions. More accurate non-normative understanding of how programs and policies would work encourages decision makers to be more innovative in suggesting change. Of particular importance is the possibility of increased empathy on the part of the decision maker for those people affected by the decision. Deeper normative understanding may encourage creative conceptualization of common denominators among the various goodnesses being sought and badnesses being avoided.

Deeper, more objective, normative understanding may make it possible to conceive of or create a ranking of alternatives with respect to their net advantages. Or, even in the absence of ability to so rank alternatives, deeper, more objective, normative and non-normative information helps decision makers and investigators to conceive of new and applicable ways of reaching decisions among conceived alternatives.

It is our thesis that a simple philosophical position, such as any of those examined in this book, is a straitjacket to people engaged in the problems of men. Although we have no panacea, we can point in the direction of a more complete understanding of rational conduct. For men who despair of a rational consideration of experience, the answers to problems are often ex ante pleasantly simple, but the pleasure that such men take in the simplicity of their answers is more than counterbalanced by the ex poste pain of their failures. History reveals no better method of solving problems than empirically grounded reflective thought; but this method can be and has been frequently misunderstood. We have tried in this book to examine reason in action, to show some of the factors that made it successful when it was successful and that made it fail when it failed.

For Further Reading

Readings Suggested by Lewis K. Zerby, Philosopher

General Works on Ethics

Frankena, William. *Ethics.* Englewood Cliffs, N.J.: Prentice-Hall, 1963. An elementary book on ethics—elementary in the sense that it concerns the elements of ethics. Not easy reading, but worth serious study.

Brandt, Richard. *Ethical Theory.* Englewood Cliffs, N.J.: Prentice-Hall, 1959. A most exhaustive study of several important ethical traditions. Particularly useful as a study of utilitarianism in modern thought.

Sellars, Wilfrid., and Hospers, John, eds. *Readings in Ethical Theory.* 1st ed. New York: Appleton-Century-Crofts, 1952. A book of selections with excellent readings on ethical intuitionism and criticism of it by ethical naturalists; the positivistic emotive theory and criticism of it by the normativist, Sir David Ross; and a group of selections on "The Problem of Justification," which includes a particularly pertinent article called "Objectivity in Morals" (pp. 681-97). In the second edition of this book (1970) this article is omitted, but an equally important one called "Emotivism and Ethical Objectivity" (pp. 276-87) has been added.

Edel, Abraham. *Ethical Judgment: The Use of Science in Ethics.* Chicago: The Free Press, 1955. An attempt to show the relationship between science and ethics. Very relevant to the position of the authors of the present volume.

Leys, W.A.R. *Ethics for Policy Decisions.* Englewood Cliffs, N.J.: Prentice-Hall, 1952. Leys argues that philosophical positions are important not for the answers they give to questions, but for calling attention to and making an examination of questions that need to be asked and considered by men making policy decisions.

Hook, Sidney, ed. *Human Values and Economic Policy.* New York: New York University Press, 1967. Of particular importance for the reader of this volume is Hook's essay entitled "Basic Values and Economic Policy" (pp. 246-55).

Murphy, Arthur E. *The Uses of Reason.* New York: Macmillan, 1943. An excellent critique of several forms of irrationalism and an eloquent defense of reason which, Murphy argues, "has proved its worth in the attainment of truth that will stand examination in the daylight, in ideals that work and have worked for human freedom, in comprehensive wisdom to which nothing is alien that contributes to the full realization of man's humanity."

Works on the Ethics of Positivism and the Emotive Theory of Value

Schlick, Moritz. *The Problems of Ethics.* Englewood Cliffs, N.J.: Prentice-Hall, 1939.

Ayer, A.J. *Language, Truth, and Logic.* 2nd ed. New York: Dover Publications, 1946.

Stevenson, Charles. *Ethics and Language.* New Haven, Conn.: Yale University Press, 1960.

Stevenson, Charles. *Facts and Values: Studies in Ethical Analysis.* New Haven, Conn.: Yale University Press, 1963.

Works on Ethics and Pragmatism

Dewey, John. *Human Nature and Conduct.* New York: Holt, Rinehart and Winston, 1922.

Dewey, John. *Reconstruction in Philosophy.* New York: Henry Holt, 1920.

Dewey, John. "Theory of Valuation." *International Encyclopedia of Unified Science.* Chicago: University of Chicago Press, 1939.

Works on the Ethics of Utilitarianism and the Interest Theory of Value

Mill, John Stuart. *Utilitarianism.* New York: Library of Liberal Arts, 1957.

Sidgwick, H. *The Methods of Ethics.* London: Macmillan, 1874.

Stephen, L. *The English Utilitarians.* London: Duckworth, 1900.

Perry, Ralph Barton. *General Theory of Value.* New York: Longmans, Green and Co., 1922.

Perry, Ralph Barton. *The Moral Economy.* New York: Scribner, 1937.

Works on the Ethics of Existentialism

Sartre, Jean Paul. *Existentialism and Humanism.* New York: Philosophical Library, 1949.

Warnock, Mary. *Existentialist Ethics.* New York: St. Martin's Press, 1967.

Readings Suggested by
Glenn L. Johnson, Agricultural Economist

Knight, Frank H. *On the History and Method of Economics.* Chicago: University of Chicago Press, 1963.

Robbins, Lionel. *An Essay on the Nature and Significance of Economic Science.* London: MacMillan, 1949. These references by two highly respected economists, one from the United States and the other from England, are commonly used to introduce advanced economic students to the work of economists.

Friedman, Milton. *Essays in Positive Economics.* Chicago: University of Chicago Press, 1953. Although the title of this reading would cause one to expect a purely positivistic article, the article does deal with monetary values and is, hence, normative as well as positive. As such, it is representative of what many economists regard as positivistic work, if not highly consistent with philosophic concepts of positivism.

Parsons, Kenneth H. "Logical Foundations of Economic Research." *Journal of Farm Economics*, November 1949, pp. 656-86.

Parsons, Kenneth H. "The Value Problem in Agricultural Policy." *Agricultural Adjustment Problems in a Growing Society.* Edited by Earl O. Heady [and others]. Ames: Iowa State College Press, 1958.

Boulding, Kenneth E. *The Image.* Ann Arbor: University of Michigan Press, 1956. Parsons is an outstanding agricultural economist and represents the pragmatic impact of

John Dewey on agricultural economics via John R. Commons and the Wisconsin institutionalists. Boulding's book reflects a substantial impact of pragmatism on his thinking.

Heady, Earl Orel. *Economics of Agricultural Production and Resource Use.* New York: Prentice-Hall, 1952.

Arrow, Kenneth J. *Social Choice and Individual Values.* New York: Wiley, 1951.

Baum, E. L.; Heady, Earl O.; and Blackmore, John, eds. *Methodological Procedures in the Economic Analysis of Fertilizer Use Data.* Ames: Iowa State University Press, 1956. The first two of these readings, while not specifically conditionally normative, as defined in this book, deal with what we have called the conditionally normative approach in this book. It should be read in relation to Parson's chapter on value problems and agricultural policy. Arrow's work is in the sequence of work which starts with Vilfredo Pareto and includes John R. Hicks. The third chapter deals almost exclusively with conditionally normative analysis of fertilizer use problems.

Bentham, Jeremy. *An Introduction to the Principles of Morals and Legislation.* London: Athlone P., 1970.

Marshall, Alfred. *Principles of Economics.* London: MacMillan, 1946.

Marx, Karl. *Capital.* Translated from the 4th German edition by Eden and Cedar Paul. London: Dent & Sons; New York: Dutton, 1957.

Mill, John Stuart. *Principles of Political Economy with Some of Their Applications to Social Philosophy.* London: Parker, Son and Bourn, 1862.

Ricardo, David. *The Principles of Political Economy and Taxation.* London: J. M. Dent & Sons; New York: Dutton, 1937. Bentham's book is utilitarian and, hence, normative in nature. While few economists have been purely normative, utilitarianism is a normative philosophy important in both legal and economic thought. Another normative philosophy prominent in the history of economics is the labor theory of value as developed by Ricardo, John S. Mill, and, of course, Karl Marx, though refuted by Alfred Marshall in his synthesis of supply (cost or sacrificed value) and demand (value) in the simultaneous determination of value in exchange, which is sometimes, but not always, a price.

Index

A

Absolutists
  normative, 225
  positivistic, 225-26
Abstract knowledge, 12
Action(s)
  in case studies: of Thailand,
    47; of farm credit, 66; of
    national recreation area,
    73; of pickle industry, 107
  as choice, 4
  definition of, 11
  expected return from, 7
  in practical problems, 221
  right
    and agricultural economists
      in credit problems, 69
    in case studies: of farm cred-
      it, 67; of national recrea-
      tion area, 92, 97, 98-99,
      100, 101; of the pickle in-
      dustry, 130; of MSU agri-
      cultural economics depart-
      ment, 144, 148, 149, 155;
      of Nigerian rural develop-
      ment, 192
    as a compromise among
      goods and bads, 70
    defined by agricultural econ-
      omists, 69
    defined by economists, 9
    defined in static production
      economies, 13
    definition of, 11
    and innovative educators,
      167
    profit maximizing, 66
    as public actions, 71
    and second-order condi-
      tions, 8
    and simulation, 198
    social scientists' involvement
      in, 67-69
    and solving practical prob-
      lems, 8
  as solutions, 4
  wrong, definition of, 11

Adelman, Irma, 199n
Adrian, Charles R., 99n
Africa, 25, 171, 172, 175, 178,
  179, 180, 201, 218. *See also*
  Nigeria
African studies at University of
  Nigeria, 169-70
Agency for International Devel-
  opment. *See* U.S. Agency for
  International Development
Agricultural Adjustment Admin-
  istration, 68
Agricultural Commission of the
  American Banker's Association, 67
Agricultural Credit Act (1923),
  59
Agricultural Credit Corporation,
  68
Agricultural development, in
  Thailand, 37-40
Agricultural economics
  compared to economics, 19
  and existentialism, 23
  and farm credit problems, 68
  is it dead, 22-24
  and Karl Popper, 17
  and positivism, 16
  and pragmatism, 21, 22
  and outright normativism, 18
  unifying characteristic of, 144
Agricultural Economics, Department of at Michigan State
  University, 62, 103, 104,
  132-66 *passim*, 221, 229,
  230, 233
Agricultural Economics, U.S.
  Bureau of, 20
Agricultural economist(s), 5, 21,
  23-24, 57, 205. *See also* Agricultural economics
  and action, 150
  and choice, 167
  and decision making, 72
  and goodness and badness, 20
  and maximization, 9
  at Michigan State University,
    132

information
in case studies: of Thailand,
30; of Kentucky, 49, 53;
of national recreation
area, 146; of sample size,
204, 212
and decision makers, 233
improvement of, 9
and normativism, 215
and objectivity, 10
inquiries and investigations,
30, 134, 143
knowledge
in case studies: of Ken-
tucky, 54; of University
of Nigeria, 179
compared to knowledge of
values, 92
and creativity, 227
its place under kinds of
knowledge, 12
problems, 202
questions
in case studies: of Ken-
tucky, 57; of MSU agricultural economics depart-
ment, 142; of sample size,
208, 211, 212-13
in defining operational problems, 59
reality, 59
statements of MSU agricultural economics depart-
ment. 136, 141-42, 143,
150, 163-64
Non-Pareto-better. See also Pareto-better; Pareto, Vilfredo
adjustment, 55-56, 68, 71
choices, 126
solutions, 192, 197
Non-Pareto optimality, of problems, 72
Nonprescriptive knowledge, 12,
13
Nordin, John, 184
Normative. See also Non-normative; Normativism
absolutists, 225
aspects of sample sizes, 204
beliefs
in credit problems, 60
and definition of belief, 11
and human error, 71
and right actions, 11
belief structures, 70

concepts
in case studies: of Thailand,
29, 30-31, 36, 37, 45-47;
of Kentucky, 49, 50, 53,
55; of credit problems,
60, 61, 62, 63-67, 69; of
national recreation area,
99; of pickle industry,
107-115, 125-26, 130-31;
of MSU agricultural eco-
nomics department, 148,
160, 164; of University of
Nigeria, 175; of sample
size, 207, 208
interdependency with non-
normative concepts, 22
and positivism, 17
and theoretical problems,
221
use of by educator, 167
and workability, 225
dimension of reality, 173
evaluation, 114
experiences, 107, 176
information
in case studies: of Thailand,
29, 30; of Kentucky, 49,
53; of sample size, 204,
212
and decision makers, 233
improvement of, 9
and objectivity, 10
and philosophers, 13
inquiries and investigation
in case studies: of Thailand,
30; of pickle industry,
106-107; of MSU agricul-
tural economics depart-
ment, 134, 143
meaninglessness of, 101
omission of, 214
issues, 92
knowledge
in case studies: of national
recreation area, 100; of
University of Nigeria, 175,
179; of sample size, 205
and creativity, 227
matters, knowledge of, 16
problems, in Nigerian rural development, 202
questions
in case studies: of Ken-
tucky, 50, 57; of credit
problems, 59; of MSU

and normative information, 13
and positivism, 15
Philosophy, and economists, 1.
See also Existentialism; Normativism, conditional; Normativism, outright; Positivism; Pragmatism
Pine, Wilfred, 188
Planning Without Facts (Stolper), 198
Plato, 2
Poincaré, Jules Henri, 15
Popper, Karl R., 17
Positive stage (Comte), 15
Positivism
  and agricultural economists, 69n, 71
  as an approach, 215, 231
  in case studies: of Kentucky, 49, 56; of credit problems, 68; of national recreation area, 101; of MSU agricultural economics department, 132, 142, 162; of University of Nigeria, 175, 180; of Nigerian rural development, 190; of sample size, 211
  described, 15-18
  and existentialism, 22
  exculsion of certain knowledge, 12-13
  mentioned, 14, 20, 22, 214
  and Pareto, 21
  and science, 19
Positivist, compared to normativist, 18
Pound, Glen, 186
Practical problem. *See* Problem(s), practical
Pragmatism
  in case studies: of pickle industry, 131; of MSU agricultural economics department, 142, 162, 163; of University of Nigeria, 176, 177, 180; of Nigerian rural development, 190; of sample size, 207, 211, 212
  described, 21-22, 215-16
  exclusion of certain knowledge, 12-13
  mentioned, 14, 215
  restrictions of, 232
Prescriptive beliefs, 221
Prescriptive knowledge, 12, 221

Principles of Economics (Marshall), 66n
Problem(s). *See also* Problem-solving
  and agricultural economists, 69
  awareness of, 202
  in case studies: of Thailand, 32-45; of Kentucky, 55; of credit problems, 58-72 *passim*
  definition of, 3
  disciplinary, 3-4, 221
  and the economist, 217
  human, 1-2, 5, 23
  and language, 3
  and the market place, 6-8
  operational, 59
  practical
    and agricultural economics, 19, 24
    in case studies: of Kentucky, 49; of national recreation area, 73, 101; of pickle industry, 130, 140; of University of Nigeria, 180; of Nigerian rural development, 202-203; of sample size, 204, 205, 212
    described, 3-4, 221
    and simulation. 220
    solutions of, 8
    and theoretical problems, 181
  and simulation, 218
  theoretical, 3-4, 181, 196-97, 198, 201, 202-203, 221
Problem solving. *See also* Problem(s)
  and agricultural economists, 214-15
  in case studies: of Kentucky, 50, 56-57; of MSU agricultural economics department, 132, 144
Production and Marketing Administration Committee (PMA), 51-52
Production Credit Association (PCA), 59, 62
Production Credit Corporation, 62
Profit-maximizing right action, 66
Projections. *See also* Simulation

About the Authors

GLENN JOHNSON has been on the faculty of Agricultural Economics at Michigan State University since 1953. He received his bachelor's degree from the University of Illinois, his master's from Michigan State University, and his Ph.D. from the University of Chicago. Before joining the MSU faculty he served in the U.S. Bureau of Agricultural Economics and at the University of Kentucky. His many contributions at Michigan State University led to his selection in 1966 as a recipient of the Distinguished Faculty Award, the highest award given by the university. In 1970 he was elected Fellow of the American Agricultural Economics Association. He served as vice-president of the American Farm Economic Association in 1962 and has twice won the Association's award for the best published research. He was the first director of the Economic Development Institute at the University of Nigeria and served as a consultant to the Ford and Rockefeller Foundations, the Agency for International Development, and numerous other organizations. Co-author of a widely used textbook in farm management, he is noted for his extensive problem-solving research relating to farm management, national agricultural policy, and economic development in less developed countries, particularly Korea, Thailand, and Nigeria.

LEWIS ZERBY received his B.A. in music and his M.A. in philosophy and English from the University of Illinois in 1939 and 1942. He was granted a Ph.D. in philosophy and psychology in 1945 by the University of Iowa. Since 1946 he has been in Michigan State University's Department of Philosophy, specializing in ethics, social philosophy, and the philosophy of law. From 1962 to 1966 he participated in the MSU program at the University of Nigeria. In 1965 he traveled extensively throughout East and West Africa studying African universities. This study was made possible by a grant from the Carnegie Foundation. From 1967 to 1972 he was professor of philosophy and chairman of the justice, morality, and constitutional democracy division in James Madison College, a residential college at MSU. At present, he is a professor in the Department of Philosophy. He has served as managing editor of the *Philosophy of Science Journal* and has published numerous articles in professional journals. His most recent publication, *If I Should Die Before I Wake, The Nsukka Dream*, is a history of the University of Nigeria which he wrote jointly with his wife, Margaret.